CHRIS
CHRISTIE

Also by Bob Ingle

The Soprano State: New Jersey's Culture of Corruption
(with Sandy McClure)

CHRIS CHRISTIE

THE INSIDE STORY OF HIS RISE TO POWER

BOB INGLE and

MICHAEL SYMONS

 ST. MARTIN'S GRIFFIN ✻ NEW YORK

www.stmartins.com

Design by Steven Seighman

The Library of Congress has cataloged the hardcover edition as follows:

Ingle, Bob.
    Chris Christie : the inside story of his rise to power / Bob Ingle and Michael Symons. — 1st ed.
        p. cm.
    Includes bibliographical references and index.
    ISBN 978-1-250-00586-1 (hardcover)
    ISBN 978-1-250-00836-7 (e-book)
    1. Christie, Chris.   2. New Jersey—Politics and government—1951–
3. Governors—New Jersey—Biography.   I. Symons, Michael.   II. Title.
    F140.22.C47I64 2012
    974.9'043092—dc23
    [B]

                                                    2012009432

ISBN 978-1-250-03126-6 (trade paperback)

St. Martin's Griffin books may be purchased for educational, business, or promotional use. For information on bulk purchases, please contact Macmillan Corporate and Premium Sales Department at 1-800-221-7945 extension 5442 or write specialmarkets@macmillan.com.

First St. Martin's Griffin Edition: June 2013

10   9   8   7   6   5   4   3   2   1

For our parents and their parents,
whose influence we never outgrow

CONTENTS

ACKNOWLEDGMENTS

The authors thank our families and friends for putting up with us as we missed events and special occasions while crisscrossing the region and country researching this project, especially Lisa, Audrey, Connor, Ron, Barbara, Mildred, Monie, and Nick, who accepted delays and cancellations with love and generous understanding. And to our Gannett colleagues for their support, especially the Trenton bureau staff, John Schoonejongen, Jason Method, and Bob Jordan, and at the *Asbury Park Press*, Tom Donovan, Hollis Towns, and Gary Schoening. George Witte, our editor at St. Martin's Press, believed in us from day one, as did the SMP team of professionals who took on this book with enthusiasm. Our agent, Roger Williams, was always at the ready for what needed doing, even when it meant showing up in front of the New Jersey State House dressed as Santa in a red convertible with antlers. Sandy McClure is a special friend and colleague who cheered us from the sidelines along with J.B., and checked in every week for progress reports and encouragement. Governor Chris Christie and his effervescent wife, Mary Pat, promised cooperation and delivered with no strings attached. We appreciate their openness and that of their extended family, close friends, and the governor's administration. We are thankful for input from fellow journalists and the many best wishes from the public who read us in newspapers and on the Internet and follow us on radio and TV as we try to make sense of it all.

FOREWORD

I knew Chris Christie as a federal prosecutor of politicians I tracked for years as a New Jersey State House reporter. He took down Wayne Bryant, the veteran state senator from Camden County who had taxpayers outfit him with a red Lincoln Town Car; he jailed state senator John Lynch, the powerful political boss who ruled the state's central section; and he imprisoned longtime Newark mayor Sharpe James, whose fans greeted him with cheers when he returned home from the lockup. Jail time for those three is something I never thought I would see.

Christie prosecuted the Garden State icons for using their positions to benefit themselves or their cronies, a long-standing tradition in New Jersey—one politicians practiced with impunity. The arrogant Bryant traded funding to the state's medical university for a low-show university job. The quick-tempered Lynch took payoffs to help a mining company get state approvals. The flamboyant James helped his girlfriend to city-owned land, which she flipped for a profit.

When Christie, a fund-raiser for George W. Bush, was named U.S. attorney, the appointment was rightfully called political. Little was expected of the Morris County securities lawyer, a former county official with no experience in criminal law. But skeptics were quieted, at least for a bit, when Essex County executive Jim Treffinger, a Republican, was arrested, handcuffed, and paraded before the press during one of the early high-profile takedowns. Treffinger, who had promised to clean up govern-ment, instead hired his hairdresser for a no-show job, among other things.

Christie, declaring his disgust for those who believed they were "be-yond the reach of the law," made an unprecedented dent in New Jersey's culture of corruption, with the convictions or guilty pleas of more than 130 public officials.

Republicans were aching for him to run for governor long before he challenged wealthy Democratic incumbent governor Jon Corzine. In a liberal-leaning state with an electorate that has tolerated fiscally, but not socially, conservative statewide candidates, Christie convinced enough residents, overburdened with high taxes and the cost of corrupt govern-ment, that change was the only way to survive. Voters pulled the lever and sent him to arguably the most powerful governorship in the nation.

As governor, he challenged an education system backed by the state's most powerful labor union, the New Jersey Education Association. He linked with some Democrats to reform a public employee benefit and pen-sion system facing bankruptcy in part because former Democratic and Republican governors raided it.

His line-item veto of budget items and his blunt, straight talk on every-thing from taxes to Hurricane Irene—when he told sun worshippers in Asbury Park to "get the hell off the beach"—made the news in every state.

At home, Senate president Steve Sweeney called the governor a bully, a punk, and a rotten prick after Christie cut Democratic favorites from the budget. Assembly speaker Sheila Oliver took the name-calling to a higher level when she labeled Christie mentally deranged, and a liar, in a spat over his contention that she sought his support to keep her Democratic leader-ship seat when a revolt was brewing.

Christie drew national attention for his ability to move ordinary people to action. With a series of town hall meetings, the governor convinced vot-ers, who pass judgment on most school budgets, to reject more than half of the proposals in 2010 in a show of support for reining in spending. Christie tapped into taxpayer frustration, and perhaps taxpayer realization, that more spending does not always equal better education.

When Republicans across the land clamored to make Christie a presi-dential candidate in 2011 he decided to stay put. Clearly, he was tempted.

But in the end, he likened such attention to smoke, saying that "You can become intoxicated by that smoke, and you can wind up losing your way." Christie's inner compass told him, at least in 2011, home is where he belonged. He made it public with customary humor: "Whether you like it or not, you're stuck with me."

Here, readers get the chance to see beyond Chris Christie's public persona. Coauthors Bob Ingle and Michael Symons, veteran award-winning journalists, offer an inside view of the hard-driving prosecutor turned governor, the qualities and the politics that brought him to where he is, the flaws and the circumstances that could hinder his reelection and elevation to the national stage.

This book offers an intimate view of the public and personal events in Christie's life. You will:

Discover why "leave nothing unsaid," is a driving force.

Find out which obsession caused big trouble during the first year of his marriage to wife Mary Pat.

Learn what poetry taught him.

Hear him challenge opponent Jon Corzine to "man up and say I'm fat."

See him accused in political ads of intervening on behalf of his brother with New York's U.S. attorney, who later received a no-bid contract from U.S. Attorney Christie.

Watch him grapple with the issue of a distant relative, a ranking member of the Genovese crime family, who attended family parties at his aunt's home.

Be in the circle with Mary Pat and their four children just before he takes the stage to make his acceptance speech as a newly elected governor.

Hear what was said at the hospital bed of his dying mother.

Bob Ingle, both respected and feared in Trenton, practices a take-no-prisoners style of journalism. But he tells a story with heart, and texture, and humor. When Gannett New Jersey bureau chief Ingle hired me for his State House crew, the first thing I investigated was why so much laughter echoed from his offices. It won't take you long to figure it out.

The other part of this team, Michael Symons, is a detail man. No minor fact of a news story escapes his view. He digests complicated government jargon and explains to readers what game is at play in a way that makes it look simple. Symons, whose institutional knowledge is sought by colleagues and competitors, cuts through bureaucratic fog like a laser beam.

Ingle and Symons will take you on a wild and funny, insightful and illuminating, educational and entertaining walk through Chris Christie's Soprano State. As Bob often says, "Don't wear your good shoes."

—Sandy McClure, author of
Christine Whitman and coauthor of *The Soprano State*

CHRIS CHRISTIE

INTRODUCTION

There is a self-assuredness about Chris Christie that could give the impression he never failed at anything, that the world is at his command, nothing stands between him and his goals, that he grew up wealthy among people accustomed to having their way and buying whatever influence was needed.

That's a long way from the truth.

Go back a couple of generations on his mother's side of the family and you'll find people coming to America from Italy on a ship, penniless, with nothing but their hopes and dreams and the promise of a new start from that big green copper woman who lifts her lamp by the golden door in New York Harbor. You know the one: "Give me your tired, your poor, your huddled masses yearning to breathe free." Christie's ancestors were willing to do whatever it took to keep themselves, and many times several relatives, fed and in shelter while looking for opportunities to give their children a better life.

They held on through disease, death, and divorce and became stronger for it, experiences that were shared with the kids in the Christie household by their mother's mother, Anne, who they called Nani. She loved Franklin Roosevelt because he led the country during the Depression and war, and was outwardly bitter at her former husband for leaving her with three kids to raise alone.

Her first child, Sondra, later called Sandy by friends and family, would grow up to marry Bill Christie, starting a family with him that eventually grew to three kids, the five of them living in a one-bathroom house. Chris, the oldest, was polite and friendly and played baseball well, excelled in school, and served as a surrogate father to his siblings when their hard-working dad was not around. Sandy—strong-willed, opinionated, and self-disciplined—confided in Chris; they talked intimately and often, right up until her life ended with him at her side.

Theirs is a story of an extraordinarily close family taking care of one another and reaching for their goals, while keeping their feet planted on terra firma. They worked hard and placed value on education. In a day of blow-dried politicians who seem right out of central casting, so careful to be politically correct and talk much while saying little, in public and private there is no pretense from Chris Christie or his extended family. They're like the people on your street who have personal triumphs and tragedies; they're open about it. They laugh a lot.

Nani was old school, a strict disciplinarian. Sandy wanted her kids to be assertive, and firstborn Chris is just that. He also is ambitious and over-reaching at times, looking for the next rung on the ladder, a maverick un-afraid of offending the powers that be, which he did as a young politician and paid a price. When he was knocked down, he picked himself up and looked for new opportunities.

He has a knack for pointing out how ridiculous is so much of what we've come to accept as routine. He parlayed a reputation as a butt-kicking U.S. attorney into a campaign against one of the richest men in politics, and won. His time as governor brought him to the attention of millions across America who think the nation needs him in Washington. When Harvard's Kennedy School of Government and *The Washington Post* jointly presented Christie a leadership award in December 2011, *Post* publisher Katharine Weymouth said, "He is not, to put it bluntly, a conventional state leader. There is no denying his ability to get results."

That kind of admiration can cause some to lose their way. But not Christie, even when polls show him with high approval numbers in a state that leans Democratic. Such polls are gratifying, but he knows in politics things change fast and in order to maintain that kind of support he must keep producing the results the people want, not necessarily making people happy with his rhetoric or style. He takes nothing for granted.

"People admit up front, 'I don't agree with a lot of what you're doing. But man, I love the way you do it,'" Christie said in an interview. "I think what people in the press corps—and by the press corps, I'd extend that out to kind of like the Trenton crowd, whether it's the lobbyists or the insider types—they don't get the way that we're governing. It's different. And I always said during the campaign it would be really different. On election night, when I said, 'We're going to turn Trenton upside down,' and people said, 'Well, he's just really excited and being hyperbolic'—I thought about that line before I gave it, well before I gave it, that if I ever won, that's exactly what I was going to say. Because that was exactly my intent, I felt like this place needed to be completely turned upside down stylistically. As a result of that, the fact that we have the popularity that we have right now is really gratifying, but I also know that if I feel like, 'Okay, phew, good. I'm at 58 percent. I want to sit behind the desk and put my feet up and go "All right, I'm done,"' I'll be at 45 percent in two months."

Christie and wife Mary Pat, who grew up as one of ten children, met in college, where he first struck her as some kind of student government geek. They have four children and strive to maintain a reasonably normal life, forgoing the stately governor's mansion in Princeton to live in their nearly as stately Morris County home so their kids don't have to change schools.

People frequently ask what the governor is like in private, away from reporters and cameras. He's the same—articulate, smart, self-assured, and funny, a natural storyteller who loves to talk. He holds listeners spellbound—sometimes laughing hysterically, other times with a lump in their throats, as when he recalls the last conversation he had with his mom.

He's demanding, he's loyal, he's combative, he's entertaining, he's mouthy—but never boring.

CHAPTER ONE

◆

Nothing Left Unsaid

Chris Christie was in San Diego late in April 2004, some 2,800 miles from home attending a conference of federal prosecutors, when he got an urgent call from his brother, Todd. Their beloved mother, who was fighting an uphill struggle against cancer, was in St. Barnabas Medical Center, surrounded by family members. Sandy was one tough patient, having survived breast cancer a quarter-century earlier and a brain aneurism in 1996, but the dizziness and headaches she'd started enduring that winter turned out to be the result of two large tumors in the back of her head. Chemotherapy and radiation hadn't worked. Now, Todd alerted his brother that things had taken a turn for the worse. Mom had only days to live. So Chris hopped a red-eye flight to New Jersey and went directly from Newark Airport to her bedside, where he found his mother fading in and out of a coma.

At one point she gained consciousness, recognized her oldest son, and began a conversation with him, as he later recalled:

"What day is it?" she asked.

"It's Friday."

"What time is it?"

"It's ten o'clock in the morning."

"What are you doing here?"

"I'm here to visit you."

"Go to work."

"Mom, I'd rather spend the day with you if you don't mind."

"Go to work. That's where you belong."

"What, are you worried that you're not getting your taxpayer's money's worth today? I'll make up the time, don't worry about it. I'd rather stay here with you."

She grabbed her son's hand. "Christopher, go to work. It's where you belong. There's nothing left unsaid between us."

Christie frequently recalls that story in a style that leaves audiences hanging on every dramatic word and pause as a way of explaining what makes him tick—and his pull-no-punches attitude. "My mother sent me to work because that's the values she taught me," he says. "There was nothing left unsaid between us because she was Sicilian—so you know there was nothing left unsaid between us. If you're wondering who I am and where I came from and why I'm doing this and why I understand New Jersey the way I do, it's because of her, because she taught me don't leave things unsaid. She taught me: Be yourself today, and then tomorrow you won't have to worry about you got it right or wrong and who you told what version of the truth to. One thing for sure: I will always tell you exactly what I think and you never will have to wonder where I stand."[1]

Expressing opinions on matters large and small is rarely a hesitation for Christie, whose say-anything style would cost him his first job in politics, draw attention to a crusade in his second, and seize the national spotlight in his third.

But it's not all flash: Sondra Grasso Christie, who died at age seventy-one just days after that bedside conversation, and her husband, Bill, infused in their children—Chris, Todd, and Dawn—a work ethic and sense of purpose from the time they were small. Sandy had no patience for complaints and no problem pushing her children socially and intellectually. "She was very opinionated. She loved to argue. You had to learn how to argue or you got run over,"[2] Chris remembered.

Sandy's independence and bluntness can be traced to her mother, Anne, who was born in Brooklyn, New York, in 1909. Anne's parents, Salvatore and Domenica Scavone, had emigrated from Sicily around the turn of the twentieth century. The family, including Anne's widowed maternal grandmother, Annie, a brother and a sister, moved in the 1910s to Camden Street in Newark's 6th Ward, where Anne's father worked odd jobs as a laborer, eventually catching on at Port Newark and then with the city.

Friends and family called Anne's mother Minnie. Her father was called, "Yes, sir," jokes Sandy's brother, Joseph Grasso.

"Grandma was this tiny, little, wonderful caring lady, and Grandpa was a real chauvinist. My grandma had to shine his shoes, iron his underwear, dump out his spittoon. When we had dinners, he'd sit there and have a jug of wine on the floor and pour it into the soup that she'd made," recalled Joseph, known by friends, family, and colleagues as Joe. "Then afterwards, we had to put on a show, all the kids. We couldn't talk though dinner. If Grandpa talked, you responded. You couldn't talk to your siblings. You didn't start a conversation with your sister. So he was a real tough cookie. Respectful as hell, but Grandma was his slave. Boy, he ruled the roost.

"Grandma was the most loving, caring little person. She would come and sit on the bed with you at night, always had the rosary beads, would say prayers," Joe said. "My grandfather just put the fear of God in everybody. If you stepped out of line, you were going to get whacked, whether you were a kid or not. I don't ever remember Grandpa showing a lot of love to anybody. He was just this staunch guy who sat in his chair—he was the king, and this is the way it was going to be."

By age twenty Anne was working as a clerk in the courthouse. She married Philip Grasso, who had arrived in Newark's 14th Ward with his parents, Santo and Santa, from Italy shortly after his 1905 birth—born on the Atlantic Ocean on his family's way to America, according to Bill Christie. It was a marriage arranged by Anne's domineering father. Philip, the second of ten children, worked a series of factory jobs—as a hatter, as head of a fur shop—and as a laborer before meeting Anne, a small woman, maybe five feet tall, with tiny hands, and a disciplinarian with strong political opinions. Together they had three children, Sandy being the oldest—then got divorced in 1941, which was unusual in that generation.

Her mother's divorce compelled Sandy to take on added responsibilities early, helping with her younger sister and brother. Anne's mother moved in with the family after Salvatore died, but for the most part Anne was raising three children—the youngest, Joe, born a year before the divorce—on her own. She had a tough time in the job market as a divorced woman but did land a few jobs—at the War Department, then working for a friendly attorney, and as a customer service representative with the IRS, a position she would hold for twenty-five years until retirement. Anne was a voracious reader, though she hadn't completed high school, and socked away $10 from every paycheck in an envelope in her drawer, enabling her eventually to sightsee her way on trips through Europe and go on cruises, and to spend time—much as her grandmother and mother had done years earlier—with her daughter Sandy's children, who called her Nani. She was at the Christies' house every weekend, allowing Sandy and son-in-law Bill to go out together each Saturday night, and often during the week. "Chris and I just sat around and listened to her talk about what it was like growing up during the Depression," Todd said. "She was blunt about when my grandfather left her and her unhappiness with raising three kids on her own."

How unhappy? Her son's given name was Philip but she refused to call him that because it was her former husband's name, and instead referred to her youngest child by his middle name, Joseph. He used his middle and confirmation names on things such as his passport, rather than Philip. And when Joe named his second son Philip in 1987, at the suggestion of his wife, Victoria, who didn't know the full backstory, Anne refused to use that name in conversation. She would call his house and ask, "How's the baby?" When her grandson outgrew the label, she dubbed him "Handsome Harry" although his middle name is Thomas. Sandy, perhaps in solidarity with her mom, referred to her nephew little Philip as "the brat."

"All I heard was all these things about him—some of them well deserved, as I grew up to find out," Joe said of his father. "She had a very difficult time dealing with the way he treated her, and why they divorced. One time he tried to run her over. I probably saw him ten total years of my life. He'd come to visit, and he'd never come on time. She was very bitter."

Philip Grasso remarried, had no more children, and died of cancer in 1969. Anne never did remarry and died in 2001 at age ninety-two. "She never remarried because she didn't want to have another man bringing us up. And at the end of the day, it was pretty sad she spent sixty years alone," Joe said.

"Look, she was the strength behind all of us and Sandy picked up all of those traits. There weren't any two ways about it. My mother was pretty calm and she wouldn't take any crap from anybody."

Sandy and Joe bracketed a sister, Minette, who had a complicated family life. She married as a teenager and had three children, two daughters and a son, in a rocky union that ended in divorce.

Minette's second husband, John, had a brother who made an unwelcome cameo in Chris Christie's eventual political career—Tino Fiumara, a ranking member of the Genovese crime family. "John really stepped up to the plate and became a real good person and gave up a lot," said Joe. "He was kind of bordered on being a wiseguy, because of his brother Tino. But Minette said to John: If we're going to get married, you can't do that. And he didn't. He never had that life, but he was kind of on the edge with Tino."

Christie said he first learned about Fiumara's line of work at age fifteen by reading the newspaper. "It just told me that you make bad decisions in life and you wind up paying a price. Really, for most of my life, he spent his life in prison. That teaches you a lot."[3] In 1991, Christie, then twenty-nine, was asked by his uncle to visit Fiumara in a Texas prison while he was in the state for a football game. "My best recollection is we updated each other on what was going on with the family," Christie told a reporter when news bubbled up about that branch of the family tree.[4]

Joe said mobster Fiumara wasn't around the family often. "It was all blown out of proportion. I can tell you, I was going to visit Tino once, I had a customer in Kansas City and he was in Leavenworth at the time. And when the papers came that I had to sign to go through all this crap I said, 'I'm not going to do it, because I don't want it hampering my career.' When I became a member of the New York Stock Exchange, I got investigated by the FBI, the whole megillah. So I didn't go and visit Tino, and he understood. The story with Chris, they all blew it out of proportion. If he saw Tino ten times in his lifetime, that was a lot."

Christie said he had seen Fiumara at large parties in his aunt's home as a youngster and ran into him once in a restaurant when Fiumara was out on parole. Fiumara was due to be released in 2002 but was indicted again by U.S. Attorney Christie's office on charges of helping another criminal evade prosecution. Christie recused himself from the plea negotiations, which ended with Fiumara heading back to prison for eight months. Fiumara was released in 2005 and died in 2010. Minette had died of breast cancer in 1991; her husband, John, the governor's uncle and Fiumara's brother, died in 2011.

Joe Grasso is a retired investment professional who manages the governor's blind trust from his home in California. He volunteers his time traveling to poverty-stricken nations for Rotaplast International. Founded by a friend, Dr. Angelo Capozzi, the organization helps treat children with cleft lip and palate anomaly who otherwise would not receive surgery. He has coached running for the Special Olympics for thirty-two years and worked for the Juvenile Diabetes Foundation. It's his way of giving back to a great country that has been good to him and his family, he says.

Once the baby of the Grasso family, then its prince, and now its patriarch, Joe rose from painting cars and houses—"You're too smart to be a grease monkey," his mother and grandmother used to tell him—to become partner in a major California-based financial firm, despite never having gone to college.

"I probably had a very unusual relationship with my sisters and my mother, that most people don't have. We talked all the time. Even when I moved here, I would call them once a week, or my mom twice a week," Joe said. "They were very protective of me, and when I grew older, in my twenties, I was protective of them. I don't ever remember us fighting and not talking afterwards. If we disagreed or argued, we never went on our merry way and didn't talk at all. We'd always resolve it, whether we agreed or not. And we'd always talk. We always, I felt, showed a tremendous amount of respect for each other, as we did for mom.

"We had a very happy family. We didn't have a lot of material things, but we had more love than most," Joe said.

Bill Christie, the governor's father, was the third child of four in a family with roots in Germany, Ireland, and Scotland that had been in New

Jersey—specifically in Newark, almost exclusively in the city's 12th Ward—for generations, for one part of the family back to the future governor's great-great-great-grandparents, who arrived around 1850.

Bill's grandfather Hugh, a coppersmith, was an alcoholic, which compelled Bill's dad, James, the oldest of what would eventually be seven children, to leave school in the sixth grade to support his family. In an era when Newark was an industrial force, Bill's father later worked making camel hair belts that were woven on looms and used in manufacturing. He never took a day off. "In those days there wasn't welfare or if there was they didn't get on it. Dad was a serious dude," Bill recalled. Even so, he took time to read the newspaper every day and keep up with events.

Bill's parents were Roosevelt Democrats. His mother, Caroline "Carrie" Winter, was the first of four children born to John Winter and Caroline "Carrie" Lott, both of whom were born in America. Like most people of that generation, John had moved from job to job—as a rigger's helper, a tacker at a leatherworks, even a stint as a brewer at the Hensler Brewing Co., according to his 1918 draft card for World War I. Carrie Lott was the third of seven children born to Zerriak Lott and Walburga Ernst, who had arrived in the United States in 1880 from Baden, Germany. John's parents, Charles and Christine, emigrated from Bavaria and were married in 1880.

The Christies lived in the Ironbound section of Newark dominated by Italian immigrants, which helped prompt Bill as a nine-year-old to adopt a baseball team from a Midwest state he'd never visited. With nearly every kid in his Ann Street School neighborhood a New York Yankees fan, driven largely by ethnic pride in their star Joe DiMaggio, as well as local interest in the club's AAA minor league affiliate the Newark Bears, Bill—in a small act of rebellion—adopted the St. Louis Cardinals during the 1942 World Series.

"I didn't want to be a Yankee fan. I didn't want to be like everybody else," he said. "So the Cardinals in '42 beat the Yankees in five, and I said, 'That's my team.'" It's a tie that remains strong today—though even in the aftermath of the Cards' 2011 championship, he kids that being a Yankee fan might have been the better way to go.

Sandy and Bill had met in the late 1940s, when they attended rival high schools—she in Newark, he one town away in Hillside, where his family had moved when he was in the eighth grade. "I was a cheerleader. She was a flag twirler," Bill recalled. "Our schools played against one other, so we got a little bit acquainted there. We didn't go out at all, but we kind of looked at each other and said a few words."

Before they would connect, Bill went from high school to Breyers ice cream company to the Army. The Korean War was being fought, but Bill's ability to type led him out of the infantry to a noncombat support job known in the service as a Remington Raider. "I became a typist and part of three warrant officers who ran the place. So touch typing was a big plus, inadvertently," Bill said. "I got all my maturity in the Army. I think every guy ought to go to the Army. I met guys in there that let me know, and I drew from them, that I had to get a college education, for sure."

That was a lengthy process. Upon returning to civilian life, Bill attended night school on the G.I. Bill—first at Columbia University in New York because he wanted to be a broadcaster and the university had a relationship with NBC. On Wednesday nights, rather than go to Columbia, Bill would go to NBC. Still, the broadcasting dream eventually faded. "I guess I wasn't ambitious enough to be a broadcaster, because it would have meant sacrifice if you wanted to start. You always went out of town," he said. Plus, the cost for classes had jumped—from $25 per credit his first semester, to $30 and then to $50. (These days, it's more than $1,000.) The tuition benefits for Korean War veterans, $110 a month, weren't as generous as the direct tuition payments made to colleges for World War II vets. "So now it was costing me bucks," Bill said.

Instead he followed a favorite uncle, one who had first impressed upon Bill the value of higher education, into accounting. "He was the kind of guy that said to me, when I wasn't going to school, pre-Army, 'How much change do you have in your pocket?' He was one of those guys that wanted to tell you that if you keep doing what you're doing, your pockets aren't going to be as full as if you go to school," Bill said. "So he was the one that inspired me to go to college, before I went to the Army. But I wasn't really ready to go to college. When I went into the Army and came out, I was serious."

It wasn't until more than a decade after they'd first met—after Sandy had been married to a nice guy but divorced—that Bill and Sandy were reintroduced by mutual friends. "We later met at a dance," Bill said. "I used to play a lot of basketball. I was a pretty good basketball player, so I used to go to West Side High School, which is where she was, and I got to know guys over there. So we met at a dance and went out for a spell. And then I said, not only do I love this lady, but she's going to be a great mom."

After a short courtship, Bill and Sandy were married in 1961, in their late twenties, and found a place to live in Newark. Money was tight, Bill said. "We didn't have two nickels to rub together. We actually took out a loan to buy furniture and that sort of thing." Bill rode the bus to his job at Breyers ice cream during the day—first calling stores to encourage them to stock the company's ice cream, as in the "Breyers calling" advertising jingle of that day, then as a sign-shop supervisor. At night he would attend classes at Rutgers University in pursuit of an accounting degree. Sandy had been working at the Kearfott Co., a defense equipment manufacturer, when she and Bill met for the second time, then worked at Remington, the company that made the typewriters Bill had used in the Army—where she made a contact that got Bill's career started on the right foot.

"She was in the office, being the gal who handled a bunch of salespeople. So Remington Rand in those days sold their equipment to Peat Marwick. And now I'm going for accounting. And Sandy said to me, 'Gee, you know I know Wendell'—and again, she made friends easy—so she and Wendell had this fun relationship, so she said, 'How'd you like to interview with Peat Marwick?' And that's how I got into public accounting," he said. Still more than a year shy of getting his degree, Bill was put on the staff in 1961 doing proofreading and other tasks. "I got to meet a lot of the other guys on the staff. So they let me get on the staff before I had my degree," Bill said. "It worked out well. Actually, I took a decrease in pay to go to public accounting. But I thought it's going to be a brighter future."

Bill Christie's 1962 Rutgers graduation photo includes a pregnant Sandy, carrying their first child—expected by all concerned to be a daughter, not because of an ultrasound, which was still in development then, but because of a needle that swung in a circle, rather than back and forth, when dangled over Sandy's belly. That old wives' tale, perhaps not coincidentally, was paired with Sandy's stated desire to have a daughter and so they prepared for the anticipated October birth with a list of potential girls' names.

The baby arrived about a month ahead of schedule on September 6, 1962. Not only did the 4 a.m. contractions catch the Christies by surprise, but the young milk deliveryman was not expecting to see anyone on the usually deserted apartment stairs that morning. "Whatever flight it was, he's coming around not expecting to see anybody, and not only did he see somebody, but there's this woman with this baby about to deliver," Bill said. "I can remember he really looked frightened."

Bill figured this might be good time to discuss alternate names with his wife. He had been skeptical about the twirling needle method of gender detection and being a practical kind of guy, thought they should be prepared for a son.

"On the way to the hospital, I said to Sandy, 'In the event there's a boy, would you mind if I named him after my dad?' And I'm not inside Sandy's mind, but I have a feeling that she said, 'What the hell? It doesn't matter, it's going to be a girl anyway. Yeah, all right, sure, name him after your dad.' I'm not sure that's what she was thinking, but Chris is born. She never reneged on anything, so we were going to name him after my dad."

Bill's father was named James Christopher, and Bill's older brother—Chris's godfather—was James Christopher Jr. His brother's wife was also pregnant at the time and he was planning to name his son James III. The governor would later say in interviews, including one on Jimmy Fallon's late-night NBC show, that his father and uncle had argued over who had dibs on the name, but that's not how Bill recalls his conversation with his free-spirited brother.

"So I called him and I said, 'I know you're the junior, but I want to name him after Dad,'" Bill said. "And he said to me, and I can remember these words, because they were important, he said to me, 'I don't care, because what's the worst thing that can happen? When we're out together, we holler, "Jimmy!" and two kids come running.' That's what he said.

"Anyway, I said to myself, 'No, that doesn't sound right.' So I switched them. That's how Christopher James came out," Bill said. "Chris used to say to us, when he was younger, 'What were you thinking?' Kids used to bust him about that, Chris Christie, so he used to ask us what we were thinking. Now he loves it. At some point in time, it got to be a good thing, right? It's kind of easy."

The governor said his mother "claims to have never thought about the nickname until they got home, and my grandmother was there. And my mother said she picked me up out of the bassinet and said, 'Look at little Chris Christie.' And my mother said she nearly passed out. 'Oh my God. Chris Christie.'"

That wasn't the only dilemma with the name. Bill's sister-in-law was named Christine Christie, so now there were two Chris Christies in the family, temporarily. "My uncle divorced her, though, so she was not a factor much longer," the governor said with a laugh. "By the way, the real kicker to the story is that my uncle had two girls. So there is no James Christopher III. There is no James Christopher of that generation."

Two years later another boy—Todd—was born to the Christies. The twirling needle got that one wrong, too. In 1967, the Christies and their two children, then ages five and two, moved out of Newark. The procession was a common one for the city's middle-class white families, as racial tensions built in New Jersey's largest city, then boiled over in that summer's riots. Bill and Sandy borrowed $1,000 each from each of their mothers to put a down payment on a $22,000 ranch-style house in Livingston, just a few towns away but seeing itself as having far more in common with Morris County to the west than the troubled urban centers to the east.

Years later, as part of his pitch for revamping public education, particularly though not exclusively in urban areas, Christie would say his parents' decision to move out of Newark was crucial to everything he'd later accomplish. "I don't think I'd be governor," he said.

Efforts to have another child, perhaps adding that daughter Sandy hoped for, proved frustrating. Three pregnancies ended with miscarriages. Finally in 1973, the Christies learned they'd been approved to adopt a girl, then two years and three months old. "She was half–Puerto Rican, so the social worker said—and I'm very socially liberal, I don't know where that came from," Bill said. "So I said, 'Puerto Rican, what the hell is the difference?' Sandy and I were on the same page when it came to that kind of stuff."

"We had an aboveground pool in the backyard," Todd recalled, "We heard my mother screaming in the house. She comes running out and said, 'Oh my God, you're going to have a sister! I can't believe it. I can't believe it.' There was this tension in the house—what does she look like, what is she gonna be like? My mom hounded the adoption agency so much from that Thursday that on Saturday a woman stopped by the house, which she wasn't supposed to do, and brought one picture of my sister. I remember the four of us sitting around this circular kitchen table and my mom taped it to the wall and we all kind of like sat there and stared at the picture and said, 'This is going to be unbelievable.'"

The addition affected the family dynamic. "We changed a lot because of the difference in Dawn's personality. We knew Mom and Dad were intense and both had tempers, and we knew where the line was in the sand and when not to cross it," said Todd. "My sister had to learn that line, so for the first year or two we'd be shooting her a look like: Oh man, please, don't go there."

The boys were extremely protective of Dawn. Both remain so now, Todd particularly. She is the mother of five children close in age to Chris's children and stays in the background, so much so that even many close followers of the governor don't realize he has a sister. Dawn is guarded, very private, and happy to remain supportive behind the scenes, such as by making phone calls on her brother's behalf in the 2009 campaign.

"In the beginning of the campaign I think it bothered her that sometimes people didn't know he had a sister," said Todd. "She is very different from Chris and me, and I sense all she ever wanted to be was a mom. My own psychological analysis of my sister is when you spent the first two years of your life in a foster home with a bunch of other kids and don't have that kind of intense love that parents can only bring in the first couple of years, I think it affects you."

Bill passed the CPA exam and had a series of accounting and finance jobs, including a stint at Arthur Andersen, winding up as an administrator in the back office of a Wall Street investment firm called Wertheim & Co. His brother-in-law, Joe Grasso, got him the job; Joe himself had gotten in at Wertheim through his aunt's friend. Joe later left the firm after a partner in the company recommended that Joe become a partner—only to be told by colleagues that Joe would never be a partner because he wasn't Jewish and lacked a college education. Sutro & Co., a San Francisco–based security brokerage house and investment manager, selected him for a seat on the New York Stock Exchange, then later made him a partner. "Two years after I was a partner, Wertheim called and asked, 'Would you like to come back as a partner?'" he said. "I said, 'I'm the same Gentile without a college education. Thank you very much, no.'"

To get to Wertheim each day, Bill would drive to a train station and ride the rails, then reverse that commute for the way home. Every day the children would ask Sandy what train he was taking so they could gauge how much time they had to play. When Dad got home dinner was almost always a family affair, often between eight and nine. Sandy was like her mom, neither liked to cook—but she always did, Bill said.

"They both were fairly strict and most dinners were not a relaxing experience," Todd said of his parents. "It was a Q&A of what your day was like, and very much a reinforcement of whatever they were trying to do. Whether it was talking to us about school, whether it was talking to us about whatever sport we were playing, whether it was talking to us about whatever flak we may have given our mom that day, which was never dealt with very well. Dinner was not like let's just sit back and talk."

The Christies were demanding parents who would clash often, with Sandy inevitably winning most of those arguments. Bill says he can only remember two times when a dispute ended with her telling him that he was right.

"Sandy and I had an argument one time when the discussion got along the way, and she says, 'Yeah, you always say you're sorry.' And I finally got sick of hearing that and I said to her, 'Well, you know, let's talk about all the sorries I said. You know why I said I'm sorry?' And she said, 'No.' 'Well do you know the number of times I said I was sorry when I wasn't, I just wanted us to continue to talk?' She says, 'No, how many?' And I said, 'I don't know, it's in the 90 percents.'

"And it's true. You get to a point, I think you can kind of determine who's madder. I know I could. And I think she could, too. So one of us got off our horse," Bill said. "We were strong, did have disagreements, but it was a great marriage."

Chris explains his parents' relationship with customary humor: "This is what you need to understand: While my father is a wonderful guy and incredibly successful in his career, my father was merely a passenger in the automobile of life. You have a Sicilian mother, she drives the car. You'll notice all the different bits of advice I'm giving you are coming from my mother. Not because my father didn't give great advice, he just couldn't get it in."

After he said that before an audience at a *Washington Post* leadership forum, he was asked who drives the car in the governor's household. "The interesting thing about our relationship is my wife's a really successful businessperson on her own, so we're really copilots."

The questioner complimented the response.

"I'm blunt, but I am not stupid," Christie replied.

While Sandy dominated a room or a marriage through force of personality, she didn't do so through intimidation, except when necessary. Typically she was smiling, making friends, and dishing out the unvarnished truth.

"My mom was obviously a very strong personality," said Todd. "My dad, similar strong personality. Now he has mellowed with age, but my dad was very strong and had, at least I always viewed, as much of an influence on us as my mom. My dad was an incredibly hard worker, very strong-willed and a big disciplinarian," Todd said. "So growing up in our house was, I think, incredibly strict. They demanded a lot out of us and truly didn't allow for much room for error. So it was a very tough, strict house."

"It was kind of like my mother's in charge, and my father—I don't know that they agreed to do it that way, but my father would just not contradict my mother, I think out of fear more than anything else," Chris said. "My parents had lots of conflict. For me, growing up, they argued a lot. And it clearly had an effect on all of us. They were both very emotional, emotive people." Young Chris found himself "mediating a lot of those disputes, between the two of them or kind of just calming down Todd and Dawn in the aftermath of them."

"Chris would be fighting with Bill all the time. He probably fought with Bill more than anybody," said Chris's Uncle Joe. "They always had this relationship, where Todd really didn't have that. I think that Chris didn't particularly like the way that Bill treated my sister, and Chris being who Chris is, it offended him and it hurt him, because my sister and Bill had battles all the time. This is not casting all of it on him, because Sandy could stir it up. But he'd just keep it up."

Joe said that shortly before Sandy went into the hospital for the last time, he saw Bill and Sandy in a heated argument. "Here she's on her dying bed, and they're battling. Let her die in peace," Joe said. "There was no compassion. And I think she probably initiated it. I can't remember; we were all sitting, and she said something, and then he just went off. Bill used to go off the deep end pretty quickly, and I think he went off the deep end with Todd and Chris a lot. And that's why they gravitated to Sandy."

At one point while working on Wall Street, Bill took a risk that strained his finances and his relationship with Sandy. "He took a second mortgage out on the house and didn't tell her and was playing the stock market," Joe said. "And she called me and told me. [My wife] Victoria and I decided that we were going to put money aside for her so she wouldn't lose the house, if it came to that, but we made it specific, and I think in our will, that it was for her only, not for him. We were that close, she'd talk to me about it. We discussed it and said, 'Don't worry about it, you're not going to lose that house.'"

While the Christies argued frequently, it was one way they related to each other, there was no doubt they also loved each other. Once, as a Father's Day gift, Sandy and Todd arranged for Bill and Todd to spend a weekend in St. Louis watching the Cardinals, Bill's team since childhood, also adopted by Todd. She insisted on a hotel room that overlooked the stadium. "It was a great, great gift. It's one of those things that shows she was special," said Bill, who gets emotional talking about it. "As you know, the governor talks about her a lot. This is just another little human story. She was definitely different and very thoughtful."

The Christie clan was a close-knit one that welcomed friends as if they were extended family. Rick Mroz, friends with the Christies since college, remembers the family as "embracing" literally and figuratively. "They're huggers." He said the Christies "treated me like I was family. They talked to me like I was a peer."[5]

That outward affection has been handed down by the last generation, said Uncle Joe. "We hugged and kissed gentlemen on the cheeks way before it became popular in this country. That is what family was always about. There's no boundaries," he said. "My one brother-in-law, John, who passed away recently, he was this tough dockworker. But he'd always hug you and kiss you on the cheek and tell you he loved you."

Perhaps none of those family ties was closer than the connection between Sandy Christie and son Chris, who says he still thinks about her every day. He quotes her advice constantly, in private and public. "She would talk to Chris about things that she wouldn't talk to anybody else about," Bill said. When she was minutes from dying, it was Chris, not Bill, who was left alone with her for a final conversation as the rest of the family cleared the room, coming back in for her final breaths after Chris let them know she was ready to let go.

The Christie home was a house divided politically. Bill is a Republican, Sandy was a Democrat. Sandy's mom, Nani, was a liberal Democrat. The political discussions between Nani and Bill were heated, Todd said, wondering in retrospect how it was that his father allowed Nani to have so much influence on the kids. "She was there every weekend and sometimes during the week," Todd said. "She was an incredibly interesting woman who had been through a lot and was someone from that generation who grew up with nothing. My memory of her is that you'd wake up in the morning, walk down to our family room, where she slept on the couch, and you'd see her saying her rosaries, every morning without fail."

Joe Grasso says Nani, his mother, never talked about politics, except at the Christies' house. She would debate about religion often, but not politics. "When Chris was growing up, they used to debate politics all the time. It was unbelievable," he said. "My mother was just gravitated to him, because he was a—we call them a *chiacchierone* in Italian, it's somebody who's always talking. She'd say, 'Oh, *chiacchierone*, this kid is going to be president one day.' She did, bless her soul."

Joe's wife, Victoria, said she sees similarities in her nephew the governor, sister-in-law, and mother-in-law.

"There are some people who can relate to other people, and there's no pretense," Victoria said. "And that's the way I see Chris and Nani. But she was quiet, she was a quiet woman. Where Sandy, I don't think she was so quiet. Not at all. And Chris probably isn't quiet, either. Some people just have that quiet strength. And Sandy had a louder strength."

In 1979, when Christie was a high school senior, Sandy developed breast cancer. She survived, thanks to early detection and treatment. Her story later became part of Christie's 2009 race for governor, when Democrats aired misleading ads accusing Christie of wanting to eliminate insurance coverage for mammograms for some women, as Democrats spun his proposal to allow insurers to sell "mandate-free" policies that didn't adhere to the state's menu of required coverages.

Both Chris and Todd were athletic. Baseball was Chris's passion, and he played organized ball as a catcher starting in Little League. He had a good bat and a good arm, rapport with his pitchers and the beginning seeds of leadership. For instance, when his Babe Ruth League team traveled to Maryland for a tournament as a thirteen-year-old, his teammates commissioned Chris to write a thank-you letter to the local paper thanking their coaches. He got home, put his bag down, and retreated to his room to write a letter—without his father knowing. Friends assumed Bill had done it until Bill set them straight. "My friends were calling me saying, 'Wow, you wrote a nice letter for Chris.' So he could write very well, too."

Todd played baseball—a catcher, like his brother—as well as football, but Chris was limited to baseball by his parents because he had injured a knee when someone ran at him when he was riding a bike, making him fall off. He eventually needed arthroscopic surgery, and they didn't want to risk permanent damage from football.

"Banged it up. It was swollen," Bill said. "Anyway, we took him to a doctor, and it hurt to the extent that it atrophied, that big muscle we have. And when you atrophy it, it even causes more strain on the knee, so then he had to go through a whole bunch of exercises strengthening them. So it was serious."

Chris became captain of his high school baseball team, the Livingston Lancers. The experience ended on a slightly sour note, though. Chris's starting role as a senior was taken away by Marty Britt, who was Essex County's best catcher and had transferred from Newark Academy to Livingston High.

"Once Marty came in, that was it," said teammate Stephen Slotnick. "But it didn't matter. Chris was a leader no matter what. His job was to keep us together, and that really is what stands out about him."

After Chris lost the starting position he remained enthusiastic and was like a cheerleader. His father recalled, "Guys who are friends from Little League were sitting with me at the Greater Newark tournament game, and they said to me, 'My kid could never have done what Chris did. No way if they lost a starting job. They probably wouldn't have stayed on the team, never mind his attitude.'"

His running was something else again. "He was never known for his speed," said Slotnick. "I remember once in junior varsity, he hit a long triple and then got picked off third base. The coach was furious and yanked him out of the game."

The 1980 team was 28-2-1 and earned a trophy for the best team in the state. At a celebratory dinner to mark that championship, as well as one captured by the tennis team, the crowd gave a standing ovation to Chris, when he was recognized—by the tennis coach, actually—for his positive attitude and leadership after losing his starting job. "I want a kid like that on all of our teams every year," a still appreciative Bill recalls him saying.

"We felt like every time we walked on the field, we were going to win. And we did, pretty much," Christie said thirty years later. "Playing baseball, I think it teaches you leadership skills, it teaches you how to be a gracious winner and loser, it teaches you all that stuff—and I still carry that with me."[6]

When they weren't playing on school teams Chris and Todd played games often—sometimes Strat-O-Matic baseball inside, or Wiffle ball or touch football in the backyard or with other kids in the neighborhood. One of their childhood friends, Harlan Coben, became a bestselling novelist.

Another childhood friend, Chip Michaels, said the governor's old friends remain amazed by his profile. "We break his chops a little bit, just saying 'You're the governor?' It's crazy. He grew up like everybody else in New Jersey, So to see him as a celebrity, it's really odd. But he's the same guy. He's a grounded guy."[7]

The Christies grew up in tony Livingston, but their lifestyle wasn't affluent. Smaller than many homes in the township, there were three bedrooms and one bathroom in the 1,343 square feet of living space at 327 West Northfield Road. The boys and Bill would crowd in the bathroom together getting ready for their day, then Sandy and Dawn shared the facility. Vacations were rare, generally consisting of three- or four-day trips to relatives' houses in Ortley Beach or Seaside Park.

"That's what we knew, so it was great. We had a blast. It was great just to have three or four days alone with my dad, because he was working all the time," Todd said.

"A lot of our friends lived in much bigger houses," Todd recalled. "If they asked their parents for something, whatever the hot thing of the day was, they were getting it, and we weren't. Whenever we hounded my mom about it she would say, 'If you go into the backyard and find a money tree feel free to shake it because I could use some of that as well.' My mom was an amazing woman in her frankness. When I hear Chris speak a lot of times it is my mom. My dad had a much better filter."

Sandy didn't want to hear complaints and would invariably respond to bellyaching with an unsympathetic "Poor you." "It was like: 'I have no time for complaining. I'm a busy woman. I have no time for complaining. Something bothering you? Do something about it,'" Chris said.

"You always knew where you stood, believe me when I tell you, whether you were family or friends," Joe said.

Sandy was bold, brassy, funny, opinionated, and on occasion profane with language and raised finger gestures.

Asked by family members what help they could provide after she had her brain tumors removed, she asked for a cigarette. When she was near death, Joe and Todd were at the hospital nearly around the clock. To

Sandy and her family, as a child Joe was their prince—and Todd, a gregarious storyteller and comic, sought to play off that image in an off-color joke to his mother, Joe recalled.

"Since we were sleeping there in the room with her, we'd go out in the middle of the night, two o'clock, to the Dunkin' Donuts down the street, get donuts and coffee, and come back. So one morning, right before she died, she wakes up: 'Where were you?' Todd answered, 'We went out, I had to get your brother a hooker.' She didn't miss a beat. 'Not my brother!' And she had the blanket over her, she stuck the finger up, and flipped him the bone. That's typical Sandy. It's the dead truth. You had to see the look on Todd's face. 'Not my brother. Maybe you, but not him.' It was perfect Sandy."

Mrs. Christie found an income-producing temporary job for the Livingston School District doing a census for the board of education. They liked her and she liked working outside the house. The census job evolved into others and eventually she became a receptionist at the board office, a position she held for the next twenty years. "She was the meeter and greeter," said assistant superintendent Eunice Grippaldi, who worked with her for years. "She always had a stash of something special for the little kids when they came in. She was an institution here."[8]

Besides her work at the school, Mrs. Christie was a volunteer with Little League and a leader of the Parent Teacher Association of every school her children attended. "Whatever we were involved in, mom wanted to be there to help," Chris said. "She was tremendously supportive. She always told us that we could be whatever we wanted to be as long as we worked at it."[9]

Ironically, Mrs. Christie was a member of the New Jersey Education Association, the teachers union that would spend millions in an unsuccessful effort to keep her son from becoming governor decades later. "She talked about the dues being taken out and wondered what she was getting for that," Todd said. Chris, too, worked for the board of education for two summers doing routine office chores. "He doesn't talk about that too much," Todd joked. "They probably do a psychological check now to try to anticipate what you're going to do a little later on." Chris's other part-time jobs as a kid included work at the Livingston ShopRite grocery, where Aunt Minette was the pharmacist's assistant.

Chris was a straight-A student, his brother and sister average. Todd was smart but a free spirit—president of his senior class but always joking and talking in class. "Chris escaped some of the wrath at home, just because some of the antics that I had," recalled Todd. Being the younger brother of an overachiever had a downside: "It was difficult following him because I always heard from teachers, 'You're not him.'"

While Todd was different from Chris, Dawn was different from both of them. Bill thinks it was primarily that girls are generally tougher to raise than boys, as he'd heard from nearly all of his and Sandy's friends as parents. Or perhaps the Christies were just used to boys. But things were different—so much so that Bill recalls being shocked by the way Dawn and Sandy related.

"Sandy had a different relationship with Dawn than she did with the boys. We all did," Bill said. "Dawn would talk to Sandy in a way that I couldn't believe that Sandy allowed it. But she did. They're different. And parents I think are somewhat different. As a matter of fact, I think the mistake I made was I treated her like a boy.

"The main thing about raising boys is you can scare them. I mean, you could. I could scare them both. I might get cross, and I'd be looking, and they said they could tell, my eyes started bulging, that it was time to be quiet," Bill said. "Sandy was the same way. Sandy was tough on them, so that made it easy for us. In any event, I could holler at Dawn and I could just see the look on her face like, 'When you stop, let me know.' There was no scaring her. So she was different. She's a great mom. She's a doting mother, different from Sandy, big-time. Of course, she's easier on her kids than Sandy or I were."

Dawn's rebelliousness as a child continued into her early adulthood, and Chris and Todd have helped her navigate a number of difficulties, including a car accident and a divorce. She has since remarried and lives happily in the same Morris County township as her brothers.

Bill, himself a middle child, thinks birth order influenced his kids' personalities, with Chris, the oldest, being the most serious, the most studious, a natural leader from an early age.

"Dawn used to call Chris her second father because she was nine years younger. If I wasn't around, Chris was watching over her," said Bill, adding, "That's what she hated about him. Todd was more emotionally friendly, emotionally with her, and Chris was more—very, very supportive but no BS. Big brother and no BS."

Chris doesn't dispute the "second father" description. "Yeah, I mean, I was. And still am, to some extent."

"That's really the start of being a leader," Bill said. "To me, he always was more serious than his friends. Not serious serious—he had a great sense of humor, but he was extremely stable, easy to raise. Look, we knew he was a leader, clearly. He was very mature. He definitely controlled his siblings. He was Todd's guardian. If we wanted to know how Todd was doing, we asked Chris."

Chris and Todd were very close. "We shared a room together, a small room, thankfully we were both much thinner than we are now," said Todd, who called his brother his best friend. "We would always talk sitting in bed at night, almost unusually close."

Like most siblings, they "fought over everything," as Todd put it—including baseball, with Chris an avid Mets fan and Todd adopting the Cardinals, perhaps as a way of sharing a connection with his father. Their parents didn't mind if the boys argued, or even occasionally got physical, although Nani didn't tolerate that. The parents' rule was it had to stay in the house. "They would say," Todd said, "when you get outside of here don't let anybody think they can get in between you."

Chapter Two

Give Me a Law Book

Chris Christie knew from childhood, at an age when most kids dreamed of being a firefighter or an astronaut, that he wanted to be a trial lawyer. When he was ten years old and his grandmother asked what he wanted for Christmas, Chris said he wanted a law book. As Todd put it: "My mom had those books you keep with report cards and stuff and I'm going to guess from second grade if you could find that book where it says what do you want to be when you grow up he said lawyer."

Chris's interest in politics and public service began at an early age— "Chris wanted to be a politician when he was a baby," said his uncle, Joe Grasso—and found focus as a fourteen-year-old at Heritage Junior High School. His local state legislator, a former Assembly speaker named Tom Kean, who was running for the Republican nomination for governor, spoke at his school and struck a chord. "If I said right now I remember exactly what he said the day I saw him appear at my school, I'd be making it up. I don't remember," Chris said. "What I'm left with more is just the impression of a guy who I thought was just smart and nice and the things he was saying, I kind of gut-agreed with. I can't give you specifics as to what it was. I don't remember. But that's the impression of it, was that I like this guy and I agree with him. And I thought it's interesting."

Whatever caused the spark, at that point Christie decided he wanted to be involved in politics, but he didn't know how to get started. After school, after he had excitedly told his mother about the guest speaker and his desire to volunteer for his campaign, Sandy, the Democrat, ordered her son into the car and drove him to Republican Kean's house at the end of a long winding driveway on a huge estate. While Sandy waited outside, her respectful son slowly and reluctantly knocked on the door. Kean himself answered it.

Kean, New Jersey's popular forty-eighth governor, remembered the visit shortly after watching Christie be sworn in as the state's fifty-fifth governor. "His mother's at the car, he's looking at his mother, nervous, and says, 'Sir, I want to get involved in politics and I don't know how to do it, and my mother says I gotta ask you.' I said, basically, 'I'm thinking of running for governor. If you want to find out, get in the car. I'm going up to Bergen County. Come with me and see if you like it."

"He was not shy," Kean said. "Although his mother was the one who forced him up to the front door. . . . I think he's got the kind of character that it takes. He knows what he believes in, he knows what he wants to do and he knows who he is, and I think that's going to help."[1]

Chris traveled that same evening with Kean, a man he had met for the first time in that day's school visit, to the Oradell VFW, where he placed Kean's campaign materials on every chair, was introduced by Kean to state senator Ray Bateman, Kean's rival for the Republican nomination, and stood in the back of the hall and listened. "I don't remember much else about the evening, except that I just knew I was in the middle of a race for governor. I was watching it happen, and I thought it was really cool," Chris said. It was February 1977—and while it's impossible to imagine a kid doing the same thing today, and not just because of the troopers protecting Christie's house at the end of the driveway, it was even far-fetched for Sandy Christie thirty-five years ago, the governor says.

"No, they couldn't get to my front door today. Nor would parents be as trusting today as my mom was to Tom Kean," Chris says. "It kind of says something about Tom Kean, too, because my mother had never met him until the day that I went up to his house, and she felt like she knew him. He had represented them in the Assembly for a while, and she felt like she knew him. The trust level of my mother—who was not the most trusting person in the world, by nature—in retrospect makes the story even more amazing, that she let me go with the guy that night. But she felt like she knew this guy. She trusted him. She liked him."

Sandy dispatched Chris to the door by himself because she wanted her kids to be assertive.

"My mother was very assertive, and she expected the same of her children. You have something to say, say it. Don't hold back. You want to do something, go do it. Don't tell me you're afraid. What's the worst thing that can happen?" Chris said. "One of my mother's favorite questions to us as kids always was, 'What's the worst thing that can happen?' If we said we didn't want to do something, or were afraid of something, 'What's the worst thing that can happen?' And she would make us tell her what we thought the worst thing that could happen was. And then, most times, she would say, 'Well, that doesn't seem so awful, does it?'"

What was awful, for young Chris, was the election's outcome. He would periodically volunteer for Kean throughout the spring—sometimes traveling with the candidate, other times brought by Sandy to events or debates. And on the first Tuesday night in June, Chris was among those at the Holiday Inn in Livingston, just down the street from his house, as Kean lost the Republican primary to Bateman. (Bateman in turn went on to lose the November election to Governor Brendan Byrne, despite Byrne's popularity having plunged after he established the state's income tax.)

In Kean's 1977 defeat there was a lesson for his young charge, who recalls "how devastatingly disappointed I was"—and how impressed he was a day later, when the candidate gathered some of his so-called Kean Raisers to say thanks and sign the high school yearbooks of the older volunteers.

"The cool story is that the next day, he invited me and the two high school seniors from Livingston High School who were the head of his youth group to his home—the morning after the primary," Chris said. "The impression I walked away with that day was he was fine. I expected to see somebody who was going to be as devastated as I was, or worse, and he wasn't. He was fine. And I remember him saying to us, 'It's just another election. It'll be fine. Maybe I'll have the chance to do it again someday. It's not the end of the world. Nobody should be all that sad.' He was just very, very relaxed and at ease. I don't know whether he was putting on an act or if he really felt that way just to make us feel better, but he was great."

Chris's father remembered something else that impressed the teenager about Kean's talk with the kids. "Chris said somebody came into the room and said, 'We need you in the next room,'" Bill recalled. Kean's response was: "'When I get through with these young men, I'll come in.' That was impressive to Chris, to think that the guy didn't just tear away. He stayed until he was done."

Four years later, Kean secured the Republican nomination in 1981 and went on to win the state's closest gubernatorial election ever—by just 1,797 votes out of more than 2.3 million cast. Four years and one economic expansion after that, Kean won reelection by the largest margin in history, rolling up nearly 70 percent of the vote and winning in all but three of the state's nearly 570 cities and towns.

Christie excelled through Livingston High School, getting good grades and being elected president of his class for four years. One of the things that made Chris a good student was being an attentive listener with a great memory—and he remains so today, such as when he corrects a reporter's version of past events or recalls a year-ago conversation.

"We took one class together in high school and I remember feverishly taking notes, and Chris was sitting there listening and pretty much sketching out outlines of whatever was being said. I thought, 'Look at this guy, he is not going to do very well.' He got an A in the course and I got a C," Todd remembered.

Christie graduated in 1980, then headed off to the University of Delaware, close enough to home for a quick visit but far enough away to be independent. Why did a Jersey boy choose Delaware? For the most practical of reasons: "Because they gave me a lot of grant and scholarship money, was the bottom line," Chris said. "My parents did not have a lot of money, and I liked Delaware. I went to visit it. But it was certainly not my first choice."

His number one pick would have taken him to Washington, D.C.

"My first choice was Georgetown, and I didn't get in. And so when the financial aid package for Delaware came through, my father, who's a CPA, said, 'You know, Chris, you start to add up these numbers, I mean, this is pretty good.' And he said, 'Why don't we go back down to Delaware and look again?'" He returned with his parents in early spring, to avoid conflicting with baseball practice, met with some political science professors, and decided he liked it. "Really at bottom it was a financial decision, but it wasn't that I didn't like the place. I liked it, and I liked it enough to apply to it, and I was happy to go there. But really what motivated it for me was more financial than anything else."

Pausing for a moment to reflect, he conceded his life would have been much different had he gone to Georgetown—for one, he wouldn't have been involved in student government and met his future wife, Mary Patricia Foster.

"Yeah, in a whole bunch of ways," Chris said. "A much different school, a much different type of education. I wouldn't have met Mary Pat. I think when you wind up marrying a person that you date in college, you often think about what made her go there and what made me go there and how did that all happen."

It happened in part through university politics, with Chris en route to a bachelor's degree in political science he would earn in 1984. His sophomore year, Chris delivered a speech on the floor of the Delaware state Senate, as part of his unsuccessful push to allow student representatives on the college's governing board. "We lost," Chris recalled. Nevertheless, he said, "It was thrilling."[2]

Of greater consequence, student government introduced Chris to Mary Pat, who grew up in Paoli, Pennsylvania, a small middle-class town on the outskirts of Philadelphia. She was the ninth of ten children in an Irish family, raised in a big drafty house built in 1899 and teeming with activity—featuring three bathrooms, which sounds better than the Christies' one-bathroom home, but still had to accommodate a dozen people. "We weren't allowed to take showers in the morning until my father took a shower," said Mary Pat, recalling the daily run on short-supplied hot water. Her father was the eastern seaboard regional sales manager for Foster Wheeler, a

Swiss energy company with its executive offices in New Jersey, selling big-scale things such as power plants.

For Mary Pat, like Chris, Delaware wasn't her first choice. While Chris, a product of the public schools, had sought a Jesuit education at Georgetown, Mary Pat, who had attended Catholic schools all her life, wanted to attend the University of Virginia. She didn't get accepted, then visited a friend at Delaware and applied to its business school.

"So my safety school ends up being great," Mary Pat said.

"We were friends for a long time in college before we ever dated," said Chris. "We were always dating other people. So it wasn't one of these kind of love-at-first-sight things, at all. It was more really elimination of our previous love interests is what it turned out to be eventually. We were just good friends."

They'd met at the university's student center in Chris's sophomore year, her first at the school. He was in the Delaware Undergraduate Student Congress, and she was the Resident Student Association's DUSC representative. She wasn't exactly bowled over by his charm. "I kind of thought he was geeky," she recalls, laughing. "Yeah, I did. I thought he was a student government geek. He was very serious but I didn't mind that. I just thought he was *really* into student government. I was really into having fun."

Mary Pat had run for high school class president, though she didn't win. She remained active in student government at Delaware. When Chris ran as a junior for student body president, she agreed to run on his ticket for class secretary.

Chris's departure to Delaware had been a downer for his brother, though it did offer an opportunity for Todd and Bill to have a closer relationship. Two years later, though, that void was fixed easily enough when Todd followed his brother to Delaware and enrolled in political science classes—only to find that looking in Chris's notebooks for classes they both took was little help, since Chris took notes in a bullet-points outline and relied on his spongelike memory. He helped Chris win election as student body president, putting up signs and drumming up support, a precursor to similar efforts in the 1990s and in 2009. And in that campus campaign, Todd thought he saw a spark between Chris and Mary Pat.

"All through the campaign I thought I was picking up on a little bit of electricity there and Chris kept saying, 'Nah, nah, nah.' Not long after the campaign he called me on a Friday night and asked, 'Can I come over to your apartment?'"

Todd lived off campus and had a date visiting that night, so he tried to fend off the interruption. "I said, 'This really isn't a great time.' And Chris being Chris he said, 'I'm on my way.'"

When he arrived, Todd said, "He was just so serious about it. 'I just wanted to tell you, you were right and that Mary Pat and I are dating.' I remember looking at him and going: That's it? 'Yeah, that's it.' You have to get out of here."

Chris rolls his eyes when hearing Todd's version of the story, noting that his brother had been hounding him for weeks about his relationship.

"Now, he makes it as if, 'Well, why are you bothering me with this?' Except he had been asking me constantly, and I just didn't feel like I wanted to share the information with him," Chris said. "And then finally Mary Pat and I were going to be out someplace together in a way that it would be obvious that it was a date, and not just we happened to be in the same place together. And I didn't want him to find out from anybody else I was dating her, because he'd been asking so much and I'd just been refusing to tell him the truth. I said, 'No, no, no, no.' So I wanted him to hear it from me. I did not know, nor did he tell me when I called him and asked if I could drop over, that he had a young woman there."

Todd liked Mary Pat—she is bright, vivacious, and personable—but was concerned Chris was overly serious, having just ended a long relationship in college after being involved in a long relationship in high school. "You ought to date a bunch of people. What's the matter with you? Live your life a little bit. Date a bunch of people. You're too young to be this serious," he said.

Chris took all his relationships seriously. Later, in a commencement address to his alma mater, Chris said he took a poetry class at Delaware to impress his first college girlfriend. Whether the ploy worked is lost to history, but the gambit had the extra benefit of meeting a professor who made poets relevant to him. "I'm not sure this has made me a better lawyer, but what it did was help to take off the blinders. It opened my mind to other things."[3]

Mary Pat's personable warmth was welcomed by Chris's parents, who led a house of huggers and were underwhelmed by Chris's previous girl-friend. "She would come into our house and not even say hello. What the hell?" Bill said. "She would leave without even saying good-bye. I didn't like that at all. Sandy and I would talk about how we'd never seen any-thing like her at all.

"So anyway, we go to visit Chris at Delaware. This has to be his junior year, because he's already going to be the president of the student body," Bill said, "So we're sitting there, and this young lady comes in just full of life, turns to us and says, 'Hi!' We introduce ourselves as Chris's parents, and she's very chatty, and she walks down into his office there. And Sandy and I turn to each other and say, 'Now why can't he go out with somebody like that?' Well, apparently he was; that was Mary Pat. She was just as she is, very outgoing and friendly. A perfect match."

Victoria Grasso, Chris's aunt, said Mary Pat, like Chris's mother, can strike up an instant friendship. "You know when you have a connection with someone that's just immediate? I had that with Mary Pat, the first time" they had an extended talk, said Victoria, who married Joe in 1985. "It was at Minette's funeral. The two us were still kind of outsiders at that point. I remember the two of us sitting next to each other and we just kind of could share things, like 'God, this family is so tight.'"

Mary Pat and Chris dated for two years—she, a year behind Chris, was student body president the year after Chris. That turned out to be a busy senior year for her—school president, heavy course load, all the while maintaining a long-distance relationship, Chris having returned to New Jersey to attend Seton Hall Law School. They got engaged before she graduated.

After college, Mary Pat moved in briefly with an aunt and uncle in North Jersey and got a job at Donaldson, Lufkin & Jenrette. They married in March 1986, during his law school spring break. After a honeymoon at Couples, an all-inclusive resort in Jamaica, their wedding gift from Bill and Sandy, their first place together was at 1B Ashwood Avenue in Sum-mit, a studio apartment over Windhorst Liquors.

"You walk up these stairs over the liquor store, and there were two apartments, one on either side. We were in the one to the left as you went up the stairs," Chris remembered. "My mother-in-law and father-in-law came for dinner four or five weeks after we got home from our honeymoon, and years later my father-in-law told me that my mother-in-law had cried two-thirds of the way home to Pennsylvania after that dinner, saying, 'I can't believe my daughter is living in such a dump.' But for us, we knew it wasn't a great place, but we were twenty-three and twenty-two. I was still in law school, and I was working part-time. She was working at DLJ in New York for $20,000 a year on the trading desk there as a trading assistant. So it was what we could afford, and we were newly married, and who knew better?"

"I couldn't believe how much we had to pay for it," Mary Pat said. "Six hundred dollars a month, and it was one room cut by a half-wall with an efficiency kitchen, like a half-refrigerator, a burner. I was just happy I barely spent any time in it."

The upside was Mary Pat could walk to the train station for a ride into Manhattan, which eliminated having to pay for expensive parking. Otherwise, it was particularly hard on her, not exactly a sports fan at the time, because 1986 was the year that the Mets won the World Series. Baseball lover Chris wanted to watch every minute of every inning. "That was a big issue in their marriage the first year," Todd said. "Here's Chris wanting to catch every inning and she is on the other side of this half-wall in their bedroom reading."

"It was like Mets fan nirvana. Never was a better year before, never has been a better year after," Chris recalled. "So it was a tough year to have your first year of marriage, and we had a lot of arguments in that first year of marriage that almost all exclusively were about me watching Mets games.

"There's a little bit of tension anyway when you have one person in the house who's a student working part-time and another person in the house working full-time who's commuting into Manhattan every day," he said. "So she'd leave at 5:45, 6 a.m. every morning. I'd still be sleeping. Then I'd roll out of bed, go to law school, work in the afternoons or early evenings at the law firm where I was working, then come home, and the first thing I'd do when I come home is flip on the game. She'd be like, 'Let's talk about our days,' and I'd be like, 'Yeah, let's talk about it while we're watching the game.' So that did not make me popular, and we had any number of dustups in that first six, seven months, that almost all involved the Mets."

The Mets obsession was a bit of a surprise to Mary Pat. The games weren't on TV every night in Delaware. And when they saw each other on occasional weekends when he was enrolled in law school and she was still in Delaware, he wasn't flipping on the game during those short visits.

"It wasn't like I would say, 'Okay, let's go grab dinner, and then I need to watch the Mets,'" he said. "I would sacrifice watching baseball for the weekend when I was with her, and it no doubt became a big shock to her when we started living together after we were married that I was watching baseball every night."

"I actually didn't even know Chris was such an avid baseball fan, honestly, when we started dating. In fact, I probably didn't even appreciate it until after we were married," she says, in diplomatic understatement.

After eleven months in Summit, Mary Pat found another apartment on the second floor of a two-family house at 247 Prospect Street in Westfield, with cheaper rent, a garage, and just two blocks from the train station. They left that for their first house, at 515 Elm Street in Cranford, which was a little bigger but old and right off busy Centennial Avenue, what the Christies called "just a more expensive dump." It needed a lot of work, which it didn't get right away because Chris was not, in the words of his brother, "the handiest man around."

"We bought a house in Cranford that was just a complete disaster. It was the typical thing you do when you're young and stupid," said Christie, who was around twenty-five years old then. "Everybody told us not to buy the house. Bad location, needs too much work, you're not going to get your money out of it. You know, all the things your parents, my parents told me, her parents told her. We said, 'No, we're buying the house. We don't care.'"

Parents know best. They paid $160,000 in 1989 for what Christie later dubbed "The Nightmare on Elm Street," put $15,000 of work in it, then sold it in October 1991 for $140,000. The Christies weren't too concerned: Chris had earned his law degree in 1987, was hired at the Cranford law firm Dughi & Hewit the same year, where he specialized in securities law and appeals, and was well on his way toward becoming a partner in 1993. Mary Pat was also doing well on Wall Street.

"We were there for about not quite two years, and we had to get the hell out," Christie said. "Plus, I had started to make some money at that point; Mary Pat had started to make money at that point, so we could afford to go. If we took a loss on the house, it was not going to be a determinative factor where we could move next."

Christie's mother suggested they look at a house her friend was selling on Kennaday Road in Mendham, a few towns west of Livingston in Morris County.

"We went and looked at the house, and we hated it," Christie said. "That was the first time I had ever been in Mendham." They liked the town, just not the house. Driving back out, they saw a new development being built that intrigued Mary Pat—so they checked it out, though Chris said they weren't going to build a house.

"We went through a model house that they had there, and we liked it. She liked it, in particular, which is the most important part of the story. She liked it," said Christie. "So then we just started looking for houses, mostly in Westfield. And every time we got done looking at a house, she said, 'Yeah, it was nice, but it wasn't like that one in Mendham.' Well after I went through four or five weekends like this, I finally said to her, 'Let's just go back to Mendham and talk to the guys.'"

With the 1991 recession working in their favor, as it made the builders anxious and eager to complete a deal, the Christies bought a vacant lot for $110,000 in March 1992 and had their home built, one of the first in the development, at what would eventually be 60 Walsingham Road.

Things were happening fast by 1993 for Christie—owner of a new home in Mendham, about to be a first-time father, ready to jump into a combative first act of his political career, and making partner at his law firm, Dughi & Hewit. The impact of his time there persists, as Christie employs in state government people he'd met at the firm. As governor, he would nominate the firm's partners who'd hired him to state boards—Russell Hewit to a paid position on the board of Horizon Blue Cross and Blue Shield of New Jersey and Louis Dughi Jr. to an unpaid position on the state Fish & Game Council. Dughi was never approved by the state Senate.

A former partner of Christie's at the firm, Bill Palatucci, who remains his closest friend in politics, said Christie made a huge impact as the firm's hiring partner. "He was kind of the glue that held the place together. I was there ten years. I barely knew everybody's first name after ten years. He knew every secretary and paralegal's name. He knew their spouse's name. He knew their children's names," Palatucci said. "It was just a great place because it was a very—fun's the wrong word, but it was just a very positive atmosphere. You enjoyed working with the governor as an attorney, and you would want to work on his cases if you were a paralegal or a secretary. You wanted to work with Chris Christie."

By that time settling into a comfortable home, one similar in size to Mary Pat's childhood home but more than twice the size of the house where Chris was raised, the Christies started their own family—son Andrew, born in 1993, and daughter Sarah, born in 1996. They then moved to a bigger house five minutes away—purchased for $775,000 in 1998, the nearly seven-thousand-square-foot home on six acres carried a property tax bill of over $36,700 in 2011. They sold their former home for $630,000 in 1999. The Christies welcomed two more children to their family—son Patrick, born in 2000, and daughter Bridget, born in 2003.

Mary Pat, who has worked most of the time since graduating high school, obtained a master's degree in business administration from Seton Hall University that she earned at night and works part-time as a bond trader in Manhattan, where she job-shares with another woman and has earned as much as $500,000 a year, even with reduced hours.

She takes part in her children's school activities and as New Jersey first lady is interested in projects involving women and children. While the governor's work schedule and political travel make family meals a bit more difficult, she said she still tries to cook dinner for the family at least four nights a week. Risotto is a favorite, as is chicken "a gazillion different ways" and a marinated flank steak from Burrini's Olde World Market in Randolph.

"I like to cook. I wish my family liked everything I cooked. I like to be adventuresome. I really like cooking," Mary Pat said. "I am sometimes exhausted, but it's also really important for me—I think it's a role that I've taken on—that my family is exposed to different foods and also that they eat relatively healthy. Because on the days that I'm not cooking—like Sunday they went to the football game, and I'm like, okay, I know that when I'm not cooking, they're eating rather poorly."

The Christie children attend Catholic schools—a point critics would use to question his sincerity about public education when he became governor, generating an angry and consistent none-of-your-business response. "That's my choice, and my wife's choice. We happen to believe that a religious education is an important part of an overall education for our children. So, we've decided to send our children to Catholic school because we believe that," Christie said. "It's no shot on the public schools. I'm a graduate of the public schools. My wife's a graduate of parochial schools. When our child became five years old, I wanted him to go to public school. She wanted him to go to parochial school. All of our kids go to parochial school. So, you can figure out who wields the power in the Christie household.

"I've come to agree with her that I think it's an important part of our children's growth as human beings. And so, we've made that choice," Christie said. "But guess what? I still pay $38,000 a year in property taxes, most of which goes to the public school system in my town. And we don't utilize it. And I don't complain about it because that's my responsibility as a citizen of my town and my state. But then don't tell me that I can't be serious about public education because I don't send my children there. Every child is my responsibility in this state. And that's the kind of liberal know-nothing thinking that just drives me crazy."[4]

The family decided to remain in their Mendham home rather than move to the stately state-owned governor's mansion in Princeton. The governor reserves many weekends for activities with the children and sports. "Our children are in a good place right now in their schools, in their life. It's a really fragile time for them. We have our priorities," Mary Pat said.[5] Some of the bigger controversies of Christie's term as governor have been rooted in those sorts of priorities—such as staying at Disney World with the kids, a Christmas trip they had been promised, instead of returning to New Jersey during a crippling blizzard, and taking a state helicopter to his son's baseball game, landing just beyond the playing field.

Christie said he and Mary Pat have tried to follow her parents' example, rather than his, and avoid loud conflicts in front of their children. "She knew about my parents and the arguing that they did and wasn't really enamored with the idea any more than I was," he said. "So we kind of made a deal with each other early on: As much as we can, if we have to have an argument, we kind of wait until they're gone to bed and asleep if we have to argue about something. It happens in our room with the doors closed. We're not yelling at each other in the kitchen or out in the backyard or anything like that.

"We want them to have both a calm and a united front among the two of us, and I think we both agree that both are important, that your children really feel threatened if they feel that you're split, that you're arguing," Chris said. "They don't know at a young age how to put that in perspective, and there's so much divorce and everything that goes on around them."

Divorce has been common in Christie's family. His grandparents got divorced in 1941, and his mother divorced her first husband. His father didn't get divorced but did remarry and move to the Jersey Shore after Sandy's death; his dating initially angered his children, who felt it was disrespectful. Sandy's sister Minette divorced once, her brother Joe twice. Both of Christie's siblings divorced. Chris and Mary Pat have been the exception.

The Christies said they try to maintain a united, common front.

"They [the children] don't try to divide and conquer anymore," Chris said. "It's fruitless, and they know it."

"We're always on the same page is how we say it," Mary Pat said. "Whether we are or we aren't that's what they think. And I think that that goes a long way to getting them to listen."

"We make it very clear to them that, like, don't try to play it," Chris said. "Because then they come to me and ask me for something, my first question is, 'Did you talk to your mother about this?'"

"And I use it in the same way when I'm not sure what I want the answer to be, and I know that this is something we need to discuss," Mary Pat adds. "I say, 'We need to talk to your father about it first.' Then we decide together."

Chris and Mary Pat decide nearly everything together, not just parenting. They regularly sit at the end of every year to assess each of their careers and map out next steps—particularly in Chris's years as federal prosecutor, when backers were encouraging him to run for office. She was involved in campaign meetings in 2009, helped raise funds for the race, took part in the sit-downs in 2011 at which a run for president was being analyzed—an equal partner in the Christie household.

"Absolutely. Underline the word equal. Underline both words, equal partner," Christie friend Bill Palatucci said. "Very smart, tough as nails, a very successful businessperson in her own right. Very worldly person, I think she's had a lot of experiences growing up in a big family, doing well on Wall Street and in the financial world all that time. So Mary Pat is an equal partner, and they make all those decisions together."

CHAPTER THREE

Run Out by Republicans

Chris Christie had a promising future in law but there was that other ambition burning inside him, a sense of public service first sparked as a teenager when former Assembly speaker Tom Kean, the future governor, spoke
to his class. In school politics Christie was successful and he yearned
for the big time. He made his own opportunity in 1990 with another
Christie—Somerset County politician Christie Whitman, a former president of the state's utility regulation board, who was urged to run against
U.S. senator Bill Bradley—Rhodes Scholar, Olympian, basketball legend
at Princeton and in the NBA for the New York Knicks. Bradley was seeking a third term after winning his second with 65 percent of the vote, and
top-tier challengers were a scarce commodity that year in the Republican
field.

One of the people urging her to challenge Bradley was Bill Palatucci,
who was preparing for the state bar exam to begin a legal career but was
already a renowned campaign veteran, having directed Kean's 1985 reelection romp and George H. W. Bush's win in the state in 1988, in which
Bush started out 17 points behind in the polls but won by nearly 14 points.
Bush visited the state eight times, including twice as the race drew to a
close, making campaign swings through Paterson, Bloomfield, Union City,
South River—atypical places for a Republican to tread. (That was the

Republicans' sixth straight win in New Jersey in presidential contests; none has won the state since.) Someone suggested to Christie that he contact Palatucci, who then put him in touch with the Whitman campaign.

"I think he wrote some white papers on some issues for them," Palatucci said, admitting he didn't remember the phone call. He does remember meeting Christie when he ran Bush's reelection effort in Jersey in 1992, the one he lost to Bill Clinton. After the defeat, Christie invited Palatucci, who had passed the bar exam but figured he'd return to political consulting and lobbying, to instead come aboard at Dughi & Hewit—and he did, part-time at first but eventually becoming a partner. "Because I'm older and my name ended up being on the firm, everybody thinks I recruited him to my firm, but it was the other way around," Palatucci said.

It marked the beginning of a friendship so close that Todd Christie said Palatucci is like a second brother for the governor. Their time together was mostly spent at work, rather than family social events or on weekends. But they have developed an innate trust and loyalty—and the same full-honesty, hammer-it-out-in-private pattern that the Christie brothers have long deployed, at their parents' insistence.

"Behind closed doors, they have arguments about everything," said Todd, who's now a political fund-raiser partner with Palatucci. "They hash it out, and once they get out, they're on the same page. I don't think I can ever recall Bill saying a bad word about Chris—I mean ever, not just since he became governor, but ever, in front of anybody. Even in terms of when he's talked to me. If he's really mad, I can tell, and he certainly tones down what he says to me. But they have a really unique relationship. I think right to this day, Bill's one of the only people that says exactly what he thinks."

Palatucci grew up thirty minutes from Christie's Livingston but a world away environmentally. His father owned a little neighborhood bar, Frank's Tavern, next door to their home, and that's where the future campaign operative shaped his attentiveness to working-class politics.

"There was a little factory in town. I vividly remember getting ready for school or having breakfast in the morning and, when the night shift let out, if [the bar] was not open right on time, there would be a friendly knock on the door: 'Frank on his way?' 'Be right there!' My dad would have to hustle over," Palatucci said, "So that was kind of my upbringing. For my politics it was a typical, blue-collar shot-and-beer place. No food, just a bar. These were Reagan Democrats, blue-collar factory guys."

Palatucci had access at a young age to a focus group every night— plumbers, carpenters, and factory workers sharing some beers, commenting on the news and the ads during the ball game. His father would work from breakfast time until past midnight, and Bill would visit him and observe from the other side of the bar.

"It gave me a great antenna for bullshit," Palatucci said. "If I wanted to see my dad, I had to go next door and sit on a stool and watch the Yankee game. And different news things would come on, or TV commercials. These guys would look at Bill Bradley and say, 'Who the hell does he think he is? I loved him as a New York Knick, but this stuff about running for president is bullshit.' Or his unwillingness to take a position on Jim Florio's $3 billion tax proposal. To me, the guys in the bar, they all had a position on hot stuff. They'd be very happy to tell you."

Palatucci's instincts were right. Political unknown Whitman came close to defeating Bradley in 1990; he decided not to run again, then made an unsuccessful bid for the Democratic presidential nomination in 2000. Whitman capitalized on her newfound profile and won two terms as governor.

In April 1993, the politically unknown Chris Christie, thirty years old and a registered voter in Morris County for barely six months, unexpectedly announced that he would challenge incumbent state senator John Dorsey, an eighteen-year lawmaker, in the Republican primary. "That was kind of his first attempt to figure it all out," said Palatucci, his friend and informal sounding board.

It was a big and brassy move because Dorsey was the Senate majority leader. Just as bold for a Republican from his conservative neck of the woods was the theme of Christie's debut: Saying "we already have too many firearms in our communities," he jumped into the race protesting Dorsey's opposition to New Jersey's ban on semiautomatic weapons. The ban was among the signature pieces of legislation passed in the first half of

Democratic governor Jim Florio's term, and Republicans—who stormed back to win overwhelming majorities in the legislature in a 1991 tax revolt—tried to repeal it but couldn't muster the votes needed to override Florio's veto.

"The issue which has energized me to get into this race is the recent attempt by certain Republican legislators to repeal New Jersey's ban on assault weapons. In today's society, no one needs a semi-automatic assault weapon," Christie said, being careful to make clear he respected the Second Amendment, but would work to prevent any "weakening" of gun laws.[1]

That first race introduced several reform themes that would be associated with Christie throughout his political career.

He pledged to propose bills against "inflated pensions" for lawmakers, calling them "inappropriate for part-time legislators."[2] He pressed Dorsey to follow stricter limits on campaign donations from political action committees and refuse donations from any companies or vendors that did business with Parsippany–Troy Hills, one of four municipalities for which the senator was municipal attorney.[3]

Bold as it was, Christie's campaign lasted just nine days, shot down in its infancy by thirty-seven names.

Petitions to run for legislature need one hundred signatures from registered voters eligible to vote in the election—meaning in Christie's case, he needed John Hancocks from one hundred Republicans who lived in the 25th District's eighteen towns. Thirty-nine of the names on his petition were invalidated because they came from people who lived outside the district, apparently not aware that Mendham Township where Christie lived and Mendham Borough had been divided in redistricting two years earlier. (Welcome to New Jersey, where the overstocked supply of municipalities includes more than a dozen pairs in which one place shares the same name as a neighbor, separated only by their "borough" or "township" form of government.) Christie asked an administrative law judge to accept thirty-seven new signatures collected the previous night, after Dorsey challenged his petition. No dice. Dorsey needled Christie, saying he didn't know the district because he'd lived there less than a year. "He may be an aggressive candidate, but he doesn't seem to understand the rules of law," Dorsey said.[4]

Christie was represented in the ballot challenge by Daniel Lindemann, an associate in Christie's law firm who also represents another recurring theme in Christie's career—trusted people around him keep getting recycled and rewarded. He is known for his loyalty and he demands it from others. Lindemann was on Christie's transition team in 2009, studying the state's bountiful independent authorities, which would become a Christie gubernatorial target, and as governor he appointed Lindemann to the New Jersey Urban Enterprise Zone Authority.

When Dorsey became entangled in a controversy about blocking the reappointment of a state Superior Court judge, Democrats approached the aggressive young Christie about switching parties and becoming their candidate to face Dorsey in November. "I was flattered, but I will continue to work through the Republican Party," Christie said.[5] The Democratic county chairman claimed it was Christie who initiated the idea.

As it happened, Dorsey lost to Gordon MacInnes, a rare Democratic victory in Morris County. MacInnes was beaten four years later and customary Republican dominance restored in a race that launched the political consulting career of Mike DuHaime, who went on to work on Rudolph Giuliani's campaign for president, then Senator John McCain's—and the next year, Christie's campaign for governor.

Like they say, when you fall off the horse the best thing to do is get back on right away. And so Christie hit the campaign trail again the next year, this time seeking to be a Morris County freeholder, which is similar to a county councilman or commissioner. He had a reform platform of eight to ten items, pledging things such as ending health benefits for part-time elected officials. "It's interesting now in hindsight because having been U.S. attorney and the kinds of things he's talked about as governor, it's pretty consistent," observed Palatucci. Again, Christie looked to oust an incumbent and fellow Republican. He was aiming for one of three seats up that year held by Frank Druetzler, Cecelia "Cissie" Laureys, and Edward Tamm.

Christie's team included Jack O'Keeffe, a feisty former freeholder director who embraced his reputation as Christie's ally and mentor. "We have had an exceptional relationship. The first day I met him . . . there was almost an immediate chemical reaction, a good feeling," said O'Keeffe, who died in 2011.[6] "He has a knack for conversing with the public about what he is doing and why. I think he's almost magical in his ability to get approval from people."[7]

They went after county management, especially regarding the slow progress in construction of a new jail. It got nasty. Christie said the incumbents were failures and an embarrassment to the party. Laureys, a sixty-two-year-old grandmother, compared Christie to Nazi propaganda minister Joseph Goebbels.[8]

Christie accused Laureys of lying when she said there were no minutes kept by a committee studying police computer systems, and demanded she step down. "I don't know why she did it, but she lied and it's not the first time she lied about the whole thing," Christie said.[9] (Remember the "lying" theme; it returns when Christie is governor.) Minutes were kept, but Laureys denied being purposefully deceitful and said she felt intimidated by Christie. He didn't ease up. "She knew damn well what I was asking for."[10]

The issue of open government (and the lack of it) dominated the race, with persistent questions about the incumbents' unwillingness—until a rejected request by Christie for information was followed by pressure from prosecutor Michael Murphy—to provide minutes of private talks regarding the $9.5 million purchase of two trash transfer stations. Christie launched an ad claiming the incumbents were the targets of an investigation by Murphy's office—referring to the prosecutor's efforts to get the freeholder board to release the trash transfer station records, a matter that included no interviews with witnesses, no detectives, and no intent to lead to a prosecution. Murphy called it an inquiry. "It's a matter of semantics," Christie said.[11]

The incumbents couldn't get a judge to block the ad, but Christie agreed to add a trailer to it indicating the investigation was over and the documents released. It took nearly a week for the change to be made. The incumbents sued for slander. Christie said the lawsuit didn't stand a chance, which is usually the case when suits are filed in the heat of political contests. "It also is very difficult to slander the reputation of people who have been called fumbling, bumbling, inept amateurs by the local press," he said.[12] He refused to apologize, even though the lawsuit would have been dropped if he did so publicly.[13]

In the June 1994 primary, Christie finished first in the nine-candidate field. O'Keeffe won, as well. The losing candidates stuck with their lawsuit. "They just can't accept that the election is over. . . . Once you get into politics, you have to expect to lose and if you do, you have to be able to do it gracefully," Christie said.[14] The lawsuit ended with a settlement in November 1996. Terms weren't disclosed, but as part of it Christie formally apologized to Laureys and Tamm in a one-page letter published as an advertisement in Morris County daily and weekly newspapers. "These advertisements were not appropriate," Christie wrote in the ad. ". . . I fully intend, in any future campaigns in which I am involved, to be much more sensitive to the impact of such tactics."

Christie saw it as a learning moment, for him and for anyone else interested in politics. He addressed it again in 1997 when discussing a potential state Senate bid: "I think if more people say they're sorry if they did something wrong, we'd have a more civil system. . . . Did I do this intentionally, knowing it was wrong? No, But it turned out the statement wasn't accurate, and I regret any damage it may have caused."[15]

During the general election campaign, when Democratic candidates called for the county to restore its former annual $35,000 contribution to Planned Parenthood of Greater Northern New Jersey, which was eliminated in 1989 after an abortion controversy, Christie opposed restoration—but on financial grounds, not ideological. In fact, he said he donated money to the group. "I support Planned Parenthood privately with my personal contribution and that should be the goal of any such agency, to find private donations," he said. "It's also no secret that I am pro-choice. . . . But you have to examine all the agencies needing county donations and prioritize them. I would consider all groups looking for funding, but there is a limit and we have to pick and choose."[16]

Christie won the freeholder post in November easily—no surprise, since in Morris County the Republican Party has captured every freeholder race, except for one at the height of Watergate, since 1910. He spent $105,000, including $60,000 of his own, and finished first. A bitter Laureys had refused to endorse him, mustered around 110 votes in a write-in campaign, then didn't voluntarily relinquish her office keys, forcing the freeholders to make a formal request for them.

After the animosity the campaign generated, Republican Party leaders considered adopting a code of conduct clamping down on negative campaigns.[17] Christie called the idea ridiculous and noted in passing that one member of the subcommittee studying the idea, Jean Dismore, had yelled at Christie's wife, Mary Pat, at a campaign stop on the day of the primary with the ultimate Garden State put-down, "telling us we are acting like Jersey City politicians."[18] (If you don't think he saw that as an insult, fast-forward to 2011 and 2012, when his campaign trail put-downs of President Barack Obama included calling him a "Chicago ward politician.") The well was already so poisoned that county GOP chairman Oscar Doyle created an ethics tribunal to review complaints about negative campaigning, but Christie never signed Doyle's ethics code, saying Doyle wouldn't explain how it would work. "I'm not going to participate in any kangaroo court that Oscar is conducting," said Christie.[19]

Christie quoted the liberal Democrat Adlai Stevenson at the January 1995 freeholder meeting where he was sworn into political office for the first time.[20] He then wasted little time making waves, asking fellow freeholders at that first session to take pay cuts and eliminate their taxpayer-supported health benefits. The idea was voted down but Christie went ahead, voluntarily cutting his $25,000 salary by 25 percent and declining to take health benefits. The money saved by those moves was applied to treatment beds for drug-addicted county residents at Daytop Village.[21] (Christie would later join Daytop's board, and in 2010 his inaugural committee directed $136,800 in leftover funds to the charity.)

Christie and O'Keeffe also raised immediate questions about the new jail contract. The board voted to look into the costs for replacing jail architect George Kimmerle, who had never designed a jail before and had been hired in a 4–3 vote without bidding, a formal procedure, or even notice given to three of the freeholders. "I'm sick and tired of people hiring their political friends," Christie said. Kimmerle had made small amounts of campaign donations to the freeholders who hired him.[22] As Christie and O'Keeffe pushed, at one point holding a rogue hearing with alternate architectural firms without the full board's consent, Kimmerle's lawyer threatened legal action. When design costs grew to as high as $46 million, after $38 million had originally been forecast, the freeholders fired Kimmerle when he sought payments exceeding his $2 million contract.

The jail contract was rebid and came in at $32 million. It now cost less—but had been made much smaller, and the per-square-foot cost was actually higher than in Kimmerle's design. Ironically, after he was fired, Kimmerle's design won an award from the American Correctional Association and an American Institute of Architects committee.[23]

Less than four weeks after taking office as freeholder in 1995, Christie said he was thinking about running for the General Assembly, the lower house of the New Jersey Legislature. One of the district's two Assembly seats was being vacated. The other was held by an appointed incumbent, Anthony Bucco, a former freeholder who'd lost freeholder primaries in 1992 and 1993 but was picked by party insiders for the Assembly when Rodney Frelinghuysen moved up to Congress. Republicans shook their heads at Christie's impatience. "He's been a freeholder for what, 20 minutes?" candidate Michael Patrick Carroll asked.[24]

Christie officially jumped into the race April 3. "I've now established the beginning of a record. When I make promises, I keep them," Christie said.[25] If he was elected to the Assembly, he promised he would quit the freeholder board—which wasn't required in New Jersey's era of multiple-office holding. Carroll challenged Christie to sign his "Contract with Morris County," but Christie derided it as a ploy by Rick Shaftan, Carroll's political consultant. Shaftan would later remain a vocal critic of Christie as campaign manager in 2009 for Christie's chief rival for the GOP's gubernatorial nomination, Steve Lonegan. Bucco was dismissive. "If all you need to be a legislator is unlimited money and uncontrolled ambition, with no record of accomplishment, then the state's in a lot of trouble."[26]

Christie pledged to cut his legislative salary and staff by 20 percent, refuse health benefits, and cut spending and taxes. Bucco, angry with Christie over his representations about tax increases at the county and municipal level under Bucco, referenced a bill moving through Trenton that would penalize candidates for distortions. "We should call it the Christie bill," said Bucco, calling him a "poster child for what everyone wants to get rid of in politics: Someone who will say or do anything to get elected."[27] He also ran an ad that depicted Christie as a diaper-clad baby.[28]

Christie finished fourth. When he extended a hand to Bucco at GOP election headquarters that night at the Governor Morris Inn in Morris Township, "he was greeted by a stare that could have chilled a jug of Prestone," as *The Star-Ledger* described it.[29] Bucco said the victory sent a message that Morris County "will not tolerate negative campaigning and character assassination."

Party insiders were pleased they'd rebuffed Christie, who had now fought the Republican establishment three straight years. Christie had dropped $45,000 of his own money into the campaign. "I feel I have learned a lot. You have to talk much more about yourself than about somebody else," Christie said.[30]

That unpleasantness behind him, Christie concentrated on his work as freeholder. Ironically, given his insistence as governor a few years later that all disagreements remain internal and that his party's lawmakers rarely stray from voting as Christie pleased, his term as freeholder was defined by public, sometimes divisive, debates. Indeed, Christie and O'Keeffe boasted that's what they'd bring—narrow 4–3 and 5–2 votes, even though the board was all-Republican. The era was defined by Christie's aggressive self-assuredness, and a dwindling tolerance for it by an establishment that felt he was out of line. "They have made this like a crusade," Joan Bramhall, the freeholder director, said of Christie and O'Keeffe.[31] A political caucus to smooth things out was scheduled, then canceled.

His zeal for making changes wasn't always shared. His colleagues voted down Christie's plan to require bidding on professional services contracts exceeding $50,000. A similar reception greeted his pitch for prohibiting county officials or workers from accepting favors, gifts, loans, or promises of future employment from anyone doing business with the county. Christie said the schmoozing is widespread—that he got dozens of offers to play golf after winning an election, after getting none while a candidate.[32]

Freeholders voted down the plan, then distorted it while criticizing it in a letter to the *Daily Record*. The following spring, freeholders who'd opposed Christie's ethics proposal pushed a plan to create a county ethics board, which Christie and O'Keeffe opposed because it could create costs, for such boards need office space and supplies and can hire employees and an attorney.[33] Freeholders voted down the ethics board plan, then unanimously voted for Christie's plan to bar officials and employees from accepting gifts of more than minimum value from county contractors, even though a state official at the hearing suggested it might be susceptible to a legal challenge. Just as with the jail contract, Christie had lost at first, only to win eventually.

Christie was the freeholder board's liaison to the county Department of Human Services, and in that role looked often to the private sector and to shared services as a way to keep costs down. For instance, the board privatized a center that helped an average of 150 alcoholics a year.

As the human services liaison, Christie worked with Family Court officials to create a new juvenile justice plan in which money would be directed on a child-by-child basis to the agency or program that met a troubled child's individual needs, rather than given in blocks to community-based agencies. "It really stands the traditional system on its head. The money will be distributed based on the special needs of the specific juvenile we want to serve, rather than sending money into community-based programs and hoping the square peg can be fitted into the right hole," said Christie.[34]

When Governor Christie Whitman proposed welfare reforms in 1996, Christie signed a letter written on behalf of the freeholder board urging changes to the plan, because, he said, the working poor could be hurt by proposed rules on subsidized child care. He suggested income eligibility be set on a county-level basis to account for the cost of living and to reconsider increasing co-pays for each child to be put into subsidized child care, among other points.

"Many working poor are at risk of losing their childcare subsidy," wrote the freeholders. "Loss of childcare may mean a parent will no longer be able to work and will have to go on welfare, setting up a vicious cycle which defeats the very purpose of welfare reform getting people to obtain and keep a job," said the letter.[35]

In July 1996, the freeholder board voted 5–2 for a resolution urging Congress to override President Bill Clinton's April veto of a bill that would have banned most "partial birth" abortions. The item was raised by Christie at a work session, though he missed the meeting where the resolution was formally adopted. "It offended me and my sensibilities. When you take a position of choice, you don't have that in mind. . . . It's an issue of how we conduct ourselves as human beings," Christie said.[36] "I'm pro-choice, but I think this procedure is reprehensible."[37]

In a 2011 interview, Christie said his conversion on the issue had occurred in 1995. It followed a doctor's visit made six months before his daughter's birth in February 1996.

"I had been pro-choice before that. And I would call myself kind of—before that, a nonthinking pro-choice person. It was just kind of the default position that I took," Christie told CNN's Piers Morgan. "And then when my wife was pregnant with our daughter, Sarah, who is now 15, we happened to go to one of the prenatal visits at 13 weeks. And they put the Doppler on my wife's abdomen, who didn't look at all pregnant at that point visibly. And we heard this incredibly strong heartbeat. And I remember we came separately. She came from her job. I came from mine. We went back to work. And I was driving back to work, I said to myself, you know, as to my position on abortion, I would say that a week ago that wasn't a life. And I heard that heartbeat. That's a life. And it—it led to me having a real reflection on my position. And when I took time to reflect on it, I just said, you know what, I'm not comfortable with that anymore. That was back in 1995, and I've been pro-life ever since."[38]

Though he'd been widely expected to forgo a reelection bid in favor of seeking the Republican nomination for state Senate in 1997, Christie—with input from his wife, Mary Pat—decided to run again for county office. "I didn't want there to be any ambiguity at all concerning what I would be doing. . . . I wanted to make it clear to the people that I want to be freeholder for at least the next four years."[39]

Not that sticking around Morris County would prove easy. Christie was selected as freeholder director for 1997, but on the night when former governor Tom Kean, his onetime mentor, came to administer the oath of office, fellow freeholder Sue Murphy Ostergaard lay into Christie during what's normally a pomp-and-circumstance reorganization meeting. She cast the only vote against him and blasted the board as "duplicitous, shortsighted . . . and lacking in credibility."[40] Recent history may have played a role in her negativity: She had been deputy director the year before and not only didn't get to move up, she was bounced from that spot in favor of O'Keeffe.

Christie said he was hurt by the remarks. "Tonight was a night for my family—my wife, mom and dad and children to enjoy. I was in the minority for a time on this board, and I never would ever have embarrassed a colleague on a night like this. She's wrong, just plain wrong, but I understand that she's angry."[41] As his term was expiring a year later, he was still stung by the attack. "It was my low point here. I never thought I would meet somebody who would be mean enough to do that to another person. Despite all the problems I had with Sue over the years, I never demeaned her publicly."[42]

Ostergaard got a job a few months later as the Port Authority of New York and New Jersey's government affairs officer at the State House and left the freeholder board. At her final meeting, she sang a reworked version of "Don't Cry for Me Argentina." Bizarre, yes. But at least, unlike Laureys, she handed over the office keys without a formal request.

On Christmas Eve in 1996, jail architect Kimmerle sued Christie for libel. He said a political newsletter distributed by Christie a month earlier to Republican Party committee members wrongfully implied Kimmerle had been illegally hired to design a new jail and then overcharged the county. The issue hovered throughout Christie's reelection campaign. Christie spent $131,000 of his own funds defending against Kimmerle's lawsuit,[43] which was dropped in 1999 with little explanation beyond a two-sentence joint statement: "The lawsuit between George Kimmerle and Chris Christie has been resolved and voluntarily dismissed. Neither party will have further comment."[44]

The freeholder board at one point voted to use public funds to defend Christie, sparking controversy, since Christie's questionable statement came in a private political mailing. Christie ultimately agreed to pay the bill to quell the controversy—which would echo years later, when he was criticized for use of the state's helicopter as governor.

Christie and O'Keeffe formally entered the race for reelection in March. Douglas Cabana, a candidate on the opposing slate, said he entered the race because he and voters were outraged by the way the board conducted itself. "Everywhere I go, Chris is the issue," said Cabana.[45] The race became a referendum on Christie, who defended the public slugfests during his time in office. "Sure, we argue and debate in public. And if we only bickered and got nothing done, it would be valueless. But this board doesn't table anything. We have not avoided any issue."[46]

Cabana and running mate John Murphy ran a fifteen-second television ad, which left viewers with the impression that public dollars were spent on Christie's legal defense, even though it wasn't true. The ad was changed to say he tried to do so. Christie lost—and one year later, or four years after he said a vanquished candidate should gracefully accept a loss and move on, sued Cabana, Murphy, and their political consultant for defamation. "Their deception cost me the primary election," Christie said. "I want my reputation back."[47] Christie's opponents settled the case in January 2001 in part by issuing a written statement in which they acknowledged running misleading campaign ads. A confidentiality agreement didn't stop Christie from gloating, "We've been able to drag them, kicking and screaming, to the truth." Cabana and Murphy were without remorse. "He couldn't deal with people on a committee level, aggravated the staff and couldn't work with people. But we were trying to rehabilitate him in the party. Now he violated the trust I had with him earlier today. I'm telling you, the gloves are off again," Murphy said.[48]

In that 1997 primary, Christie finished last. O'Keeffe also lost. The loudest ovation of the night at the Republicans' party at the Hanover Marriott was for Laureys. "When someone takes away your reputation, it's something you never get back," she said. "Republican voters of Morris County not only put me back in office, but they restored my good name."[49]

Christie showed up at the hotel around 11 P.M. to make his concession speech. As he stood behind the podium, the audience continued to talk, paying him practically no attention.[50]

"There was a kind of a unity among the party regulars there that they were thrilled that this concession speech was having to be made," Christie said. "And their way of dealing with it was they literally ignored me. I was giving my speech, and no one was listening. They were just talking to each other. Nobody quieted down, they just kept talking to each other."

It was not spontaneous.

"There's no question in my mind it was a planned thing among a group of them, and then it kind of caught on. And then when I got done, I got down off the stage, and as I was walking off the stage, there was a guy standing by the stairs to get off the stage," Christie recalled.

The man was Charles "Chuck" Dawson, a Roxbury Township council-man and former mayor, and one of the few people listening to Christie's speech—though not for charitable reasons. He'd become friends with Bucco, who defeated Christie in the highly contentious 1995 primary. Christie said he tried to avoid eye contact with Dawson—"a nasty person, a terrible guy, who didn't like me"—but couldn't once Dawson tugged at his arm as he left the stage.[51]

"So he was standing by the steps, and as I was walking down the steps, he was making kind of a kissing noise with his lips as I was walking down the stairs," Christie said. "And I kind of looked and him and I said, 'What now, Chuck?' And he goes, 'That's just me kissing your fucking career good-bye.'"

Dawson didn't live to see Christie elected as New Jersey's chief executive, having died in 1998—thirteen years to the day, actually, that Christie told that story for this book. His wife, Barbara, however, not only saw it but helped Christie get there.

"Ironically, his wife was one of my most active volunteers in the gubernatorial campaign," Christie said. "She said to me any number of times, 'I loved Chuck, but he was wrong about you.' Not just when I was running for governor, but before that. And she was one of my most active volunteers. She was at headquarters all the time phone banking. Barbara was an incredible help."

Christie did not take the defeat in Morris County with the gracious acceptance his mentor, Tom Kean, did when he lost his 1977 bid for governor with the fourteen-year-old Christie at his side.

"No, no," Christie said. "I pretty much decided I would never run for anything again. It had been a very tumultuous three years, and I thought to myself, you know, maybe I was not cut out for this. That was kind of how I reacted to the loss. Maybe I have to find another way to be involved in public issues and public life. It wasn't that I was going to abandon doing that, but I was thinking to myself that maybe I'm just not cut out for elective politics. Maybe I have to figure out another way to do this because the elective thing doesn't seem to be working too well for me.

"It was a very difficult time," Christie said. "Really, the more difficult time was between June and January, because in Morris County the primary is everything. You lose the primary, or win the primary, and you know the result of the election. I was director of the board at the time, so here I am the lame-duck director of the board, having to run the county government for six more months, with everybody kind of like really not paying attention to you because they know you're going to be gone. Yet you still have the authority, statutorily, to run the government. You have to run the meetings. The much more difficult time for me was that six-month period of relative irrelevance, yet you still have to show up for work. That was a really rough period. Once January came, it was like, 'Okay, packing up my boxes and I'm going, and I'll figure something out.'"

In a five-candidate race where three people won, Christie finished in the running in only seven of Morris County's thirty-nine towns. "Our opponents didn't disagree with us on the issues," Christie said. "This election was all about personalities, and that made it a most personal type of defeat. That makes it most difficult to accept." Christie said he was the victim of "a $250,000 two-by-four of negative campaigning." "I have to accept this; I have no choice. When you place yourself in this arena, you have to know this can happen," he said.[52]

Palatucci, Christie's friend and informal political adviser, said the loss was difficult but Christie didn't dwell on it. He said Christie and O'Keeffe lost not because of what they failed to do but because of their success, for being antagonistic rather than collaborative.

"That was part of the problem, was the success, that they got those things done," Palatucci said. "The old boys' network did not appreciate all that, and I think the governor has admitted that. There was a bit of a young man in a hurry dynamic to that time in Morris County. He wasn't defeated because of anything he said or anything that the voters would have found unpopular. It was kind of rubbing the old boys' network the wrong way."

Christie left office six months later admittedly devastated but unapologetic for taking on the establishment, though he conceded that the way he conducted the 1995 Assembly campaign was wrong. "The most politic way for me to have proceeded would have been to blend into the background and not make waves. But I was elected because I espoused a certain set of ideas and people said, 'Yeah, that's what we want our government to do.' I felt a moral obligation to pursue those ideas . . . even if it was politically better to back off," he said.

The backlash came from the establishment, not the grass roots, he believed. Letters to the editor hammering at him weren't spontaneous but organized by the local Republican Party, he said. "They wrote horrible, vicious things. They said I was the Pillsbury Doughboy, arrogant, a liar, deceitful. It got difficult at times to accept. But I know when I look in the mirror that I'm a good person and have not profited a nickel from my service here."[53]

Most of those ugly wounds opened in Morris County have healed— time and success are great medicine. Ostergaard encouraged him to run for the White House in 2012. Bucco says nice things about him. Christie attempted to nominate former critic Carroll as a state judge, though the nomination was withdrawn when a local bar association said it wasn't given enough time to vet the candidate. Christie even presented a leadership award to Murphy, quite a long way from suing someone for defamation.

"I think it was a combination—there was some effort on my part, even afterwards, although not immediately afterwards, with some of them," Christie said. "But I think much more it was two things: the passage of time and becoming U.S. attorney. I think once I became U.S. attorney, and I was having success, all those people who were focused on being my enemies became just as focused on becoming my friend. Which is kind of the nature of politics."

CHAPTER FOUR

◆

Bush to the Rescue

After his defeat, Chris Christie returned full attention to work at Dughi & Hewit, the law firm where—unlike back on the Morris County political battlefield—he was treated like everyone's big brother. Still wanting to stay involved in public policy, even though his career in elective politics appeared shredded, he joined with Palatucci to launch the firm's new, two-person Trenton lobbying division in 1998.

State records show that by the time Christie left the law firm in 2001 for his next job, they had built its lobbying shop into the fifteenth biggest in Trenton, with receipts approaching $1.25 million over those four years. Their biggest client was the University of Phoenix, the for-profit college that at the time was pursuing a New Jersey campus, accounting for roughly 25 percent of their revenues. Bill Palatucci was later appointed as a member of the board of trustees for its Jersey City campus.

Hackensack University Medical Center, as well as the hospital's foundation, paid the firm around $250,000 during Christie's lobbying stint. That client is of particular interest because it was later the focus of an investigation that was pure Soprano State. State senator Joseph Coniglio funneled more than $1 million in state funds to the institution after it gave him a high-paying job as a consultant—on plumbing. He was convicted of extortion in the federal case, an investigation launched while Christie was

U.S. attorney. Convictions on five counts of mail fraud were overturned on appeal.

"Chris has no hesitation to play both sides of the street," Coniglio's attorney, Gerald Krovatin, said during the 2009 trial. "And this notion that he's going to be a different kind of Trenton politician and that there's going to be fundamental change if he were elected, that's fundamentally inconsistent with his record."[1]

Dughi & Hewit's third biggest lobbying client was Edison Schools, the for-profit private operator of public schools, whose clients included charter schools in Jersey City and Trenton. Edison's corporate management team at that time included Christopher Cerf, who started as its general counsel in 1997, as its chief operating officer in 1999, and finally as its president. Cerf was later appointed by Christie as his second education commissioner; in 2011, the pair proposed to create public-private partnerships to run some New Jersey schools.

In 1999, in his capacity of representing Edison Schools, Christie lobbied the Assembly Appropriations Committee, without success, asking that changes be made to a school choice pilot program that would allow parents to send children, tuition-free, outside their home district to districts that volunteer to take them. The bill capped the number of students who can leave a district for charter schools at 7 percent of enrollment; the New Jersey Education Association led the charge for the cap. Christie was there representing the Granville Charter School in Trenton, a city where 8 percent of public school students had already escaped to charters. Christie asked that the cap not apply to the thirty-one districts, most of them poor and urban, that were covered by a long-running school-funding lawsuit, since otherwise Trenton might not be able to add more charters. "For our school in particular, we had 500 kids who enrolled, but there were 1,000 families that applied for the spots," he said. "There is a real desire in places like Trenton to have different types of educational opportunities for their children."[2]

Dughi & Hewit's lobbying efforts became fodder during the 2009 campaign. *The Star-Ledger* reported, "Christie's firm lobbied against some bills supporting school choice programs—including one that would have required the state to help pay to send children to charter schools—while favoring other school choice proposals." As a candidate he promoted vouchers that students in failing schools could use to pay tuition at private schools or a different public school. He also wanted to add more charter schools in cities. When that contradiction came up as an issue during the campaign, a campaign spokeswoman said Palatucci did over 90 percent to 95 percent of the lobbying work.

Palatucci said it was even more when asked about it in 2012. "I did 99 percent of the lobbying. In New Jersey, it's always prudent to err on the side of more disclosure, not less disclosure, so it was just to make sure that nobody ever accused lawyer Chris Christie of being in or around my lobbying activity without registering. He went to maybe a handful of meetings where he was simply in the room where I was doing work on behalf of my clients. But he did no independent lobbying himself. Those were my clients, it was largely my work. Some of it had a real legal element to it, either through drafting of language or understanding ultimately related litigation. But he was never in Trenton on his own, on behalf of clients, to my memory never attended a legislative hearing or testified on his own. It was more an effort to make sure we were covering our bases and fully disclosing. Maybe in hindsight it would have been completely proper not to have registered him, but then he could have been accused of lobbying without being registered. So damned if you do, damned if you don't. You over-disclose to meet the letter and the spirit of the law."

The firm's other clients included Community Education Centers, which later employed Palatucci as a senior vice president until he left in 2012; Jersey Central Power & Light, the second largest electric utility in the state; and the Securities Industry Association, which paid the firm $15,250 over two years—at a time, as critics later pointed out, visions of negative campaign ads in their heads, that Bernard Madoff headed its trading committee. The firm was hired to get securities fraud exempted from the state's consumer fraud protection act.

You may be wondering how a lobbyist came to be a gubernatorial candidate, when usually elected officials become lobbyists *after* they leave office. First off, it's not that unusual, at least in New Jersey, where a handful of former lobbyists now serve in the legislature. And, at the time, it appeared that Christie had run his last campaign, his life in elective politics over at age thirty-five. He'd kept an eye on Morris County's freeholder politics and tried to help his former ally on the board, Jack O'Keeffe, mount a comeback that fell short. In a missive that hinted at the crusades he'd wage years later against independent authorities and perceived wasteful spending, no matter how minuscule, he wrote a letter to the editor criticizing the Morris County Municipal Utilities Authority for agreeing to pay a public relations firm $15,000 to, among other things, design a new logo. "Why then, you might ask, are the freeholders silent when they can take steps to cut your taxes even further? Instead of 'rocking the boat' and asking the tough questions, they choose to sit by silently while the MUA wastes your money on a new logo and a fancy public relations firm," he wrote.[3] But he wasn't among the fourteen candidates who ran for freeholder in 1998 and didn't seek county office again.

That didn't mean the door was slammed on a career in public service. A new portal opened when he volunteered as a campaign lawyer for George W. Bush, arranged through Palatucci, who had won the confidence of Republicans at the highest level through work in New Jersey on campaigns for Ronald Reagan and George H. W. Bush. Together Christie, Palatucci, and wealthy real estate developer Jon Hanson pooled their fund-raising efforts and raised more than $500,000 in 1999 and 2000 for George W. Bush and the Republican National Committee, enough to merit "Pioneer" status in the fund-raising apparatus the campaign had set up that year. "To be relevant, to be important to the Bush guys, yeah, we raised a bunch of money," Palatucci said. They would much rather have run Bush's state campaign than raise dough. "We were kind of forced into fund-raising because the [Governor Christie] Whitman team wouldn't let us do the politics. Being second bananas, we got stuck with doing the fund-raising."

Palatucci had organized and attended the first visit by nine New Jersey Republicans, including Christie and a cadre of high-level elected officials, to Austin, Texas, in January 1999, part of a series of visits by folks from various states while Bush's presidential campaign was being prepared. "I didn't ask Christie Whitman's permission. I didn't need to, I knew him [Bush] from the old days."

Palatucci's relationship with George W. Bush, whom he called Junior, dated to 1988, when he was running the state campaign for Bush's father; Bush's son would come to New Jersey as a surrogate. Palatucci frequently picked up the younger Bush curbside at Newark Airport's Terminal C, then home to the busy Continental Airlines hub. "I didn't even bother to get out of the car to get him and he's the vice president's son at that time. He'd come walking out of the terminal and hop in my Honda," he said. "Bush would get in, put his cowboy boots up on the dashboard, put a cigar in his mouth and say 'Let's go.'" The future two-term president spent hours in New Jersey in 1988, most of it in Palatucci's silver Honda.

Palatucci ran into Bush in New Orleans in November 1998 at a Republican Governors Association convention. He, Bush, Florida governor Jeb Bush, and an aide to the Texas governor wound up in an otherwise empty room. "Come to lunch in Austin" and bring some friends, Bush told him, cryptically and without explanation. The aide, Palatucci soon learned, was political adviser Karl Rove.[4]

Palatucci and several of the movers and shakers in New Jersey Republican circles went to Austin first in January 1999—the least known among them a defeated county politician named Christie. There were three trips in all, each with more people than the last. By the time it was over, Bush had the Jersey Republican leadership behind him for president.

Christie volunteered to do legal work for Bush in his presidential campaign, but he didn't limit himself to that role. In January 2000, for instance, he represented Bush as a surrogate at an American Legion hall debate in Flemington, New Jersey, where he was identified as Bush's state campaign coordinator.[5] He appeared on several Court TV shows discussing the Bush-Gore presidential election dispute.[6] Christie later got a thank-you note from Bush for his fund-raising support, which he framed and hung on his office wall as U.S. attorney.[7] He also got a nickname, as Bush liked to assign—"Big Boy." Christie and Mary Pat also gave nearly $29,000 to Republican federal candidates and committees between 1999 and 2001.[8]

Christie's performance—and an aggressive campaign in which he secured the backing of prominent Republican leaders and fund-raisers in the state[9]—eventually garnered him Bush's nomination as U.S. attorney, the top federal law enforcement office in the state. Christie later acknowledged that he began eyeing the job in the summer of 2000. "I gravitated to it immediately, immediately," he said. "I just kind of thought that I would be perfect for the job. Now, I don't know in retrospect whether I really had any basis for that or not, but I just—my sense, my gut was I could do that really well."

Palatucci smoothed the way. "I take his résumé, put a cover on it, and mail it to Karl Rove," he said, along with letters of support from the state's top Republicans—politicians on all sides of an intramural GOP war, with antiestablishment Bret Schundler taking on Governor Donald DiFrancesco and Representative Bob Franks in the 2001 gubernatorial primary. "We wanted the president's people to know that this person's got a lot of support from all quarters of the party."

In spite of the shared Honda experience in 1988, Palatucci said he never spoke to Bush personally about Christie or the U.S. attorney post or any other job. Christie didn't want to go to Washington because he had three young children at home, but a local appointment would be attractive. Palatucci wrote to Rove on Christie's behalf. "You don't send your own résumé to the White House, nobody does. At least anybody who really thinks they can get a job at the White House. You have somebody else do it," he said. He emphasized two Christie traits: "He was a really good lawyer and I knew he was a very effective communicator."

Christie acknowledged the role his support for Bush's campaign played in getting the job. "In the context of political life in this country, the way you get to know these people is by supporting them and being involved in their campaigns," he said.[10]

Speculation he'd get the job first made it into print a mere three days after the Supreme Court decided the Bush-Gore election.[11] By March he'd been pegged as the favorite,[12] though at least the names of ten other prospects were also being bandied about in the press, including Palatucci. By late summer, he'd seemingly edged out Rosemary Alito—sister of future Supreme Court justice Samuel Alito, himself a former U.S. attorney in New Jersey.[13] While Christie had support from the Republican political leadership at the State House, South Jersey GOPers were pushing for state gaming enforcement chief J. P. Suarez, a former assistant federal prosecutor who would later become a senior vice president for WalMart Stores Inc., as were state and national Hispanic groups. "As far as I can tell, Mr. Christie's claim to fame is that he jumped on our president's bandwagon and he and his people raised a considerable amount of money for the campaign. I applaud that, but it doesn't qualify him for the U.S. attorney's position," said Dr. Antonio Gines, state chairman of the Republican National Hispanic Assembly.[14] Bush settled on Christie and formally extended the job offer through White House counsel Alberto Gonzales in a 4:30 p.m. phone call on Monday, September 10, 2001.[15] Christie left his office where he worked as a securities attorney and took the next day off.

Sixteen hours later, the parameters of the job changed significantly, as hijacked airliners, one of which took off from Newark, began smashing into the World Trade Center towers and Pentagon and a field near Shanksville, Pennsylvania—that last one after a passenger revolt aboard United 93 led in part by Cranbury, New Jersey, resident Todd Beamer, who with the rallying call "Let's roll," attempted to take back the hijacked craft, which was believed headed for Washington. Nearly seven hundred New Jerseyans died in the terrorist attacks. Christie was home when it happened, but his wife and brother, Todd, were at work in lower Manhattan. Christie was talking with Mary Pat on the telephone when she saw the second plane hit the South Tower on the TV in her office about four blocks from Ground Zero. It was the last communication they had for hours.

"My immediate impression was I thought there was an accident," she said. "The guy to my left had been in the World Trade Center on the '93 bombing and he thought it was an attack right away." All doubt was erased a few minutes later. "One of my traders hadn't gotten to work yet, and she called screaming on the phone, saying, 'It's an attack!' She had Cantor trade tickets falling on her hair. And that's really how I knew."

Cantor Fitzgerald is a financial services company whose offices occupied floors 101 through 105 of One World Trade Center; it lost 658 employees in the terrorist attack, two-thirds of its workforce, more than any other tenant. Mary Pat at the time was working at the Seaport Group, an investment bank and a client of Cantor, so she knew many traders who died on 9/11. She later worked part-time for Cantor, as a managing director in its high-yield corporate bond department, but left in 2012 to become a full-time managing director of the New York private-equity investment firm Angelo, Gordon & Co.

On the morning of September 11, Mary Pat had followed her regular commute into Manhattan—driving into Jersey City, taking a PATH commuter train through the World Trade Center, and walking to her office. Then came the attacks, followed by bedlam. Mary Pat couldn't get through to her husband in New Jersey but was able to reach her mother in Pennsylvania and tell her she was fine. When the Twin Towers fell, smoke enveloped her building, so thick no one could see out the windows. Fire marshals forced everyone to the basement—"That's when everyone finally started listening" to them, she said—and that's where she stayed for more than two hours. It was dark, someone was having a diabetic attack, and a group of them wanted out.

"Eight of us from my office got T-shirts, wrapped them around our faces, and kind of did a human chain to get out. When we got out, it was desolate by then. Everything's covered in white where we were," she said. "We start walking north, and then it wasn't until we got towards the Brooklyn Bridge that there was another panic going on. Someone said someone's blowing up the Brooklyn courthouse. And there was a mass of people coming across the Brooklyn Bridge into Manhattan."

The bridge is about a mile away from the World Trade Center. Thwarted in their event to escape Manhattan, they changed direction, eventually walking more than two and a half miles to Pete's Tavern in Union Square, on East 18th Street. "At Pete's Tavern, we went upstairs and started watching TV. They were still showing footage at that time of people jumping out of the towers," Mary Pat said. "We were helping serve food. We were really just helping, because people were streaming in. And I was able to get through to Chris because somebody there had a Sprint phone card, and we were able to use a pay station. That's the only reason I got through to him, through Kansas City."

Christie had stayed home from work, after learning the previous afternoon he'd been chosen as New Jersey's next top federal prosecutor. In the end, his office played a role in the 9/11 investigation, because one of the planes used in the attack took off from Newark. But all that could wait: That chaotic morning, his priority was helping his wife get off Manhattan island—which was also the goal of hundreds of thousands of people trying to cross the Hudson River into New Jersey.

"When we were on the phone," Chris said, "I went on the Internet, and they were saying that the lines on the West Side were from like 33rd Street up to in the 70s. Then I went on the Internet to look at the ferry that went from the East Side to the Atlantic Highlands. And they were saying on the Internet that there was no wait. So I said to her, 'Go over to the East Side, and get on that. I'll come down to the Highlands and pick you up.'"

Atlantic Highlands is in Monmouth County, which is the top of the Jersey Shore—but close enough to see the Manhattan skyline roughly twenty miles due north. It's around a sixty-mile one-way drive from the Christies' home.

"That ferry ride was really surreal. It was packed by that time. And it was obvious that I had been downtown because I was pretty covered in stuff—just from the walk, not that it had fallen on me. I wasn't one of these ghost-looking people, but I clearly had it all over my feet and on my pants," Mary Pat said. "So I got down to Atlantic Highlands—if you were contaminated, you went one way, if you weren't contaminated, you went another way. So I went with the contaminated people, and they hosed you down. They just didn't know what they were dealing with."

Chris stood on the corner, watching passengers walking from the boat slip, seemingly in a trance. Every other person was soaking wet after firefighters had hosed them down. He actually did the trip to Atlantic Highlands twice that day, returning later to pick up Todd, who also worked on Wall Street and returned via the same ferry line.

Mary Pat's employers at the Seaport Group told her and her colleagues they didn't need to come back right away, but she returned the following Monday. "We really felt as a group that we needed to come back, and that we needed to be there to do the work that all those friends of ours that we knew died couldn't do," she said. So each day, she commuted to work past the acrid, smoldering ruins of what was now called Ground Zero. "That was pretty powerful, when you got back those first couple of weeks. I definitely am affected by it. I'm not scared. It didn't make me scared to be in

New York, like it did some people. If anything, I kind of felt emboldened to carry on."

The Christies spent days attending friends' funerals and waited to see what would come of his job offer. It would be two weeks before the White House called back because there were no available FBI agents to do background checks. Christie was summoned to the office of Democratic U.S. senator Robert Torricelli, who told him, "You wouldn't have been my first choice, but you are the president's choice, and we can't screw around with this," Christie recalled. "He was very serious about this. It was a very emotional thing for him."[16]

After Christie's background check, Bush publicly announced his intention to nominate Christie on December 7. Christie had no experience in criminal law; his legal background was in securities and appellate law. The executive committee of the Federal Bar Association of New Jersey, without mentioning names, urged Bush to nominate someone with law enforcement credentials.[17] The executive committee of the New Jersey state bar association, prompted by lobbying from at least two former U.S. attorneys, mulled over whether to propose the same. Backers and skeptics alike said he'd better assemble a strong staff. Former U.S. District Judge H. Curtis Meanor compared the position to that of managing partner within a major law firm and said criminal trial skills are secondary to organizational skills, administrative ability, and the ability to negotiate with the U.S. Justice Department. "You've got plenty of guys in that office who can try cases. You've got to run that office like a big law firm."[18]

Jonathan Goldstein, a Republican who was U.S. attorney for New Jersey from 1974 to 1977, noted that everyone who had held that job for the past thirty years had either moved up through the U.S. attorney's office or had helped lead state law enforcement agencies and worried Christie's appointment was too political. "The United States attorney is the chief federal law enforcement officer in New Jersey, coordinating complicated and difficult investigations into allegations of political corruption, business fraud and other serious wrongdoing. The office requires that the United States attorney remain independent of any outside influences. You want the public to have total confidence in that office."[19]

Detractors scoffed he would be a failure, including many of New Jersey's newspapers. *The Star-Ledger* ran an editorial cartoon in which Bush, looking over a paper that said "No law enforcement experience" and "Fund-raiser for Bush 2000," told Christie, "That's one heck of a résumé, young man."[20] The *Asbury Park Press* questioned his qualifications in an editorial: "The ability to raise money for candidates should not be a qualification for the top federal prosecutor for New Jersey. Yet that seems to be what has made a Morris County securities lawyer President Bush's choice to head the U.S. attorney's office in Newark." The paper suggested that the nomination be blocked, adding that because Senator Torricelli was under federal investigation for fund-raising efforts, the state's other senator, Jon Corzine, "should use his veto power . . . to force Bush to look at other candidates."[21]

Corzine, who would face Christie later in a nasty gubernatorial contest, and Torricelli, who became so bruised by a campaign financial scandal he abandoned his reelection campaign in 2002, could have blocked the nomination but didn't. "We have met with Chris Christie and feel that he will be a competent and committed public servant," the senatorial duo said in a joint press release. "In light of current events and the need for strong and immediate actions by the U.S. attorney's office in the war on terrorism, it is important to honor President Bush's choice for this position."[22] Christie was confirmed December 20, 2001, in a voice vote. That night he saw Torricelli at a Christmas party. "He came over and shook my hand and said, 'You've been on the job for an hour and a half, what have you done?'" Later, Christie said, Torricelli put his hands on the newly minted U.S. attorney's shoulder and told him, "Don't ever disappoint me." Attorney General John Ashcroft also called Christie, saying, "Congratulations. Remember over 700 people in your district were murdered. It's the single largest loss of life in any district in the country. It's your job to make sure it never happens again."[23]

Publicly, Torricelli said, "Chris Christie has put together a strong team of law enforcement officials. I have every confidence that the new leadership of the U.S. attorney's office will meet the responsibilities of protecting our citizens during this current national crisis and that they will perform with distinction."[24]

In a case of no good deed going unpunished, Christie's campaign later frequently used Corzine's support against him in the day-to-day skirmishes of the 2009 campaign, countering any criticisms about Christie's freeholder days or Bush fund-raising by saying Corzine knew of all that back when he supported Christie's nomination. Corzine said in 2009 he regretted supporting Christie's nomination because the prosecutor politicized the job and used it as a launching pad back into politics. "New information, new conclusion," he said.[25]

Christie's critics didn't know him well enough, or were not smart enough, to realize that while he lacked law enforcement experience he had the basic skill set to rise quickly in the job—he is tenacious, fearless, blunt, intelligent, and supremely confident, a leader since childhood. And, just as important, he also knew how to get media attention to reinforce the image of a new sheriff in town, making good use of the "perp walk"—where the newly arrested are paraded before previously alerted news media—and press conferences. Both were big hits with media and the public.

Christie became New Jersey's fifty-third U.S. attorney in January 2002, telling people his career in elective politics was in the rearview mirror. "I won't consider running for office again. The door is shut," he said.[26] It was the nation's seventh largest office with around 120 lawyers at the time, a number that would grow to nearly 140. Mike Brey, men's basketball coach at the University of Notre Dame and a Christie friend, said Christie emailed him for advice "about inheriting a situation where you're [supervising] people you didn't hire."[27]

A short while after Christie's confirmation, Bush visited New Jersey. At the foot of the stairs when Air Force One rolled to a stop was Governor Jim McGreevey, who greeted the president, then ran behind the line of glad-handers to the end where Christie was standing. "Mr. President," McGreevey said, "this is our new U.S. attorney, Chris Christie." Bush responded, "I know. I nominated him."

While Christie had never practiced criminal law, he had endured an early brush with political crooks and law enforcement in 1980. Christie went on a trip to Washington, one of two high school seniors from each state to do so in a William Randolph Hearst Foundation project called the United States Senate Youth Program. They were to divide part of their time between each state's senators, in Christie's case, longtime lawmaker Harrison Williams and former basketball star Bill Bradley, then beginning his second year in the Senate.

"They put you up at the Mayflower Hotel for a week. You meet with everybody's who's important in Washington," said Christie—including President Jimmy Carter, Secretary of State Cyrus Vance, and the chairman of the Joint Chiefs of Staff, General David Jones.

Christie and his fellow students arrived on a Sunday—one day after NBC News broke the story of the FBI's Abscam bribery ring, in which agents posing as a mysterious Arab sheikh and his entourage were targeting members of Congress in a sting operation. Williams, New Jersey's senior senator, was among them, as were a congressman representing the Trenton area and a New Jersey state senator. Williams wasn't arrested and in fact didn't get indicted until nearly nine months later—but he had made himself scarce in the wake of the NBC report.

"You're supposed to split the week between Harrison Williams and Bill Bradley, who was a brand-new, just sworn-in United States senator, and so as it turned out, we had to spend the whole week in Bradley's office," Christie said.

Maybe Williams did Christie a favor. Instead of the usual sanitized civics lesson, the future crime buster got a reality check as a seventeen-year-old about political corruption and the black eye a state gets because of it. The Garden State kids were "ashamed, and we got made fun of all week," Christie said. A yearbook produced each year for the event includes a gallery in the back with two pictures of each state's pair of students, one with each senator. "We were the only ones who had just one senator," he said. "We just had our picture with Bradley, but Williams was 'unavailable.' There was a mention of him in the book. He was listed in the book, because he was still in the United States Senate, but we had no photo of him because he was otherwise detained."

The other New Jersey high school senior on that Washington trip, Bob Guarasci, went on to make an impact on his state, too. He founded and remains the chief executive officer for a nonprofit in Paterson, the New Jersey Community Development Corporation, which seeks to transform lives through initiatives in housing, education, and community building. He also founded a charter school. Governor Jon Corzine appointed Guarasci to William Paterson University's board of trustees. He was later reappointed to the position by Christie, who had suffered through the week of embarrassment in Washington with him.

Career prosecutors in the U.S. attorney's office joined political enemies in doubting the newcomer Christie, but undaunted by that he went about building a team led by first assistant Ralph Marra Jr., who had joined the office in 1985 and worked in the public corruption prosecutions division. Christie increased the size of his corruption unit, led by James Nobile, from seven to fourteen attorneys, intentionally building it to a larger size than it had ever been before. He quickly added a new post for a deputy United States attorney for New Jersey's southern counties, which had often complained they felt neglected by the Newark-based office, and hired Camden County prosecutor Lee Solomon to head the new Camden and Trenton offices. Christie and Solomon were friends who first met during the 1992 reelection campaign of President George H. W. Bush.[28]

Four months into his term, having met with all 119 assistant U.S. attorneys and observing how the operation worked, he restructured the office by merging the criminal, fraud, and strike force divisions into one large criminal division with eight subunits, including a unit that focused on drug prosecutions, a terrorism unit, and a securities and health fraud unit. "I feel that this structure will permit the office to be more aggressive in the type of cases we prosecute and way we prosecute them," he said.[29] He quickly turned at least some of his critics around—including Goldstein, the former U.S. attorney who'd been skeptical about the selection. "Chris Christie deserves enormous praise," he said in late 2002.[30]

U.S. senators Corzine and Torricelli wanted Walter Timpone, who had been a federal prosecutor for eleven years and headed the corruption-prosecution division, to be hired as Christie's top aide, but a meeting Timpone had with Torricelli may have doomed that wish. Timpone represented former Hudson County executive Robert "Bobby J" Janiszewski, whom federal investigators had apparently tapped to secretly tape conversations with Torricelli. Timpone angered those investigators after visiting Torricelli at his home while the senator was under FBI surveillance as part of a probe of personal and campaign finances, which closed without criminal charges. Janiszewski pleaded guilty to accepting bribes after the FBI got the goods on him. Christie didn't choose Timpone, though he heaped praise on him—and in 2010, appointed him to the state's Election Law Enforcement Commission. "Wally Timpone is a lawyer of great integrity who once served this office well. He is among a group of excellent lawyers under consideration for first assistant," he said before choosing Marra. A spokeswoman for Torricelli made it sound like Timpone had the job in a statement that said he "believes that Chris Christie made an excellent choice in Walter Timpone for first assistant and his selection is consistent with Sen. Torricelli and Sen. Corzine's desires to have a highly competent and professional staff."[31]

The U.S. attorney's office in New Jersey had a solid reputation before Christie arrived for prosecuting corrupt political figures,[32] although Christie said he felt rooting out political corruption had taken a backseat since the days that Michael Chertoff, Fred Lacey, and Herbert Stern held the office. In 1997, Special Agent William Megary created the FBI's second public corruption squad in Newark; at that office, at that time, nearly two dozen agents were investigating graft in Essex, Hudson, and Union counties alone. Agents in satellite offices handled other counties. "I'm sure if I had another FBI squad, I'd have even more cases," Christie said. "So many of these people are just so stupid."[33]

Under Christie, that reputation was taken to new heights. New Jersey political corruption is like a small lake full of fish, where a dedicated prosecutor need only cast a net to gather a basketful of potential criminals. Christie rightly gave credit to his Democratic predecessors who launched some of the cases he later completed, but takes all the credit for the aggressive tone of his operation and doubling the anticorruption unit, some at the expense of other programs. On a single day in 2002, a contractor was sentenced for paying a $9,000 bribe, a municipal authority employee pleaded guilty to bribing contractors, a housing authority executive was indicted, and a federal prosecutor revealed that three county workers were likely to plead to corruption charges in advance of a major trial. "You sit here where

I sit and you shake your head," said U.S. District Judge Joel Pisano. The court "has so many cases that deal with public corruption that we literally can't count them anymore."[34]

Palatucci credited Christie's "great management skills" and noted that his friend mostly relied on existing federal prosecutors, not newcomers from the outside, as his top lieutenants. "He had Murderers' Row. No one knew it, because it had had a succession of different issues at the U.S. Attorney's office. But one of the reasons I think they were successful there is because of his management style and morale went through the roof," Palatucci said. "He took one person to the U.S. Attorney's office, Jeff Chiesa. Everybody else was there. Stu Rabner was there. Charlie McKenna was there. Michele Brown was there. Paula Dow was there. Ralph Marra was there. It was Murderers' Row. They just needed Miller Huggins, and he appeared. One of the reasons they were productive, besides a very talented crew, was they had a leader and an effective communicator. They had somebody who knew how to manage and build a strong office."

Shortly after Christie took office, Paterson mayor Marty Barnes was arrested for handing out contracts in exchange for personal luxury gifts. That investigation, of course, had been in the works long before Christie got there; he actually had a meeting about the case twenty minutes after he was sworn in on January 17, 2002, in which his approval was sought for a grand jury indictment.[35] But Christie knew how to make the best of it in the media. He held news conferences hammering politicians from Democratic Hudson County, Republican Monmouth County, and other places. "There is no question in my mind that public corruption is happening in every corner of the state," Christie said.[36] "I knew coming in there was a problem," he said. "I knew it wasn't good, but I didn't know quite how bad it was."[37] His reputation started to sprout. He became the subject of newspaper, radio, and TV interviews.

Then it blossomed with a big fish, Essex County executive Jim Treffinger, a fellow Republican and at the time a leading candidate for the party's U.S. Senate nomination. Treffinger had also envisioned himself as U.S. attorney, angling for the appointment that ultimately went to Christie. Treffinger bragged to a friend that after he got the post, he could make investigations go away. After all, he rationalized, "Plenty of mobsters to go after; you don't have to go after all those poor politicians plying their trade."[38]

This guy was so confident in his ability to manipulate the system that he put his hairdresser, Cosmo Cerrigone, on the payroll in what prosecutors called a no-show job.[39] The well-coiffed Treffinger was sanctimonious, too. Claiming some Italian ancestry, he wouldn't allow the TV show *The Sopranos* the permits needed to film a gunfight on county-owned property, the Associated Press reported. Treffinger said he didn't want to perpetuate harmful stereotypes. David Chase, creator of the program, got the last laugh. In the final episode of the show, he inserted a reference to the prosecution of a county official named James Treffolio.

Being the butt of a joke in a popular HBO program was the least of Treffinger's worries. When Christie got the U.S. attorney post, Treffinger's career took a big detour to the Big House. Christie had no sympathy for the poor ol' pols plying their crooked trade at taxpayer expense. Treffinger was indicted on twenty counts but signed a six-page plea agreement and eighteen of the counts were dropped. He was sentenced to forty-one months.

Even as Christie was piling up conviction after conviction, questions percolated about his style and his motives. He cut a far more public figure than previous U.S. attorneys, popped up frequently to swear in local elected officials, visited newspaper editorial boards, zinged the state's "culture of corruption."

The Press of Atlantic City ran an editorial on June 28, 2003, that said: "Last week, Christie called on Gov. James E. McGreevey and Attorney General Peter Harvey to step up their efforts to weed out official corruption. 'I'm prodding. I'm not criticizing,' Christie said. 'I've heard them say it will be a priority. I'm saying, "Let's see it." . . . I hope the governor shows leadership.'" The paper found that unusual, "particularly the direct, personal mention of the governor," even though the editorial said that the state could do more to fight corruption.

The paper also found it unusual that Christie's office set up meetings with newspaper editors around the state, "something you would expect from a politician—but not from a federal prosecutor." It was also concerned that Christie had dinner in a Trenton restaurant with South Jersey Democratic power broker and party boss George Norcross III. "This dinner meeting . . . has fueled speculations that Christie is a potential candidate for governor and that Norcross plans to abandon McGreevey and support the Republican.

"Christie, for his part, has said he has no plans to run. So was he just being exceptionally accessible when he sought those meetings with editors? Maybe. When he called on McGreevey to be more aggressive on political corruption, was Christie just being a dedicated prosecutor? Maybe. But to the truisms that corruption is bad and prosecuting it is good, we feel the need to add one more: Little is scarier to those who value liberty more than a politically ambitious U.S. attorney. The office comes with immense resources that can be misused—that is, used for political advantage—without much difficulty.

"So far so good with Mr. Christie," the newspaper concluded. "He's putting crooked pols in jail. But on the question of his ambitions and how they will affect his tenure as U.S. attorney, the jury is still out."

Christie said the high profile was strategy as much as it was his personality.

"I just thought that what that office had done and what I wanted to try to make it do was under noticed and undervalued by the public. And I thought that given what was going on in New Jersey, and what I had seen go on in government in particular, that people needed to know. And that maybe they were disgusted about certain things about their government or some of the corruption or whatever that they assumed was going on, but my view was we were the people who could make that happen, who could make something special happen, and the public should know about it," Christie said. "There was some bit of design in it, but there was also, kind of, that's me. It's hard for me to tell where one started and the other ended. But there's no question in my mind that as I thought about the job, that I thought about the fact that done correctly that this job, this office, could be really important in the consciousness of people's public lives, but that it had to be done the right way."

Every week seemed to bring a new development, a perp walk or leaked word of an official being subpoenaed. After he had been in office a year, the media and people on the street were suggesting Christie should run for governor. Christie was asked about running in 2005 nearly every day.[40] He always dismissed it, saying he was uninterested—a precursor to 2010 and 2011, when admirers fell in love with his YouTube videos and opined he should go for the White House. Christie told *The Jersey Journal*'s political writer Peter Weiss in 2003 that he had no interest in running for governor. "I don't miss politics all that much," he said.[41]

By year's end, though, he seemed to be leaving the door open. When the McGreevey administration imploded, his allies made "keep your powder dry" calls to GOP politicos in advance of a possible run in 2005. Christie later acknowledged that he consulted the White House. County political leaders were hoping he'd make the run; the party had a large field of seven candidates shaping up, none of whom excited voters—another harbinger of the 2012 please-run pleadings. But a few weeks after Bush's reelection, Christie announced on November 19, 2004 that he'd stay put, having reached his decision the night before following a long discussion with wife Mary Pat, brother Todd, and his father, Bill. "After a great deal of thought and consideration, I have decided that the best way for me to serve the people of the state of New Jersey at this time is as the United States Attorney. As I have said many times, I love this job."[42]

"Chris was always the kind of candidate that wanted to govern and really to make something happen," Mary Pat said. "And when he was on the freeholder board, he really did make things happen and shake things up, and they weren't ready for it. As opposed to '04 and '05, when he was in a position where he was really making great changes. So he was already changing the public good in the job he was doing. I think that had a lot to do with why he didn't run."

"What Mary Pat said is absolutely right," Christie said. "I didn't feel the burning desire to do it."

Christie similarly passed on potential runs for U.S. Senate in 2006 and 2008. Party leaders patiently waited. "Chris Christie has the most precious commodity in public life: Credibility," said Tom Wilson, then the Republican Party state chairman. "If this [seeking elected office] is something that Chris decides he wants, I think there would be a large group of people who would be eager to support him."[43]

The only way to maintain that support, fend off the critics, and ensure options were available in the future was to continue doing a credible job as U.S. attorney. Toward that end, every year from 2002 through 2007, his office recorded more criminal convictions than the year before. There were more than one thousand convictions for violent crime, including eight hundred convictions of felons illegally using firearms. He used RICO (Racketeer Influenced and Corrupt Organizations Act) against street gangs, working with state and local prosecutors.

He originated two highly publicized child pornography cases. In one, a Belarusan ring of child pornographers led to 1,500 arrests worldwide. In another, Superior Court Judge Stephen Thompson of Camden County in South Jersey was convicted of traveling to Russia to have sex with a boy. That originated with the Camden County prosecutor and the state attorney general's office but Christie took it over.

He took on corporations and institutions: Former Cendant Corp. chairman Walter Forbes was sentenced to prison for an accounting scheme that overstated income. After another accounting scandal, he worked out a deferred prosecution agreement with pharmaceutical giant Bristol-Myers Squibb in which the drug company had to hire an independent monitor for two years and follow the monitor's recommendations. He brought to light the financial relationships between physicians and makers of hips and knees affecting doctors' recommendations, and appointed an overseer for the University of Medicine and Dentistry of New Jersey after corruption was found throughout. Christie gave UMDNJ a choice: Accept an overseer or face criminal charges of Medicare fraud. He also engineered a $265 million civil settlement against the state's largest health care system for Medicaid fraud.

He put terrorists away—no small thing in a post-9/11 environment where law enforcement was so fearful of another attack that New Jersey investigators even charged three Arab grocers for an eighteen-month-old theft of a tractor trailer filled with Kellogg's Corn Flakes, so they could be questioned in the ensuing terrorism dragnet. In 2002, he established a terrorism unit with eight assistant U.S. attorneys to focus on domestic terrorism[44] and said frequently that terrorism, not corruption, was his office's top investigative priority.

Hemant Lakhani, a Pakistani-born FBI informer who was a British citizen, was sentenced to forty-seven years in prison for attempting to sell shoulder-fired missiles to alleged terrorist groups. Brian Ross of ABC News, however, reported much of the alleged missile plot was a government setup. "For example, Lakhani had no contacts in Russia to buy the missiles before the sting and had no known criminal record for arms dealing, officials told ABC News." Ross quoted military analyst Pavel Felgenhauer as saying, "Here we have a sting operation on some kind of small operator . . . who's bought one weapon when actually, on the gray and black market, hundreds of such weapons change hands." The reporter noted that court documents showed much of the case was based on the government's key cooperating witness, an informant seeking lenient treatment on federal drug charges.[45]

From his Texas ranch, President Bush said the arrest was evidence to undercut criticism that his administration was doing nothing to fight terrorism: "The fact that we're able to sting this guy is a pretty good example of what we're doing in order to protect the American people."[46]

The case was noteworthy for the cooperation among intelligence agencies in countries that had been enemies. The magazine *The Economist* noted, "The degree of coordination among three intelligence services—Russian, British and American—has been called unprecedented. Rarely are Russia's security services—the FSB, successor to the KGB—known to work so closely with their former cold-war antagonists. Their co-operation in this case may be a product of the close relationship between Mr. Bush and Russia's president, Vladimir Putin."[47]

Christie's team's work also led to the high-profile indictment and conviction of the "Fort Dix Six," who planned to attack and kill soldiers with automatic weapons at the military facility. That case began in early 2006, when a clerk at the Circuit City electronics store in Mount Laurel, Brian Morganstern, was alarmed by a ninety-minute, 8mm video he'd been asked to convert to a DVD that showed six Muslims in Pennsylvania's Pocono

Mountains shooting guns, playing paintball, and praising Allah. The clerk called the cops, who alerted the FBI, which got an informant named Mahmoud Omar to infiltrate the group. Neighbors of theirs in the Cherry Hill area didn't report anything sinister; the three brothers among the six had shared vegetables grown in their yard with them, and the only things people found unusual and worthy of complaint were a few farm animals in the guys' suburban yard.[48]

Authorities learned they were planning to attack military personnel at Fort Dix, which one of the plotters had gotten familiar with after delivering pizzas. Omar was no saint, having pleaded guilty to bank fraud five years earlier, declared bankruptcy, and been the unsuccessful target of a deportation effort. The authorities eventually arrested the plotters in 2007, a day after another FBI informant posing as an arms dealer provided them inoperable AK-47s and M-16s. Defense attorneys tried to suggest Omar had censored his recordings of the conversation to mask that he'd tricked the others by suggesting the plot. It didn't work; by the end of 2008, one had pleaded guilty to weapons charges and the other five were convicted of terrorism. Christie said using a cooperating witness like Omar was a necessity. "The only way to find out what's going on inside rather closed or private communities is to get people in there to infiltrate them," said Christie. "Would I rather have a trained law-enforcement officer as a witness? Yes. That's not always possible."[49] Christie would later tell children at a Cape May school that the Fort Dix Six case was the case he felt "the most gratification about" in his whole term.[50]

Christie has defended the Patriot Act, including one highly controversial portion of the law that allowed the government to investigate what materials people had taken out of public libraries. "The USA Patriot Act is, I believe, the single biggest reason why we have been able to prevent another terrorist attack in the last five years," he said in 2007.[51] As prosecutor, he approved tracking people's locations through their cell phones without a "probable cause" search warrant in nearly one hundred cases. When the Justice Department in 2007 recommended that prosecutors seek warrants to secure the most precise GPS data, rather than court orders issued for tracking information relevant to an investigation, it took Christie eleven months, and nineteen warrantless searches, to change the policy in

New Jersey. "There was no action of the U.S. attorney's office that was done without the consultation and approval of the court. Any suggestion to the contrary is ill-informed," Christie said.[52]

Christie's experiences in terrorism-related cases led him as governor to nominate a lawyer who had defended wrongly detained Muslims after the 9/11 attacks as a state judge, attracting attention for running counter to the prevailing mood among many in his Republican Party.

In July 2011, Christie said the FBI inappropriately detained many people after 9/11. He did so as part of a forceful defense of appointing Sohail Mohammed as the state's first Indian American and second Muslim judge. Conservative bloggers and some lawmakers had questioned Mohammed's loyalties because of clients he'd represented and a more general fear that he'd follow Islamic Sharia law before the Constitution. "This Sharia law business is crap. It's just crazy, and I'm tired of dealing with the crazies," Christie said. "It's just unnecessary to be accusing this guy of things just because of his religious background. . . .

"Ignorance is behind the criticism of Sohail Mohammed," said Christie, lauding Mohammed as "an extraordinary American" and citing his efforts to get Muslims in New Jersey to cooperate with federal investigators, in part by setting up dozens of meetings between law enforcement and community leaders. Later that same day, he attended Mohammed's formal swearing-in, an appearance typically reserved for former employees who became judges, at which he delivered a moderated version of his fiery comments and embraced Mohammed in a lengthy hug.

Carolee Adams, president of the conservative Eagle Forum of New Jersey, said Christie was the one who was ignorant—of Sharia law. "He's come under attack and in his typical fashion he will attack the attacker without answering it in a very intelligent and knowledgeable way. That's his style," she said.[53]

That press conference caught many progressives by surprise. MSNBC's *The Last Word with Lawrence O'Donnell* devoted a large segment to it and the program faded to black with O'Donnell and his crew giving Christie what O'Donnell said was the show's first standing ovation.[54]

Antiterrorism stings and white-collar financial cases aside, it was Christie's emphasis on public corruption that became his calling card. Treffinger's downfall in the opening months of his tenure showed his critics that Christie meant business. It also showed them that party affiliation was no guarantee of safety from prosecution, which was useful to Christie when Democrats argued that his crime busting was politically based. Not true, he'd say, pointing to Treffinger and others, including a wave of arrests in reliably Republican Monmouth County, which he described as infested by corruption.

Nevertheless, Democrats still complained they were singled out. It comes with the territory, said Herb Stern, who took down a number of Democrats on corruption charges as U.S. attorney in the early 1970s. "When I was in office they said I was on a witch hunt, too. But you'd be amazed how many sons of witches we caught," Stern said.[55] Speculation that Christie was targeting Democrats to raise his political profile were so widespread that in a 2004 corruption trial, defense attorney Gerald Krovatin asked a former police chief testifying about conversations secretly taped six years earlier, "And do you know that Chris Christie is running for governor of this state?" Two federal prosecutors leapt up to object, and U.S. District Judge Joseph Greenaway struck the question from the trial record. "We don't need to go there or near anything like it," the judge said.[56]

In 2004, when a scandal touching Jim McGreevey erupted in Piscataway, local Republicans—with help from a campaign contribution from Christie's brother, Todd, and an assist from money raised by pal Bill Palatucci for the state GOP—tried using the issue to win a mayoral race. "This is the most despicable thing to come out of the U.S. attorney's office in my life," longtime Democratic pol and big-time McGreevey supporter John Lynch said. "And he wants to be governor? Let's get it on."[57] Those were words Lynch would come to regret.

Not every Democrat felt that way. "I'm—like everybody else, Republicans and Democrats—sick and tired of reading about all this crap," Jon Corzine, at the time a U.S. senator running for governor, said of New Jersey's penchant for corruption. "I want it to stop. I have no problem with what Chris Christie is doing. I have no problem. God bless him."[58]

Still, it was easy to see why some would think political bias was at play, since the list of Christie takedowns could have doubled for the flow chart of Who's Who in New Jersey Democratic Party circles:

There was Robert Janiszewski, a longtime official in Democrat-controlled Hudson County, who pleaded guilty to taking more than $100,000 in bribes. He was sentenced to forty-one months and the judge cited "corruption of unbelievable depth and duration."[59]

Senator Wayne Bryant, who collected salaries from as many as four public jobs he held simultaneously as well as being a partner in a law firm that did well with government-related clients, was indicted for corruption involving a job at the University of Medicine and Dentistry of New Jersey that prosecutors dubbed a "low-show job." Bryant would report to work, primarily to read newspapers. He was convicted on all counts and sentenced to four years. Two years later, while serving his sentence, Bryant was indicted on separate charges for allegedly taking bribes in connection with building projects.[60] He was acquitted by a federal judge in August 2012 and released from federal prison four months later.

(Of note here, Paul Fishman, who was appointed by President Barack Obama to succeed Christie as U.S. attorney, had to recuse himself from the second round of Bryant indictments because Fishman, before he took office, represented one of the building projects. The U.S. attorney in Manhattan handled the case. After following Christie into the office, Fishman, in what was seen as a petty put-down, said he didn't endorse the idea he worked in the "most corrupt" state in the nation and that such crazy talk can be "demoralizing" to people who live in New Jersey.[61])

John Lynch spent twenty years in the state Senate, which included time as Senate president and Democratic leader when the party was in the majority and when it was in the minority. He also was a longtime mayor and undisputed party boss in Middlesex County, which is in the middle of the state. Lynch might have run for governor except for an incident involving his brother-in-law. Louis Auricchio, brother of Lynch's wife, Deborah, was an admitted mobster. He shot and killed mob capo John DiGilio.[62]

Lynch did help others get to the governor's office. He was a longtime backer of Jim McGreevey and aided his rise from Woodbridge mayor, although when McGreevey became governor his young and inexperienced staff had little use for the old-time pol. Lynch admitted in 2006 that he accepted tens of thousands of dollars from a contractor while lobbying to help him develop state parkland. The former kingmaker and son of a prominent state senator was sentenced to thirty-nine months.[63]

McGreevey's largest campaign donor was real estate mogul Charles Kushner, one of the richest people in New Jersey, whom McGreevey planned to name chairman of the powerful Port Authority of New York and New Jersey, which operates New York–area airports, tunnels, and bridges in addition to controlling hundreds of millions of dollars in real estate development contracts. McGreevey used words like "integrity," "decency," and "commitment to the highest ethical standards" to describe Kushner. But GOP senator Bill Gormley, who cochaired the Senate Judiciary Committee, had concerns about possible conflicts in the real estate development area and called Kushner before his committee. Kushner resigned rather than make the appearance. But conflicts of interest weren't anywhere near the biggest of Kushner's problems.

Christie was investigating tax filings and campaign contributions by Kushner's companies. In an attempt to keep witnesses from cooperating, including his family, Kushner hired a prostitute to engage in videotaped sex with his brother-in-law, William Schulder, and sent the tape to his sister, Esther Schulder, just before a family party. The feds said he wanted to send it to his sister's children, but the guy he hired refused to do so. Christie charged Kushner with witness tampering, obstruction of justice, and promoting prostitution. Under a plea agreement, he was sentenced to two years in federal prison.

After his release—which was earlier than expected because Kushner got credit for tending to a substance abuse problem nobody realized he had—there were happier family occasions. Kushner's son, Jared, who runs the *New York Observer* newspaper and the political Web site PolitickerNJ.com, married Ivanka Trump at a golf course in Bedminster owned by the bride's father, Donald. The *New York Post* reported that McGreevey was at the wedding.[64]

While McGreevey himself never was indicted, a case involving him gives insight into how Christie brought some of his sharp sense of humor into law enforcement.

Farmer Mark Halper asked David D'Amiano—Democratic fund-raiser, waste-recycling operator, and old chum of McGreevey's—for help with dealing with the governments of Piscataway Township and Middlesex County, which wanted to seize Halper's dairy farm for a park by using eminent domain. Halper thought he should be getting more money than was offered. D'Amiano worked out a deal with Halper where Halper would donate money to Democrats in exchange for assurances that officials would give him more money for his land. To let Halper know which officials were aware of the scheme, they would use a code word, "Machiavelli," in conversations.

On February 18, 2003, D'Amiano introduced Halper to McGreevey at a fund-raiser in the East Brunswick Hilton. The governor said to an aide, identified by sources as Amy Mansue, that Halper should read Machiavelli's *The Prince* to learn how to deal with farm negotiations, a strange and hardly logical recommendation, but not as humorous as the source of the code itself. Halper had gone to federal officials earlier complaining of extortion and wore a wire for eighteen months. The Machiavelli code word people were asked to use originated not from farmer Halper, but from prosecutor Christie. One can imagine the laughter in the room when the undercover taped conversations were played.

It certainly garnered guffaws later when the story was recalled. Former governor Brendan Byrne, known for his quick wit, spoke to the New Jersey delegation at the 2004 Democratic convention in Boston and mentioned the secret Machiavelli tapes. "Somebody suggested that my history as a speaker is so bad, that I mumble so much that they never could have wiretapped me," Byrne told the Democrats.[65]

When it went public, McGreevey insisted the utterances were a coincidence, that he used Machiavelli a lot in conversations. On the day Byrne spoke in Boston, McGreevey also addressed the audience, ending his talk with a quote from Tennyson's "Ulysses," which many took to be an attempt to reinforce his contention he often used literary references, although no others could be recalled.

Fund-raiser D'Amiano was charged in a forty-seven-page indictment with eleven counts of shaking down farmer Halper. He pleaded guilty to two counts of mail fraud and was sentenced to twenty-four months in prison. McGreevey was not mentioned by name in the indictments, though as unnamed "State Official 1" he was referred to eighty-three times. No one but D'Amiano was indicted. Christie's FBI agents, however, visited McGreevey at the governor's mansion and played the taped conversations. McGreevey hired lawyer William E. Lawler III of Washington after subpoenas were served on his offices. Lawler said McGreevey answered questions and discussed the roles other staffers played in the dairy farm matter.[66]

Democrats felt Christie's efforts had reached a tipping point and organized a political counteroffensive asserting again that Christie was using his political office for political gain. "I talked with [McGreevey's] office about these issues, expressed my concern, and volunteered to consider how to advise them during this process," said Timothy Carden, a former state human services commissioner. "Nobody's hired me. I'm not expected to be hired. This is an issue of a Democrat who's a citizen who's concerned about the office performing effectively under enormous pressure."[67] McGreevey, in a twenty-minute response to the charges against D'Amiano, said the indictment resembled a "political novel" intended to hurt him and boost Christie's political prospects through "conjecture and innuendo."[68] "It is, regrettably, an effort to smear my personal integrity, my character, and my reputation," McGreevey said.[69] State senator Joseph Kyrillos called McGreevey's attack on the U.S. attorney "unfortunate and inappropriate, not to mention not particularly bright."[70]

A few months later McGreevey revealed an affair with a male aide and announced his departure in the infamous "gay American" speech designed to make him appear the victim of prejudice and blackmail.[71] The aide had been appointed to a key homeland security post for which he lacked qualifications. Which raises the question: Was McGreevey in pedal-to-the-metal prosecutor Christie's sights? In the early 1500s one of the earliest political scientists advised leaders new to power, which one could argue was Christie's situation, that it is better to be feared than respected. His name was Niccolò Machiavelli.

Bret Schundler—McGreevey's Republican opponent in 2001, unsuccessful candidate for the gubernatorial nomination in 2005, and later a key player in one of the big controversies of Christie's gubernatorial term—said, "McGreevey wants people to believe he resigned from office because of a gay sex scandal. In truth, he resigned to cover up his administration's corruption and also, quite possibly, to avoid indictment."

The idea of sting operations in political corruption cases wasn't new. Similar stings had been run in New Jersey for years—including the Bid Rig investigation that began before Christie's arrival but hit publicly, in two separate waves, on his watch.

Wave three began in April 2006, when a real estate investor named Solomon Dwek rolled up to a PNC Bank drive-up window to cash a fraudulent check.

For more than $25 million.

Twice.

Dwek, looking to extricate himself from a long prison term, promised federal prosecutors he could become an undercover informant that would help them infiltrate an international money-laundering operation among his community of Syrian Jews along the Shore and in Brooklyn, New York. That evolved into a two-track investigation that focused on development and bribes, primarily in Hudson County but also touching on Bergen and Ocean. Dwek, a fast-talking con man wearing a hidden camera, went to hundreds of meetings over three years and talked up fake, outlandish construction projects. The risks of working with Dwek were evident from the start—"Do I really want to get in bed with this guy?" Christie asked deputies[72]—but prosecutors forged ahead, building a sting entirely based on Dwek's high-wire-act meetings that grew to forty-four arrests by its July 2009 execution.

On top of the forty-four people arrested in the initial wave, two additional people—a Jersey City councilman and the executive director of the barely existent Ocean County Democrats—had pleaded guilty by the end of 2009. Thirty-one of the forty-six were from the public corruption side of the operation, fourteen from the money-laundering angle, including five rabbis, and one in the headline-grabbing, black-market kidney scheme.

Charges against some of the corruption defendants were later thrown out when U.S. District Judge Jose Linares, backed up in early 2011 by a federal appeals court, ruled in May 2010 that candidates who don't hold public office can't be charged under the Hobbs Act with public corruption—"legal alchemy," he called it. Prosecutors argued they were selling their future influence—"The gist of the crime lies in the goal," assistant U.S. attorney Christopher Gramiccioni said in a brief in the case[73]—but the courts didn't permit it. Some candidates in Jersey City, including mayoral hopeful Louis Manzo and City Council running mates, had been among those accused. Some charges were tossed, others added in revised indictments with less punishing charges.

"We felt it was an overreaching government prosecution from the beginning, and this decision is a validation of that belief," said Manzo's attorney, John Lynch.[74] Separate from the legal arguments, Manzo also launched a spirited political defense, even holding a gone-rogue news conference without his lawyer's consent to level accusations that Christie engineered the case to boost his campaign and that loyal aides carried it out when they did for maximum impact. "It's obvious, when you connect the dots, there was an attempt to use a government sting as an effort to help Christie's election," Manzo said.[75] He pointed out that Gramiccioni and his family—including wife Deborah, who later worked in Christie's governor's office—gave $1,250 to the Christie campaign. The contributions were allowable under federal guidelines. And he noted how many former Christie subordinates got jobs in Trenton. Michael Drewniak, Christie's spokesman as a prosecutor and as governor, called Manzo "deluded." "He appears to be just another official in New Jersey charged with corruption who wants to divert attention from his own conduct," Drewniak said.[76]

A week later, Manzo's lawyer took the same argument into court. "Lou Manzo was indicted for a headline," Lynch told Linares in March 2010.[77] "This was in the middle of a campaign in which the man was running for governor of the state of New Jersey, and this indictment helped him."[78]

Criticisms of the case had gone beyond aggrieved defendants bitching about their fate into actual arguments in court and, by extension, into the newspapers. Law enforcement noticed, and Christie's successor, U.S. Attorney Paul Fishman, defended the amount of time and energy poured into the case.

"There has been much discussion in the press about the integrity of the government's case and the government's witnesses, but in the end, it really comes down to the cold hard facts of the case," said Michael Ward, special agent in charge of the FBI's Newark office, when Dennis Elwell, the mayor of Secaucus, was convicted in July 2011. "Those facts prove the guilt of Dennis Elwell."[79]

"There is no question that a number of attorneys were tied up for the last two years on cases that have emanated out of Bid Rig. That meant they could not put their time into new investigations. But we have the same commitment of resources to corruption that we always have," Fishman said.[80]

By the time Fishman said that, the case had cost his office its eleven-year undefeated streak in political corruption cases, one that Christie bragged about often on the campaign trail.

Ridgefield mayor Anthony Suarez, who had refused exhortations by Governor Jon Corzine to resign when he was charged with plotting to extort $10,000, was the first to beat the rap. He refused Dwek's cash and didn't cash a check, but he did take a $2,500 donation to his legal fund from a codefendant that he says he thought was clean. A jury acquitted him in October 2010. "When you know in your heart that you didn't do anything wrong and you maintain your innocence from the beginning, I always had faith that people will see the truth here," said Suarez. "Thank God that the jury saw the truth."[81]

Michael Critchley, Suarez's attorney, had shredded Dwek on the witness stand. He said prosecutors might have been "blinded by the thought of the mother lode" in deploying Dwek, a con man he called "detestable" and "rotten to his core." "It's one thing to send out a witness like Dwek when crime is actually occurring. It's fair game if someone's involved in ongoing criminal matters," he said. "I get a little concerned and frightened when you send someone like Dwek out to entice people into committing a crime."[82]

The prosecutors' losing streak was extended a few months later, when L. Harvey Smith, a former state senator and assemblyman snagged while he was running for Jersey City mayor, was acquitted on all six charges against him connected with $15,000 in alleged bribes. Dwek, his usefulness on the stand shattered, was kept on the sidelines. A former housing commissioner named Edward Cheatam, who had pleaded guilty within two months of being charged in the case as a bribe-carrying middleman, instead took the stand—and apparently didn't make a good impression.

"The public, juries representing the people out there, is getting a little sick and tired of Solomon Dwek and what he did," said Smith's attorney, Peter Willis.[83] "It's easy to lose your reputation when you're accused of something like this and it's hard to get it back," Smith said. "I never expected my life would be in this position at this time, in this age."[84] Willis suggested the case was tied to Christie's political plans. "He had his own ambitions. You can draw any inference you want from that," he said. Drewniak said such comments denigrate the work of prosecutors and FBI agents: "I guess a solid trial victory isn't enough for Mr. Willis, so he has to conflate it into this sort of cocky nonsense."[85]

"It's about time somebody gives the government a comeuppance," said defense attorney Jack Arseneault. "They really overreached in many of these cases. The climate is such that if you're a politician, there's a presumption of guilt."[86] Fishman, who wasn't the one who decided to use Dwek, and who inherited the cases upon taking office a few months after the sting, defended the case. "We use undercover informants all the time. Some come with more baggage than others," Fishman said.[87] "Law enforcement often uses cooperators who are themselves criminals," he said. "Their behavior is carefully supervised."[88]

Dwek's bail on the bank fraud charges was eventually revoked in June 2011, after he lied to the FBI about his arrest involving a rental car in Baltimore, where his wife and children now live, that wasn't returned by the other person authorized to drive it. Charges were dropped by Maryland prosecutors when the bill was paid. An exasperated Linares revoked Dwek's bail, calling him a "consummate defrauder and extremely cunning liar."[89] He was sentenced in October 2012 to six years in federal prison.

Corzine said after having lost the governor's race that he didn't think Bid Rig III was the cause or that the case was a political ploy. "That would be an extraordinary abuse of power. The election was lost because unemployment was 10 percent. People were hurting," he said.[90]

As of mid-March 2013, three of the forty-six cases remained unresolved. Two were on the public corruption side, after charges were dismissed in February against Louis Manzo, who had been indicted, seen charges added, got charges dismissed, was indicted all over again, and led the chorus asserting that the investigation was designed to boost Christie's gubernatorial chances. Nineteen of the thirty-one accused in the corruption side of the operation had pleaded guilty, and four others were convicted at trial. Five had been cleared—Smith, Suarez, and three whose charges were dropped, Richard Greene, an aide to Smith, Joseph Castagna, a Jersey City health officer, and one whose conviction was later vacated, Michael Manzo. And one, political consultant Jack Shaw, died of a prescription drug overdose within days of his arrest.

One unresolved case was on the money-laundering side, involving one of the alleged cash couriers—Yolie Gertner, who was a fugitive believed to have fled first to Israel and then to London. Thirteen others had pleaded guilty, include Long Branch synagogue leader Eliahu Ben Haim, whose five-year prison sentence handed down in January 2012 was the longest the investigation had yielded to date.

The case also yielded the first-ever conviction in the United States for black-market trafficking of human organs. Levy-Itzhak Rosenbaum, who brokered real estate while not brokering kidney transplants, pleaded guilty in October 2011 and admitted to having brokered three kidney transactions, each time netting at least $120,000. He was sentenced in July 2012 to two and a half years in prison.

Two weeks after Obama won the 2008 election, Christie announced his resignation. Plum jobs like U.S. attorneys turn over sooner rather than later when the White House changes hands, and rather than linger as a holdover Christie headed for the doors and, a few months later, his long anticipated return to elective politics. Ralph Marra, who had been his top assistant, became acting U.S. attorney.

Had U.S. senator John McCain won the presidential election in 2008, Jon Corzine might have had two terms as governor.

"If John McCain won and I had gotten a signal from the McCain transition that they were willing to keep me, I probably wouldn't have run," Christie said. "Because there was a lot of great stuff we were working on, and Mary Pat knows how much I loved that job. I probably would have looked at it and said, 'Well, I'm making a difference here. I could make a difference there.' But once the president won, once President Obama won,

I knew I was going to be out. And I felt like, all right, if I want to continue what I've been doing, then I almost have no choice but to run."

In his November 17, 2008, resignation letter, Christie said, "These 143 men and women serve with quiet dignity, determination and a commitment to public service that is so admirable in today's society. I will always be in their debt for all they have shared with me and all they contributed to the cause of justice."

At the time his tenure ended on December 1, 2008, Christie had more than 130 convictions of elected and appointed political officials, and no acquittals, under his belt. That included five New Jersey legislators, two county executives, four other county officeholders, eighteen mayors, and fifteen municipal county members, among numerous "public servants" who, like Harrison Williams of Abscam fame, served themselves first and foremost.

The guy that many laughed at in late 2001 and early 2002 departed as the longest serving and arguably most successful U.S. attorney in New Jersey history. He certainly left on a higher note than he came in on and he never forgot it. He kept in his office in the Peter Rodino Federal Building—named for the New Jersey congressman who presided over Richard Nixon's impeachment hearings—that editorial cartoon from the early days, showing Bush impressed by Christie's thin résumé because of his fundraising prowess. Christie said he kept it to show "I don't take myself too seriously."[91]

CHAPTER FIVE

―◆―

Tossing Mud at Mr. Clean

While Chris Christie's U.S. attorney days are generally considered productive and beneficial by Democrats and Republicans, he has detractors who allege politics, favoritism, and expensive tastes sully his name.

President George W. Bush adviser Karl Rove reentered the Christie story when word spread from Washington that Rove and other officials in Bush's White House played an active role in the firings at the end of 2006 of seven United States attorneys, all appointed by Bush. Among them was the U.S. attorney in New Mexico, David Iglesias. Materials made public by the House Judiciary Committee showed that Rove and others working for Bush gave particular attention to complaints from Republicans in New Mexico that Iglesias failed to aid their election prospects by prosecuting alleged instances of voter fraud.

The seven were dismissed in midterm on December 7, 2006, Pearl Harbor Day. Allegations arose that they were fired because they did not initiate investigations that would damage Democratic politicians. They were replaced with interim appointees under provisions of the USA Patriot Act, which eliminated the 120-day term limit on interim appointments of U.S. attorneys made by the attorney general to fill vacancies. That provision allowed appointees to avoid a confirmation vote in the Senate. In 2007 the provision was rescinded by Congress, unhappy the legislative branch was being denied its advise and consent role.

At least twenty-six U.S. attorneys had been on the hit list at some point, including Christie.

The heads that rolled did so after a slow-motion review the Bush administration began when the president won reelection in 2004. It's common for those offices to be vacated when the occupant of the White House changes; upon taking office in 1993, President Bill Clinton fired every U.S. attorney except for one—Michael Chertoff of New Jersey, who'd eventually become Department of Homeland Security secretary. Clinton kept on Chertoff at U.S. senator Bill Bradley's request.[1] Indeed, that to-the-victors-go-the-spoils pattern is how Christie left federal office in late 2008 when Barack Obama replaced Bush. But it was unusual for such a move to be made midway through a president's term.

Responding to an email from the White House in January 2005, in which Rove through an intermediary inquired about the plan for how the U.S. attorneys were to be let go, Kyle Sampson, chief of staff to incoming attorney general Alberto Gonzales, outlined the legal and political ramifications. "As an operational matter, we would like to replace 15–20 percent of the current U.S. attorneys—the underperforming ones. (This is a rough guess; we might want to consider doing performance evaluations after Judge comes on board.) The vast majority of U.S. attorneys, 80–85 percent, I would guess, are doing a great job, are loyal Bushies, etc., etc." Sampson cautioned that home-state senators would likely resist the turnover. "That said, if Karl thinks there would be political will to do it, then so do I."

It was eventually learned that over two dozen of the nation's U.S. attorneys, more than a quarter of the total, were targeted for removal at one point or another during the review. Among them was Christie—twice. On New Year's Day 2006, Sampson drafted a memo to White House counsel Harriet Miers in which he identified eleven U.S. attorneys to replace. He shared the draft with Monica Goodling, at the time a counselor to Attorney General Gonzales; she recommended removing two of Sampson's targets. They were removed from the memo emailed to Miers a week later—and found their way onto "Tier 1" of a list of potential additional targets marked "others," as did a U.S. attorney from Arizona that Goodling had included under the category of "other problem districts." And so did Christie. That Arizona prosecutor, Paul Charlton, ultimately lost his job, as well as a prosecutor who'd been on "Tier 2" of Sampson's January addendum, Daniel Bogden of Nevada.

Nearly ten months later, Christie's name popped up again shortly before the firings were about to be executed. A November 2006 memo from Michael Elston, chief of staff to the Justice Department's deputy attorney general, to Gonzales's chief of staff Sampson—subject line: "Other Possibilities"—included Christie on a list of five potential additional targets that Elston said "have been suggested to me by others." No reasons were given, no sources for the suggestions. Elston told congressional investigators that Sampson had asked him to check around the Justice Department asking people if there were other U.S. attorney "problems." He made what he deemed "casual inquiries" with four or five officials, primarily in the tax and criminal divisions, including the assistant attorney general of the criminal division, Alice Fisher, and her chief of staff, Matthew Friedrich. He said he and Sampson agreed none of them warranted removal. Sampson told investigators he thought Elston's list was created differently but thought none of the people on it should be let go.

Christie talked with Elston in March 2007.

"I know who put me on the list, but I don't know why. It was a guy named Mike Elston, who was chief of staff to the deputy attorney general, Paul McNulty. He called me while I was on vacation, I was in Florida, and he called me before the list was going to be going out and said to me, 'There are going to be documents released today to Congress, and I assume they're going to be leaked, and they're going to show that you were on an early list of people we considered to be fired.' I said, 'Really? How did I wind up on the list?' And he said, 'Oh, well, I put you there.' And I said, 'Why?' And he said, 'I don't remember.'"

Christie wasn't buying what Elston was selling.

"I think, from my interaction with Mike Elston, he always came across to me as kind of a liar," Christie said. "I said, 'Listen, I don't want to talk to you. Tell the deputy attorney general to call me back.' He said, 'Well, he's really busy.' I said, 'You tell Paul to call me.'"

McNulty called Christie that night, and Christie offered to quit.

"I said, 'Listen, if you want my resignation, you can have it, because I'm not going to do this job looking over my shoulder.' 'No, I don't want your resignation. Please don't resign. You're one of my best people. I don't know how this happened.' I said, 'Well, ask your chief of staff how it happened, he put me on the list. How did it happen? How did I get on the list? How did I get off?' And he said, 'I don't know,'" Christie said. "The only impression I could come to is that they were under siege. They were all battening down the hatches down there. Nobody was going to give me any information, in part because they probably weren't giving anybody any information. And, two, because I'm sure on their part there was a real fear that I'd talk about it."

How about the Kyle Sampson memo that listed Christie as well?

"Sampson told me that he basically took what the deputy's office had put together, that he didn't have his own list, that basically he went to the deputy, who was the one who was really overseeing the U.S. attorneys, and said, 'Put together a list of people,'" Christie said. "Sampson told me that there was no way he was going to let my name be on that list ultimately, because he thought that I was doing a good job. But no one ever would tell me when I got on, when I got off, how I got on, how I got off."

While there are several theories about what caused Christie's name to drop off the list, Christie thinks the answer is not so complex.

"Everyone's looking for something nefarious. And you know what I think it is? Pure incompetence," he said. "Pure incompetence with a tinge of politics."

Rove said the White House didn't compile a list of candidates to be removed and didn't order the Justice Department to add any names to the list.[2] He acknowledged that he passed along complaints about one name on the list, David Iglesias of New Mexico, in part for lack of action on a voter fraud allegation and bungling, with an eye on a future political campaign, a high-profile corruption case by interfering with career prosecutors handling the case. And he said every prosecutor removed was axed for a justifiable reason, such as the U.S. attorney for Southern California, Carol Lam, for not giving enough priority to prosecuting immigration cases. A 2007 email between a Justice Department official and a White House official assessing the U.S. attorneys who'd been fired suggests two were let go in part because they'd engaged in significant travel outside their district.[3] Finally, Rove added, Bush could have fired them for any reason at any time. "Under the Constitution, the president's power over the U.S. attorneys is absolute. He could remove them if he thought they parted their hair on the wrong side—and Congress couldn't stop him," Rove wrote in *Courage and Consequence.*

Congress closely examined the U.S. attorney purge, starting in 2007, questioning whether the offices were being used by the White House for political purposes. When word surfaced that Christie was on a version of the hit list, even fiercely partisan Democrats such as New York's U.S. senator Charles Schumer were stunned. "It's befuddling," Schumer said at a Capitol Hill news conference. "I was shocked when I saw Chris Christie's name on the list last night. It just shows a [Justice] department that has run amok."[4] Fellow federal prosecutors shared the sentiment. "It's astounding," said Patrick Meehan, the U.S. attorney in Philadelphia. "Among his peers, Chris stands out as one of the most admired. If you were to create a list of the U.S. attorneys who have had the greatest impact, Chris would be one of the top two or three names I'd put on it. This defies explanation."[5]

Christie foes had an explanation for his removal, and it had to do with an investigation of U.S. senator Robert Menendez.

The Democratic senator was well connected to Jersey's political bosses, including by extension the granddaddy of all of them, Frank "I Am the Law" Hague, who ruled out of Jersey City from 1917 to 1947. In 1946, Hague backed William Musto for the state Assembly, where he served nineteen years, followed by seventeen in the state Senate. Among the people Musto mentored was Menendez. When Musto was indicted for racketeering, fraud, and extortion, Menendez testified against his old friend, who was sent to prison for seven years in 1982. When Menendez ran for the U.S. Senate in 2006, that testimony was presented as a young Menendez doing the right thing by turning on Musto, though not all old-timers in politics agreed. *The New York Times* quoted Menendez opponent Bob Haney as saying Menendez worked his way up through the machine, then took over.[6] *Star-Ledger* columnist Tom Moran wrote, "Menendez is the boss in Hudson County, which is ground zero for the state's corruption problem."[7]

Menendez had done well in politics as Union City mayor and member of the New Jersey Assembly and Senate and congressman—always pointing to his Cuban heritage and joining South Florida residents in their hatred for all things Castro. He said his parents fled tyranny in Cuba. *Star-Ledger* columnist Paul Mulshine tried to get the full story but wrote he couldn't get a straight answer. "Menendez was born on Jan. 1, 1954, exactly five years to the day before Fidel Castro came to power. By timing of his birth, it's possible they left Cuba during the regime of Fulgencio Batista. One problem: Batista was a right-winger. You don't make points with the Cuban-American community by railing against right-wingers."[8] A July 2006 Star-Ledger story said Menendez's parents left under Batista, "seeking economic and political freedom." Other bios only said his parents were immigrants.

Many saw Menendez as a Hudson County political boss. Even though he was in Congress, *The New York Observer* said Menendez used his "fierce and unforgiving muscle to paralyze the government of Jersey City. And why? To teach a lesson to the mayor, a man named Glenn Cunningham, who had run afoul of Mr. Menendez."[9] Later, Cunningham, a former cop and Marine, took on the establishment in the Democratic primary for state Senate and beat old-time pol Joe Doria and his colleagues endorsed by the Hudson County power brokers on the Menendez team. Cunningham won the election, but five months after he was sworn in, died of a heart attack. Jersey City shut down and four thousand people went to the funeral. It was made clear to Menendez he shouldn't be among them. Christie delivered the eulogy.

Jon Corzine appointed U.S. representative Menendez to finish the rest of his Senate term—eleven-plus months—after Corzine became governor. Menendez then ran for a full term. Two months before the Senate election between Menendez and Tom Kean Jr., son of Christie mentor and former governor Tom Kean, Christie's office launched an investigation of a nonprofit organization that rented property from Menendez.

Menendez collected more than $300,000 in rent from the nonprofit and, while a member of the U.S. House of Representatives, helped the agency for which he was landlord get federal grants. Employees of the nonprofit, the North Hudson Community Action Corp., contributed $33,450 to Menendez campaigns.[10] It also named him its "man of the year" in 2001 and named the lobby at its headquarters the "Congressman Robert Menendez Pavilion." Its lease stated the agency's ability to pay rent was dependent on the agency getting certain federal or state funding.[11]

"I think it's a conflict of interest for a congressman to do outside business with an organization that receives so much federal money," said Alex Knott, political editor for the Center for Public Integrity. "The bottom line is that the congressman and his colleagues indirectly control the purse strings of this organization."[12]

Menendez said he had received permission to enter into the lease in 1994 from Mark Davis of the House Ethics Committee.[13] But a Capitol Hill publication said Davis didn't work there then and he couldn't be questioned about it because he died the year before. A Menendez spokesman said it must have been someone else who gave permission.[14]

Bob Perry, the Texas tycoon who helped finance the "Swift Boat" ads against Democratic presidential candidate John Kerry in 2004, funded a TV ad for the New Jersey Senate race that showed a mobster in a black leather jacket talking on a cell phone in an alley. "We got a problem . . . our boy down in Washington, Bob Menendez, he's caught in this federal investigation . . . right . . . feds start looking into these fixed contracts, bada-bing, we're in but deep."[15]

At a convention of Democrats in Atlantic City, Menendez accused Kean of working with Christie. "Tom Kean Jr.'s entire playbook has been straight out of the Bush-Rove playbook and now's he's even gotten the U.S. attorney involved."[16]

U.S. senator Frank Lautenberg, no friend of Christie's then or as governor, called the probe "quite a coincidence. The timing raises a question mark."[17] Corzine said it was unfair to publicly reveal subpoenas sixty days before an election. Christie said sixty days had been his office's informal rule since before his arrival; the calendar showed the Menendez subpoena dropped just a few days before that deadline. "Every year we have elections in New Jersey. If I shut us down for a longer period, we'd be in the freezer half the year," said Christie.[18]

Lautenberg and Menendez didn't like Christie, and when they announced their support of the nomination of Paul Fishman to replace him as U.S. attorney in 2009, a slap in Christie's face was included. Menendez said the office should spend more time pursuing gangs, which some took to mean less time chasing political crooks. Fishman immediately made a fool of himself by saying he didn't think New Jersey had a corruption problem and that referring to the state in that way was demoralizing. A Rutgers-Eagleton poll released in November 2009 showed 65 percent of state residents thought there was "a lot" of political corruption and 26 percent thought there was "some."[19]

Fishman himself had a tangled history with public figures that on occasion affected his role. As a private attorney, Fishman represented Corzine's former girlfriend and union leader Carla Katz and developer Encap Golf Holdings, both of which were investigated by Christie's office. The U.S. attorney in New York had to take over the Encap probe after Fishman recused himself.

The Star-Ledger reported that investigators were seeking union records connected with Katz's management of Communications Workers of America Local 1034. Quoting unnamed sources, the paper said the authorities were focusing on an internal CWA probe that recently accused Katz of misappropriating union money.[20] Fishman transferred the Katz probe to the federal prosecutor in Philadelphia, *The Star-Ledger* said.[21] As of February 2012, no charges have been filed against her.

Menendez won the 2006 Senate race, helped by a national wave of anger over the Iraq War in extending a Democratic senate-winning streak that dated to 1976. Five years later, in an October 5, 2011, letter to Menendez's lawyer, the U.S. attorney for the eastern district of Pennsylvania, Zane David Memeger, wrote, "After review and consideration of the matter transferred to me, I have decided to close the file."[22]

It was transferred to him by Fishman, who in a procedure becoming rather familiar for his tenure, recused himself again because Menendez had backed him for the office. The letter was cosigned by assistant U.S. attorney Richard P. Barrett.

The Star-Ledger obtained a copy of the letter and said it indicated that Menendez's lawyer, Marc Elias, had pressed Memeger in phone calls for an update on the investigation.[23] On October 25, after weeks of silence, Menendez told Gannett's Raju Chebium in Washington he felt vindicated: "As I said almost five years ago, during the height of my first campaign for United States Senate, there was no merit to this investigation and there never was. This official letter—though long delayed—finally confirms this fact."[24]

When word emerged that Christie had been on, then gotten off, the Justice Department hit list, his enemies contended he survived by going after Menendez and other Democrats. "This spreads all over," Lautenberg said. "It causes people to look under the hood."[25] *New York Times* columnist Paul Krugman wrote, "Menendez's claims of persecution now seem quite plausible."[26]

Christie said nobody at the White House or Justice Department ever tried to get him to start or stop a corruption investigation. "Never once," he said. "I've never heard from the White House that way ever. And I've never been called by the Justice Department to try to move me one way or the other on a political corruption case. It's just never happened. They don't even know what we're up to in that area most of the time."[27]

The timing of the Menendez-related subpoena doesn't line up right to support the critics' theory. Christie made the list twice; he got off the list the first time before looking into the Menendez landlord agreement, then got back on the list a second time after starting the investigation. Christie bristles at the suggestion, stands by his actions, and says politicians and the media often misstate the story.

"There's lots of stuff that I can't talk about, because of grand jury rules. So I've got to be careful. But here's what I'll say about that: I don't have one second thought about the decision that we made to serve that grand jury subpoena on one entity sixty-five days before the election," Christie said.

Christie said the issue came to his office's attention through a story in *The Star-Ledger*. Ralph Marra, a registered Democrat who'd become a Christie loyalist, approached Christie with the article in hand, as Christie recalls the exchange:

"We've got to serve a subpoena on this right now," Marra said.

"Come on, it's sixty-five days before the election," Christie said. "I don't wanna."

"It won't leak," Marra responded. "It's not like we're serving Menendez. We're serving North Hudson Community Action Corp."

"Ralph, I'm really reluctant. I'm really reluctant. You know, people are going to think you're trying to play in this," Christie said.

"But you're not. You need to think about this. I'm going to come back and talk to you about it some more," Marra replied.

"Later that day he came back with Jim Nobile, chief of special prosecutions, and the two of them argued vigorously to me that because it was in the press that there was a real likelihood that documents were going to be destroyed that might prove the theory of the case, and that we needed to serve a subpoena immediately so that we would either prevent the destruction of documents or create a case for obstruction of justice for destroying the documents," Christie said.

"And I still was kind of—I wasn't committing, I was just sitting there listening, kind of shaking my head no. And Ralph stood up and said to me, 'If you don't do this, you're being political. The only reason you wouldn't do this is because you're afraid of the way you'll be perceived. And if you don't do this, you're being political. You're being just as political in the opposite direction. How about just doing what's right?'" Christie said. "And as Ralph often had the ability to do, he talked me into it. Now, I don't back away from the decision one bit. I think it was the right decision."

Kean spent the rest of the campaign saying Menendez was under "federal criminal investigation"—a phrase still being kicked around by Republicans in 2011, before the all-clear letter was finally sent by prosecutors in Pennsylvania. Christie said he's confident his office didn't leak word of the subpoena because doing so had the potential to undermine the investigation.

"We had no incentive to leak it because we were trying to prevent destruction of documents and destruction of evidence," Christie said. "I think we proved over the years we didn't want things to get public. I often said that we operate best in secret. We operate best in the dark, until we're ready to turn the lights on."

Doing that, however, opened him up to personal attack, giving his enemies ammunition for years.

"I have no second thoughts about it. I knew what the risk was. But I never had a feeling in my mind that that was inappropriate to do," Christie said. "I knew the risk. And I had operated really well in that job for four and a half years at that point by just figuring out what the right thing to do was and doing it. If I started thinking, 'Well, if it's misperceived, it could hurt me and it could hurt the office'—if I started making decisions on that basis, that's kind of a slippery slope and I don't know where it stops."

Christie's defenders when the political accusations started flying included Walter Timpone, the lawyer who'd nearly been named his top assistant at the U.S. attorney's office before his ill-timed visit to Senator Robert Torricelli doomed his prospects. "To attack Christie's integrity and infer that he is but a puppet of Rove belies six years of nonpartisan, effective corruption prosecutions of high-level Republicans and Democrats alike. It also sullies the reputation of an office that has always demanded and continues to demand the highest ethical standards," Timpone wrote in a letter to the editor of *The Star-Ledger*.[28]

By 2009, when Democrats controlled Congress and the White House, the House Judiciary Committee finally got to interview Rove and Miers, under oath but behind closed doors, under a deal brokered by Barack Obama's White House. Transcripts of Rove's interviews show he was asked about Christie and said he has no idea how New Jersey's federal prosecutor wound up on or off the list including whether the Menendez probe played a role. He conceded the Menendez investigation and leak probably favored Republicans in the 2006 election. "I would suspect so. Again, I don't know enough about New Jersey politics and how widely it was covered to make a comment," Rove told the committee.

While Rove told the House Judiciary Committee he never talked with Christie about his duties as U.S. attorney, he did create headaches for Christie in the midst of the 2009 governor's race by acknowledging that they talked about the prospect that he would run for governor—including once while Rove was still working at the White House, a job he left in August 2007, at a time when Christie was supposedly the apolitical prosecutor.

"I talked to him twice in the last couple of years, perhaps one time while I was at the White House and once or twice since I left the White House, but—not regarding his duties as U.S. attorney, but regarding his interest in running for governor, and he asked me questions about who—who were good people that knew about running for governor that he could talk to," Rove said. ". . . He may have said, I am really enjoying the job and, you know, I have got a whole bunch of cases that I am prosecuting and, boy, maybe you have been reading about me. But no; about the sum and substance of it, no."[29]

In October 2011 Senator Frank Lautenberg signed off on President Obama's nomination of U.S. magistrate Patty Shwartz—a former attorney under Christie—to the U.S. Third Circuit Court of Appeals. But Menendez did not, although Shwartz got a strong rating from the American Bar Association. It marked the first time a fellow Democrat had blocked one of Obama's judicial nominees.

Many in the legal community thought it was personal vendetta, since Shwartz, who worked in the U.S. attorney's office in Newark from 1989 to 2003, lives with Nobile, the head of the special prosecutions unit that in 2006 began investigating the Menendez landlord arrangement.[30] At first Menendez refused to comment but when media speculation grew hot, he issued a statement saying he would not have opposed a nominee because of a connection to the U.S. attorney's office. He said he was not fully satisfied with answers to his questions to her. The Obama administration stuck by its nominee and Menendez finally consented after a second interview with her.

Questioning Solomon's Wisdom

Another Christie controversy involved South Jersey, where Democratic Party boss George Norcross III has controlled all things political for years despite never having been elected to office. Lee Solomon was a Republican legislator who lost his seat to a Norcross-backed candidate, Louis Greenwald, in 1995. Republican governor Christie Whitman tried to name

Solomon the Camden County prosecutor but Norcross-affiliated Democrats blocked it, so he was named acting prosecutor. When Christie became U.S. attorney, he appointed Solomon a federal deputy prosecutor for South Jersey. During Solomon's tenure there was a huge roundup of teenagers awaiting trial in Camden County. Superior Court Judge Louis Hornstine, who was acting judge in juvenile court, noticed an unusually large number of teenagers, all minorities, brought in for no apparent reason and called for an investigation.

Hornstine and others wondered if the roundup had to do with a ridiculous situation in which federal funding for detention was determined by the jail population on one day of the year. The arrests were made just days before the annual census on October 15. Many of those picked up were wearing electronic monitors at home. Most were released shortly after the count. Insiders told the *Courier-Post* in Cherry Hill that filling the detention center just before the annual count was routine.

Central to the investigation was whether the center's director, Mary Previte, was aware of the possibly illegal sweep. A nonstop self-promoter, she cultivated an image for herself as a child advocate, even wrote books about her experience with troubled teens. In addition to that job, she was a member of the state Assembly from Camden County, which made her a cog in the Norcross machine as well a double-dipper at the public trough.

It would seem a violation of federal law to round up kids for no other reason than to boost detention occupancy for federal funds, the kind of thing Christie would pursue with vigor. Hornstine called the state attorney general's office, but his call was not returned. He called Solomon, too, who showed up the next day with an FBI agent. Even though federal issues were involved, Solomon, in what has to be one of the dumbest moves in New Jersey law enforcement, passed the investigation to state attorney general Peter Harvey, infamous for lackluster results where public officials were involved.

Harvey's record was questioned almost daily by the media. He was sued by three New Jersey state troopers for failing to pass on to the Senate Judiciary Committee a report containing allegations that the head of the state police was friendly with mob figures who loaned him money. State senator Bob Martin questioned Harvey's handling of a land deal for a trash transfer station in Linden. Martin also revealed he had information on the case of Angelo Prisco, a mobster who got an unusual early release from New Jersey prison—which resulted in a subpoena for Martin from Harvey's office. Curiously, the subpoena came after Martin cast the lone no vote after Harvey's confirmation interview.

"I was personally alarmed and disturbed by the actions of the acting attorney general yesterday, actions which I believe were based on retaliation and intimidation," Martin, a law professor, told Gannett reporter Sandy McClure.

Harvey had requested confidential police informants to go on record and take lie detector tests, which as anyone who ever watched a cop show on TV knows is ridiculous. They're called confidential informants because they're undercover. Harvey was the first attorney general fined by the state ethics commission. He had to pay $1,500 for taking free ringside boxing tickets in Atlantic City.[31]

Previte left the detention job and decided not to seek reelection to the Assembly. Two years later, the state attorney general's office said no wrongful acts occurred because no individual benefited financially. Previte and the woman in charge of electronic monitoring, Eva Johnson, did not cooperate, demanding immunity from prosecution, which the state refused to give.

Later, Christie delivered a blistering seven-point critique of Harvey's handling of a different case that also involved Norcross. There was growing public demand for Christie's office to take over the case but Christie said it had been so badly mangled by Harvey's office it couldn't be saved.

After Solomon handed the youth center investigation to the state and not long after he was beaten out for a federal judgeship, he was nominated for a state Superior Court appointment. It won swift approval without Democratic opposition, unlike when Governor Whitman couldn't get him named county prosecutor. He served as a Superior Court judge until Christie became governor and named Solomon head of the Board of Public Utilities. In November 2011, Christie nominated Solomon to return to the judicial bench in Camden County. The state Senate confirmed him in December 2011.

Christie critics ask why he allowed Solomon to hand over a federal investigation to an attorney general's office that was a laughingstock—in fact, a target of Christie's verbal barrage—and whether it was about currying favor with Norcross, the Democratic boss who was in a position to help Christie later in a governor's race.

State Senate president Steve Sweeney is supported by the Norcross organization—they went to high school together—though he does not live in Camden County, but in neighboring Gloucester. Sweeney's father and Solomon were friends before Sweeney got into politics. "Lee's just an honest, honorable guy," the senator said. And why would he give up a superior court judgeship he had lusted for? "I talked to Lee. He's extremely loyal. The people that Chris has around him would kill for him. Really, they would kill for him. Lee told me; 'I got the call, Steve. I couldn't say no. He's done a lot for me in my life.'"

When the Hippocratic Oath Turns Hypocritical

The nation learned a lot about the medical industry's darker side when Christie initiated an investigation into potential kickbacks to doctors from the sellers of hip and knee replacements. A trusting public took it for granted that physicians always did what was best for their patients. But the investigation uncovered hundreds of consulting arrangements—some of them in excess of $1 million a year—between physicians and medical supply companies. Federal officials said four hip and knee companies paid out about $800 million to doctors from 2002 through 2006. Paul Ginsburg, president of the nonprofit D.C.-based Center for Studying Health System Change, said, "In theory, the physicians are using their best judgment about what's best for the patient but, to the extent they're given these consulting arrangements, it's something that could clearly distort their incentives."[32]

"It was never our suggestion that for all the doctors who received compensation, that the compensation was unlawful," Christie spokesman Michael Drewniak said. "Most of them were quite legitimate compensation packages for research or product development or royalties for products."[33]

Nevertheless, after Christie's probe and an investigation in Congress, reforms were instituted and New Jersey's U.S. attorney was riding high. Four of the top hip and knee replacement companies agreed to pay $311 million to settle the probe. A fifth company, which had cooperated, paid no fines but agreed to disclose consulting agreements. None admitted wrongdoing. Rather than face criminal charges they agreed to be overseen by federal monitors. They would pay the monitors instead of fines to the government.

The case then took an unexpected turn, with the crime-busting Christie finding himself under the microscope and the target of accusations of conflict of interest. He personally chose his onetime Bush administration boss, former attorney general John Ashcroft, as one of the attorneys overseeing the settlement with the five companies. Ashcroft's firm was due to earn between $29 million and $52 million over eighteen months for monitoring Zimmer Holdings.

Other monitors raised eyebrows as well:[34]

- David Kelley, a former U.S. attorney in Manhattan, investigated a stock fraud case involving Christie's brother, Todd, but didn't prosecute him. Kelley was chosen to monitor Biomet Orthopedics.
- David Samson, the former New Jersey attorney general, was named monitor for device maker Smith & Nephew. Samson and Christie became close when they ran the federal and state prosecutors' offices in New Jersey in 2002 and 2003, and Samson was chairman of the New Jersey Domestic Security Preparedness Task Force, which works with federal agencies to coordinate counterterrorism efforts. "We enjoyed a death threat together. That brings you together," Christie joked, referring to a 2003 threat by the Latin Kings gang. Samson was counsel to Christie's campaign for governor, then chaired Christie's transition committee. The law firm he'd founded, Wolff & Samson, employed Christie's friend and future chief counsel, Jeff Chiesa, as well as Christie's first community affairs commissioner, Lori Grifa, who was Samson's chief of staff when he was attorney general.

- Debra Wong Yang, a former U.S. attorney in Los Angeles and Christie colleague with ties to former U.S. attorney general Alberto Gonzales, was picked to monitor Deputy Orthopedics.
- John Carley, former Cendant Corp. vice president and Federal Trade Commission lawyer under President Ronald Reagan, oversaw the nonprosecution agreement involving Stryker Orthopedics. He later was on U.S. senator John McCain's New York fund-raising team in 2008.

In addition to those, there were two other unrelated deferred prosecution agreements that came under scrutiny.

A $300 million fraud settlement Christie negotiated with Bristol-Myers Squibb included a provision that the company endow a professorship at Seton Hall Law School, Christie's alma mater.

Herbert Stern, the former U.S. attorney who had advised Christie about becoming a federal prosecutor, got a $10 million contract to monitor the University of Medicine and Dentistry of New Jersey, which was accused of double-billing for Medicare-covered services. John Inglesino, a partner in Stern's law firm and a close friend of Christie's, was paid $325 per hour for his work for the monitorship. Stern, Inglesino, another partner, and their wives later gave $23,800 to Christie's run for governor. They were matched $2-for-$1 under New Jersey's campaign finance law, bringing the total to $71,400.[35]

Democrats, who feared Christie was going to run for governor the next year and that they lacked ammunition to use against him, saw an opportunity. For his part, Christie issued what would become a familiar denial then and later when he was governor: "I am not a candidate for anything other than finishing this job."

Democratic U.S. representative Frank Pallone Jr. said in a letter he released to the public he wanted to meet Christie to discuss the "seemingly unfettered discretion"[36] in appointing monitors. He added, "There's no politics involved."[37] Shortly thereafter, another Democrat, U.S. representative Bill Pascrell Jr., called for the House Judiciary Committee to look into the matter. And, he added, "There is nothing partisan about this and for anyone to make it partisan they are either lying or drunk."[38]

State senator Bill Baroni, a Republican named in 2010 as an executive at the Port Authority of New York and New Jersey, defended Christie. "Democrats in New Jersey have been looking for something to beat up our great U.S. attorney with and they think they've found it," he said.[39]

A House Judiciary Committee subcommittee called in Ashcroft, who denied there was a conflict of interest in his monitoring contract and defended Christie as an outstanding prosecutor in sometimes acrimonious testimony. "No law that I am aware of has been violated," Ashcroft said. Representative Linda Sanchez, D-Calif., who chaired the hearing, labeled Ashcroft's contract "a backroom, sweetheart deal."[40] Ashcroft left the hearing midway to catch a flight, but not before implying that New Jersey pols were concerned about Christie's political ambitions. Pascrell and Pallone said they would demand that Christie come to Washington and explain himself while continuing to deny they were playing politics;[41] nobody believed them. They also said they were disappointed Ashcroft didn't show up with detailed receipts and invoices. "There is no reason to believe that [Ashcroft] had particular expertise in these health matters. The fees are exorbitant," Pallone said.[42]

Back in New Jersey, editorial writers were having a field day. Tom Moran of *The Star-Ledger*—the journalist Christie called "thin-skinned" in a YouTube video that went viral in 2010—wrote, "This is just the sort of conflict he has warned about for years. He gives speeches these days that come about a half-inch from being campaign stump speeches. The theme is that voters must show zero tolerance toward politicians with conflicts of interest. Only then, he says, will the state really clean itself up."[43]

The Press of Atlantic City opined: "Should Christie run for governor, his friend Ashcroft would be a valuable political ally. And one with a nice new pile of money. Again, Christie has done a good job battling corruption in New Jersey—which makes this deal with Ashcroft all the more unsettling. Christie either didn't know how this deal would look or didn't care. Neither possibility is very comforting."[44]

Those who know Christie didn't find it unusual that he would choose people he knew and trusted or with whom he shared a bond of loyalty. Christie said, "You either trust me to have integrity or you don't. It concerns me how this is being framed."[45]

Christie was invited before a Democrat-dominated House Judiciary subcommittee, which Republicans objected to because it was scheduled for two weeks before the June 2 gubernatorial primary. His testimony was postponed until late June. Nobody could remember the last time a gubernatorial candidate was called before a committee run by the opposing party. "It's obviously political, but that doesn't mean it's illegitimate," said University of Virginia political scientist Larry Sabato. "He's running as the clean, untouched, unblemished alternative to Corzine. Well, then you touch him, you blemish him. It's a perfectly legitimate subject. He's a legitimate witness, but it's political."[46]

Christie went to Washington and defended his record. There were heated exchanges with U.S. representative Steve Cohen, a Tennessee Democrat who argued that the corporations weren't free to object to monitors recommended by the prosecutors.

"You made them an offer they couldn't refuse," Cohen said.

Christie disagreed. "You were not in the room," Christie answered. "It is an ethnically insensitive comment by you, first of all, to an Italian-American. Secondly, you were not in the room when the negotiations took place, sir, and I was. And these folks came back and were not under duress."

Cohen said he didn't know Christie was of Italian descent. Christie said that agreements with the manufacturers allowed workers to stay on the job and patients to get needed equipment. Furthermore, he said, the monitors were paid by the companies, not taxpayers.

That Bristol-Myers Squibb payment to Seton Hall's law school for a business ethics program, Christie said, originated with the company and its lawyers. The only other law school in New Jersey, at Rutgers University, already had an endowed ethics chair. "It was not my idea. It was not my initiative. It was something they asked for," said Christie.[47]

Christie wasn't subpoenaed to come to Congress. He was sent a letter of invitation, which he responded to by telling the committee on the day they wanted him he would need to leave by 1:30 p.m. The panel's lawyer said that was acceptable—but then the meeting started late and Democrats had more questions when Christie's departure time drew near.

"I don't think, when I was sitting there, that other than a kind of gotcha follow-up to try to nail me on something I had said with another panel member that during that two hours or so, roughly, that they asked anybody else any questions," Christie said. "There was a whole panel up there of people surrounding me on either side, but there was no question who they wanted to talk to."

After being there for two and a half hours, Christie reminded the committee that he was leaving at 1:30 to catch a train "because of pressing business that I have back in New Jersey."

"What time is your train?" Cohen asked.

"My train is a little bit before 2:00, sir, and I have to go," Christie said.

"You are not going to make a 2 o'clock, so," Cohen said, starting another round of questions.

"Well, sir, I am," said Christie—and he left, along with Mary Pat and campaign manager Bill Stepien.[48]

"Man, I can crawl on my hands and knees from the Rayburn Building to Union Station and get there in a half an hour, so I knew I was getting there," Christie told us. "I think Mary Pat was really surprised that I really did get up and leave. But there was no chance that I was going to stand there and continue to take all that bullshit from those guys, who obviously had no idea what we had done with deferred prosecution agreements."

To this day, Christie remains appreciative of the assistance U.S. representative Steve King of Iowa provided that day. King, with an assist from a colleague, noted in the record that Cohen had secured an $800,000 earmark for one of the medical device companies Christie's office prosecuted in the case. Four of the six Republicans on the committee spoke at the hearing, but it's King that stuck in Christie's mind—to the point that he returned to Iowa in 2011 for a fund-raiser for him.

"Yeah, he stood up for me. He was the only Republican who stood up for me," he said. "I don't agree with everything Steve King does. He and I philosophically are not always in alignment. But on that day, when it was clearly a political circus, and they were just out to create a campaign ad for the Corzine administration, Steve King stood up and was counted. He didn't leave the room. If you look at that video, Republicans—there were almost no Republicans sitting there. They left me swinging out there, almost by myself. Except for Steve King. A guy who stands up for me like that, when he knows that I'm just getting hosed, anything he asks me to do within reason I'm going to do for him. That was not a pleasant day."

When Christie left the room he told reporters it was a "political circus" that was orchestrated by Corzine's allies.[49] Later, a Corzine ad with video of Christie leaving implied Christie stormed out of the hearing, refusing to answer questions, as if there hadn't been a prior agreement about his departure.

Pascrell and Pallone testified after Christie left. Pascrell noted one monitor submitted a two-hundred-page bill to its company, but Ashcroft sent a one-page bill with no billable hours or expenses, just an amount due. "This is a ransom note, not a billing statement," he said. Pallone said that at a New York University Law School forum on deferred prosecution agreements, "There was no question that the poster child for abuse was Mr. Christie." An exasperated Representative Trent Franks, R-Ariz., said he wished he had time to try to "correct all the nonsense that has been put forth here from these two New Jersey members . . . there is always a witch hunt on this committee." The hearing was adjourned because the House was calling for a vote.[50]

Despite all the denials of politics, shortly after Christie testified the Democratic National Committee issued a statement saying, "It's clear that as U.S. attorney, Christie used his position to help his friends, and now those very friends are helping him fill his campaign coffers. Chris Christie's repeated ethical lapses demonstrate that he's just not up to the task of serving as governor of New Jersey."[51] The timing suggested it was written before Christie testified.

The following April in a hearing before the House Appropriations Committee, Attorney General Michael Mukasey said the Justice Department had reined in its prosecutors' authority by requiring future agreements to be approved by the number two official in the Justice Department. "The examination of monitorship contracts was a department concern well before the stories hit the newspapers," he said.[52]

Expense Account Questions

Another controversy involved Christie staying in hotels with rates that exceeded the daily cap the federal government placed on him when he was U.S. attorney.

The Justice Department's inspector general issued a report in 2010 that found fifteen of twenty-three vouchers for lodging Christie submitted between 2007 and 2009 exceeded the government rate. Christie "provided insufficient, inaccurate or no justification" for fourteen of the fifteen trips, it said. When the issue first surfaced in the gubernatorial campaign, Christie said he stayed in more expensive hotels only when less expensive ones were not available. "We always went for government rates first. I don't think there were a lot of stays in five-star hotels over seven years."

Twelve of the fourteen trips in which Christie's hotel cost exceeded government rates involved the medical device investigation. His spokesman, Drewniak, said that in the trips Christie "addressed the companies, their boards and senior management numerous times on their obligations and compliance with the deferred prosecution agreements." Auditors found Christie took a car service on a four-mile trip to and from the Boston airport costing $236. It also said "In another example of excessive transportation costs, his car service from a London airport to his hotel in central London cost $562 round-trip."[53]

One of the places he stayed in Washington was the legendary Willard Intercontinental, which cost taxpayers $449 for one night plus tax. First built in 1816, it's two blocks from the White House. Julia Ward Howe wrote "The Battle Hymn of the Republic" there and Abraham Lincoln stayed on its second floor until his inauguration. Ulysses Grant liked to walk there for an after-work cigar and brandy and his ghost is said to still make the trip. As Grant was often approached for favors in the Willard's lobby, the myth is that's the origin of the word "lobbying." Research shows it's an interesting story but not accurate. The word dates to 1837, long before Grant was president.

The bill for the Willard was accompanied by a memo from Christie:

"During my stay in Washington November 17–18, 2004, I was unable to locate lodging at the government rate. The only available lodging was a rate of $449.00 at the Willard."

Inspectors said the memos submitted by Christie contained misleading statements, saying "that the government lodging rate was not available in the particular city on the particular dates. . . . According to the U.S. attorney's secretary the language of the memoranda did not literally mean that there were 'no hotels available at the government rate in the particular city' but that the government rate was not available at the hotel or hotels that fit her criteria—a 'decent' hotel at or near the meeting site."[54]

Angela Delli Santi of the Associated Press's Trenton bureau wrote about the issue, too, noting the records that formed the basis for the story came from Corzine's campaign camp and that the AP's request for the same records hadn't been fulfilled. She reported that on trips in 2007 and 2008, Michele Brown, who was Christie's executive assistant U.S. attorney and counsel, also "exceeded the guidelines after Christie approved her requests for rooms in the same five-star hotels where he was booked." She wrote: "The vouchers show Christie and Brown stayed at the NineZero Hotel in Boston on Oct. 16, 2007, and each billed taxpayers for $449 plus taxes and fees for their rooms, more than double the government allowance for a Boston hotel room at the time, according to a General Services Administration travel reimbursement table."[55]

The New York Times provided a more complete in-depth account, also including full disclosure that the raw material came from opponent Corzine's campaign, but the *Times* analyzed it and—a significant difference—reported that staffers in addition to Brown often traveled with Christie: "Ms. Brown accompanied Mr. Christie on sixteen trips, the bulk of them in 2007 and 2008. They were often accompanied by a junior prosecutor, Kevin O'Dowd." Brown and O'Dowd also went with Christie and Mary Pat to London, where Christie spoke to compliance officers at a company involved in the artificial limbs investigation. Christie paid for his wife's airfare "but the government covered the couple's and Ms. Brown's $401-per-night lodging. Mr. O'Dowd declined comment."[56]

"I remember us complaining at the time that the AP story was incomplete. I remember us complaining at the time: 'Now wait a second, there were a number of trips that were analyzed where Michele Brown wasn't on the trip, where it was just me and Kevin O'Dowd. And then there were some trips where it was just me and Michele Brown, and then there was the majority where it was me, Michele, and Kevin,'" Christie said. "The only thing that was offensive in *The New York Times* to O'Dowd was that he was called a junior prosecutor, which offended him. Still does to this day. But other than that, I just saw—I remember us complaining at the time to the AP editors that the story was incomplete.

"I thought the whole thing was overdramatized, anyway. Clearly it was a political hatchet job by the Obama administration, too," said Christie.

Four other U.S. attorneys were included in the report; none was named. Chris Christie was "U.S. Attorney C." One of the other U.S. attorneys tagged in the report was running for Congress in Pittsburgh, Christie noted. The report was easy to link to Christie, as the details were identical to travel data released in 2009 under a Freedom of Information Act request. The report cited Christie as the one "who most often exceeded the government rate without adequate justification" and for offering "insufficient, inaccurate or no justification for most of the excessive costs in 2007 and 2008."[57]

The amount in the report is relatively small, $2,176 over two years, but Christie was quiet about it and *The Philadelphia Daily News* editorialized, "Christie hasn't made a public comment about the report—he wouldn't even meet with the inspector general—but if he wants to retain his credibility as a 'smaller government, less spending' leader, he should come clean. The only thing worse than out-of-control government spending is remaining secretive about it."[58]

The Star-Ledger commented: "No, this isn't a lot of money. But the governor rails against public employees who take smaller perks—like a free E-ZPass, or a sports ticket, or a lobster dinner. So it's no wonder he is not commenting on this one. What could he do, blame it on the teachers union?"[59]

In all, Christie put in for more than $20,000 in mileage reimbursements during his seven-year U.S. attorney tenure, "including many trips that his public schedules indicate were made for personal or political reasons. A die-hard Mets fan, Mr. Christie put in for $73 in mileage costs for a drive to Philadelphia on a night his schedule noted an away game against the Phillies."[60]

One of the other four U.S. attorneys in the report was on the hit list of twenty-six U.S. attorneys to be fired, and two who were let go in that purge were cited in part for excessive travel out of their district. Could it be that Christie's travel habits were the real reason someone at Justice, possibly a government bean counter, nominated him for replacement?

Despite the fireworks, Christie said nobody in Washington told him to make changes. He says his secretary would secure him rooms, and if none was available below the prescribed cap, he'd tell her to get him a place near his meeting site.

"No one raised it with me because they all understood, and when they signed off on it, they would speak to Nancy about it. 'Okay so how did this happen?'" Christie said. He'd have to sign a form and get it cosigned.

Travel rules were changed after the audit, and the Justice Department in Washington now reviews travel requests. "I'm sure there's an exception for emergency travel, which if there's some poor schnook who's the U.S. attorney right now who does emergency travel but winds up paying more than the government rate and if he or she runs for office, they'll get tagged, too," he said.

When Christie was running for governor, he said as governor he'd allow his top advisers to travel with fewer restrictions than under the Corzine administration. "I would want my cabinet to follow the same rules I followed as U.S. attorney," he said. "If they were traveling and they could find the government rate, they should use the government rate. If they couldn't, they shouldn't sleep on a park bench. They should find the best rate they could."[61]

Phone Hackers Here and There

Two incidents involving Rupert Murdoch's News America provided fuel for Christie opponents, who believed he had a too cozy relationship with Fox News.

In 2005, reporter Jonathan Weil traveled to Princeton to talk to two founders of Floorgraphics, a small marketing company that was trying to get federal attention for what it maintained was a hacked entry into the company's computer system. The company placed ads for packaged goods on grocery store floors so customers would see them at point of purchase.

Weil, now a columnist for Bloomberg, wrote that company executives learned from a client that Rupert Murdoch's News America had detailed knowledge of a new store program Floorgraphics had been planning. They said News America had accessed Floorgraphics' computer system eleven times in a five-month period.

The executives, George Rebh and his brother, Richard, gave reporter Weil contact information for the Secret Service and the FBI agents they had contacted. One of them said an FBI agent told him the case was dropped because it didn't meet the $5,000 minimum damage threshold.

"The Rebhs eventually got some help from three New Jersey congressmen. U.S. Representative Rush Holt, a Democrat, sent a letter in April 2005 to then-U.S. Attorney Chris Christie (now the governor of New Jersey) asking his office to look into Floorgraphics' allegations."[62] Christie's commercial crimes chief, Deborah Gramiccioni (now Gov. Christie's deputy chief of staff for policy) responded that the case was under review by Assistant U.S. attorneys in the Commercial Crimes Unit. "Because the above-references matter may involve fraud, we are also forwarding copies of your letter and the attached information to the Federal Bureau of Investigation for review," she wrote.[63]

Letters from Senators Corzine and Lautenberg to Attorney General Alberto Gonzales didn't seem to garner attention, wrote Weil, adding that his own investigation turned up nothing. "Maybe federal investigators had dropped the ball. Perhaps there hadn't been enough evidence. Or maybe they didn't want to take on a sister company of Rupert Murdoch's Fox News."[64]

Weil changed jobs and all but forgot about Floorgraphics until news broke that one of Murdoch's newspapers in England had hired hackers to get phone messages from the phones of dead victims of notorious crimes. Murdoch called it "deplorable and unacceptable" and closed the paper.

Floorgraphics had been in the news, too. In a 2009 civil trial, a lawyer for News America, Lee Abrams, told jurors that News America's computers were used to access Floorgraphics' secure Web site.

"The complaint stated that the breach was traced to an I.P. address registered to News America and that after the break-in, Floorgraphics lost contracts from Safeway, Winn-Dixie and Piggly Wiggly," Weil reported. Much of the lawsuit was based on the testimony of Robert Emmel, a former News America executive who became a whistle-blower. After a few days of testimony, the News Corporation had heard enough. It settled with Floorgraphics for $29.5 million and then, days later, bought it even though it reportedly had sales of less than $1 million."[65]

"In an e-mail this week, a spokesman for News America, Suzanne Halpin, said, 'News America Marketing has condemned this conduct, which is in violation of the standards of our company.' Where there was ever any proof of a crime is another matter, of course. Too bad we may never know,"[66] wrote Weil in a column headlined "News Corp., Hacking Claims and the Story I Missed."

After allegations that News Corp. hacked into the phone records or voicemails of American 9/11 victims, Christie nemesis Lautenberg in July 2011 wrote to Attorney General Eric H. Holder Jr., bringing to his attention the attached letter he and Corzine had written to Gonzales in 2005. "As the department of Justice and FBI examine the recent hacking allegations involving News Corp. and its subsidiaries more closely, I wanted to make sure that you were fully aware of the case of Floorgraphics and News America, as it may relate to your current investigation."

A Fox News connection to Christie surfaced again when *New York* magazine reported that Christie and wife Mary Pat had dinner at the home of Fox News president Roger Ailes and that the network executive tried to persuade Christie to run for president in 2012. Ailes denied urging Christie to run, but reporter John Cook, who works for Gawker Entertainment, sought correspondence between the governor and his staff and Ailes under New Jersey's Open Public Records Law. He was denied. The American Civil Liberties Union of New Jersey filed a suit on behalf of Cook.

In a letter to the ACLU, an attorney for the governor said no record existed except for a calendar entry. We may never know what was discussed with Ailes, but Christie said he had no interest in running for president in 2012 even after a groundswell of encouragement from media commentators, political figures, and prospective voters.

CHAPTER SIX

Swine Flew

Jon Corzine, a hard-driving former Wall Street titan who leveraged his personal fortune into a U.S. Senate seat, centered his 2005 run for governor on a reform platform. He promised voters he was "unbought and unbossed," and a corruption-weary populace in the Soprano State didn't mind he had borrowed the slogan from Shirley Chisholm, a New York representative who was the first black woman elected to Congress. The tall, balding, bearded, and bespectacled man who grew up on an Illinois farm near Taylorville seemed just what this bluest of states needed—a smart, accomplished financial expert who was unbeholden to the entrenched interests. Although a champion of private enterprise and a big-time player in the go-for-the-jugular world of high finance, his boyhood observation and experience taught him government has a key role in civil society, a Democratic Party principle. His grandfather had been a successful farmer and active in Republican politics, but lost everything in the Great Depression.

Born January 1, 1947, from childhood Corzine saw the benefits of public programs, like road construction and telephone and electricity services. His family enjoyed federal farm price support and loans and crop-planting guidance from land-grant colleges. His father ran the family farm and sold insurance, his mother taught. He and his brother worked on their farm and the farms of neighbors. He sold hot dogs and ran a dance hall at the county fair. An overachiever, Corzine was senior class president, basketball team captain, and football quarterback. He paid $225 a semester to attend the University of Illinois at Urbana-Champaign, where he forced his way onto the basketball team without benefit of a scholarship, and in 1969 graduated Phi Beta Kappa. During summers, he worked construction jobs, helping build a nuclear power plant. After his senior year, he married his high school sweetheart, Joanne, and together they had three children, Jennifer, Joshua, and Jeffrey. He joined the Marines Corps Reserve in college and after graduation, faced with the draft, enlisted in the Marines and served a tour in Vietnam. He was in a platoon largely made up of high school dropouts.

"Once they shave your head, put on a green suit, you don't know who's who. . . . It's classless, you're all in it together. In a way for me [the Marines] reinforced my instincts toward being a Democrat,"[1] Corzine recalled.

After Vietnam, he enrolled at the University of Chicago where he earned a master's degree in business administration in 1973, then after a short stay at an Ohio bank, Corzine headed to Wall Street and a home in the North Jersey suburb of Summit—three minutes away from the Christies' first shabby apartment, though in far nicer digs.

Intelligent, dedicated, and hardworking, Corzine climbed the corporate ladder at Wall Street's giant global investment banker Goldman Sachs, going from bond trader in 1975 to chief executive officer in 1994. He pushed for and eventually took the company public in 1999—a decision years in the making, resisted by many of Goldman's longtime partners, some of whom quickly pushed him out in a palace coup while he was on a skiing trip. Since he reaped as much as $500 million in taking Goldman public, he didn't need unemployment checks or an income-producing job—but did have a lot of time on his hands. During his corporate days he met scores of favor-seeking politicians and from them learned two valuable lessons: Money talks loudly in politics, and when elected to public office you can go to the Aspen slopes without fear of being overthrown. Indeed, the retiring U.S. senator he would replace in Washington in 2000, Frank Lautenberg, got sworn into the Senate from the Colorado slopes in 1982.[2]

When running for the U.S. Senate, he got into trouble with jokes about Jews and Italians but knew how to overcome that. He apologized—and dropped about $35 million of his own money to beat former governor Jim Florio in the Democratic primary. In the general election, he beat Representative Bob Franks by 96,500 votes, 50 percent to 47 percent, by dumping more of his fortune into the campaign. By the time he was en route to Washington, Corzine had spent about $63 million on the election, more than $60 million of it from his own checkbook.

The spending spree didn't stop there. Corzine—as he had since 1999, when he first started to grease the wheels for his entry-at-the-top-floor into politics—continued to pour millions into Democratic campaigns, including some to benefit New Jersey's notorious political bosses whose influence he said he wanted to curb. They might not have owned him, but he helped enable them to own others.

In the Senate, Corzine was an advocate of universal health insurance and overhauling public education, neither of which came to fruition. "I just didn't expect George Bush to be on the other end of Pennsylvania Avenue,"[3] he told Gannett's Jonathan Tamari.

He opposed Bush's Social Security privatization plan, voted against Bush's tax cuts, favored stricter gun control, improved worker safety standards, and sought to increase the minimum wage. He was among twenty-three senators to oppose authorizing the use of force in Iraq in 2002—a vote that became a key reason why years later, when as the new governor he got to choose his Senate replacement in 2006, Corzine opted for Representative Robert Menendez over other prospects such as Representative Rob Andrews, a South Jersey congressman who supported the war authorization.

Given his history as an achiever, it's understandable that Corzine would be frustrated by the pace of Washington. He said he would have to be in office until he was eighty to get the authority of a committee chairman, the real power in Congress. (Given the recent upheaval in Congress, he could have already ranked thirty-third of one hundred in seniority in 2013. Even more ironically: The senator he appointed to replace him, Robert Menendez, already chairs the powerful Foreign Relations Committee.) He called pursuit of the presidency unrealistic for him and came to the conclusion that his best option to get things done was to win the governorship of New Jersey, considered the nation's most powerful, where he would again be a chief executive and "can set an agenda, work to execute that agenda, deliver on it."[4]

That's what he did. He first considered challenging Governor Jim McGreevey in the 2005 primary, then didn't have to when McGreevey's tenure collapsed in an avalanche of controversies, culminating with his nationally televised "gay American" speech—which followed just days after Corzine told a breakfast crowd at the Democratic National Convention in Boston he was proud McGreevey was his governor. (Also addressing New Jersey's Democrats that week was a young Illinois state senator Corzine was helping win a seat in the U.S. Senate, Barack Obama.)

The replacement governor was Senate president Dick Codey, an affable longtime politician who had expertly worked at retail politicking in Essex County and political jujitsu in Trenton's back rooms since the early 1970s. Codey liked being governor, though perhaps not running for governor—particularly against Corzine and his millions. Codey stood down. In 2009, when asked about that by Neil Cavuto on Fox News, Codey noted that his favorability ratings were higher than Corzine's. He said he had been railroaded—not necessarily by Corzine "as opposed to party bosses and I would say bullies."[5]

Republicans had no shortage of candidates wanting to run against Corzine. Former Jersey City mayor Bret Schundler, the 2001 nominee routed by McGreevey, made another run, deemphasizing his conservative credentials and playing up a reform agenda. Bogota mayor Steve Lonegan happily grabbed the party's right wing and mustered a third-place finish. Republicans opted to nominate Doug Forrester, a moderate, wealthy former state pension and benefits director who'd made millions selling prescription drug coverage plans to government entities. Forrester had been the party's nominee for U.S. Senate three years earlier, when he surged to an early lead against the incumbent, Robert Torricelli, who had so many ethics challenges that he was compelled to quit the race. Democrats maneuvered successfully to pluck Lautenberg out of retirement, which the state Supreme Court allowed even though the deadline for adding him to the ballot had passed. Voters returned Lautenberg to Washington, sending Forrester packing to West Windsor, a well-to-do suburb of Trenton.

A few years later, Forrester was back as the party's pick for governor. The attraction, in part, was his willingness to spend millions from his own pockets—and his willingness to use that money to sully his opponent. Near the end of the 2005 campaign, after Corzine's ex-wife told *The New York Times* in an interview that Corzine would probably let New Jersey down just as he had his own family, Forrester—running out of options—bought TV ads quoting her, which seemed to do Forrester more harm than good. In the end, Forrester was a pale imitation of Corzine—with less money to spend and an even less inspiring speaker. Corzine won the election handily by nearly 240,000 votes, 53 percent to 43 percent.

Corzine's experience is exactly what they mean when they advise, "Be careful what you wish for." His inaugural speech repeated the themes of reform and an end to political corruption. On the way out of the Trenton War Memorial, the theater where he took the oath, he ran into two Democratic state senators who said to him, basically, "Who do you think you are?" Either that scared him or he realized in Trenton, as in Washington, it's impossible for the CEO to get a program through without help from the legislative branch. Whatever the reason, his zeal for reform was never the same. Those two senators, incidentally, were sent to prison later by crime-busting U.S. Attorney Chris Christie.

It was more than the status-quo-loving crooks in government that slowed Corzine. Insider Democrats—including but not limited to Codey, the fill-in governor who couldn't compete with Corzine's wallet—never accepted him because he was not one of them. He didn't start out as a school board member or by driving the car for a higher-positioned politician, as they did. He didn't pay his dues. His first elected office was U.S. senator, which most of his detractors could only dream about when they weren't looking for ways to line their pockets and the pockets of their supporters with taxpayer money.

The Democrats loved Corzine's cash but wouldn't accede to his wishes, which left him talking a good game about things like ethics reform while his own party did nothing to enact it. He would back down or accept watered-down versions of his proposals. Corzine called for an end to the quintessential New Jersey practice of allowing people to hold more than one elected office—for instance, mayor and state senator, allowing them to consolidate power, dissuade would-be rivals, and feather their pension nest. Lawmakers passed a ban with not just a grandfather clause but a great-grandfather clause—it allowed people already holding multiple offices to keep doing so as long as they could keep winning reelection and it gave pols one more election season to add to their collections. Corzine's push for an airtight government reform barring so-called pay-to-play contracts to political donors—where campaign contributions are rewarded with public contracts, usually at a handsome return on the investment—was met by half-measures and stalling.

For a guy who had been a successful high-powered executive he applied the powers of his office unevenly and sometimes in ways that left even his supporters scratching their noggins.

On one occasion, there was a special session to pass a state budget because the July 1 constitutional deadline was not met. In political theater rare for him, Corzine rolled a cot into his office, closed down the government, and said he'd stay in the State House until there was a budget. Few people noticed. The biggest problem the shutdown caused was that state casino inspectors weren't working, meaning the casinos couldn't operate. The shutdown lasted nearly a week—including the Independence Day holiday weekend, much to the casinos' dismay. When it ended, Corzine paid state workers for the time they missed. No such make-good was available for the casino workers.

Later, in mocking Corzine during and after a 2010 showdown with Democrats over taxes, Christie said if the state government ever shuts down because there is no budget he wouldn't drag a cot into his office. He said he would go to the governor's mansion, order a pizza, open a beer, and turn on the Mets game, then tell lawmakers to call him when they were ready. Earlier that same year, sending an unmistakable signal on his first full day in office that he'd begun preparing for a budget fight, Christie signed an executive order deeming casino regulators as essential employees like the state police and emergency personnel, erasing some of the only Democratic lawmaker leverage the general public would notice if a shutdown were ever again needed.

Corzine did make some changes, such as having state employees pay 1.5 percent of their salary toward their health benefits, which before that were free of charge to current employees and retirees and their families. The bill for the health plans, which could cost as much as $24,000 per employee, had been completely paid for by taxpayers. Even part-time workers got in on the retirement deal. Some had several part-time jobs, each with benefits.

Just when it appeared Corzine was headed in the right direction he would do something bizarre. He spoke at a huge union rally outside the State House, raised his fist, and shouted in what pundits called his Norma Rae speech, "We will fight for a fair contract!"[6] Fight who? Corzine seemed to be oblivious that in union negotiations, he represented the people of New Jersey, not the unions. Perhaps he meant both sides would fight, but no one took it that way.

Ironically, while Corzine was acting like a union leader, Senator Steve Sweeney, who had been in the ironworkers union most of his adult life, was telling state employee unions they had to act more like private sector unions and accept realistic compromise. Democrats pushed ahead with some pension reforms based in part on one of the many studies of how to reduce New Jersey's outrageous property taxes. To block their effort and kiss up to the unions even more, Corzine announced all reforms should come through collective bargaining and any legislation to the contrary would be vetoed.

Sweeney's fellow Democrats abandoned him. Five years later, as he stood with Republican governor Christie, who shared his dedication to restructuring health care benefits and pensions for state workers, Sweeney would recall how bad he felt being the target of organized labor, which he was trying to help. "I am not making one apology for saving the pensions for 800,000 people."[7]

Trying to be all things to all sides never works. In the end neither the reformers, who didn't like the weak, watered-down attempts at improvement, nor the unions that resisted any change, accepted Corzine. State unions didn't like having to pay even a little bit for their benefits, and they were annoyed that Corzine took away the day after Thanksgiving as a paid holiday. It was never a legal holiday, but for as long as anyone could remember, state workers were granted it. Throw in the highest average property taxes in the nation, and year after year being cited as among the worst climates for business in America, and the anger in New Jersey crossed socioeconomic boundaries.

The point at which things seemed to go south for good was in 2007, when Corzine's state trooper bodyguard rammed a state SUV going 91 mph in a 65 mph zone into a guardrail on the Garden State Parkway. Corzine shattered his femur, eleven ribs, sternum, and collarbone. He lost about half his blood and was knocked out. He woke up strapped to a stretcher and freaked out, thinking he was paralyzed. Transferred to a helicopter for evacuation, when he felt himself rising he thought he was dying and going to heaven. A friend later told him he should have known he was not dying because if he were "you wouldn't be going up."[8]

He hadn't been wearing a seat belt. That wasn't the only stupid thing about this accident. It wasn't exactly an emergency. The governor was racing to Drumthwacket, New Jersey's governor's mansion in Princeton, for a meeting with the Rutgers University women's basketball team and radio talker Don Imus, who had just been fired from WFAN in New York for calling the team members, many of whom were black, "nappy-headed hos."[9]

After eighteen days in the hospital, ten of which were in a medically induced coma, Corzine curiously paid the huge medical bill out of his own pocket, then was driven to Drumthwacket—in a van clocked at 15 mph over the speed limit.

That news was small potatoes compared to stories about Carla Katz, a union leader who had been Corzine's girlfriend after Corzine and Joanne divorced. There were stories about expensive gifts and forgiven loans and $10,000 given to Katz's brother-in-law after he was forced from his state job. Skeptics wondered if the relationship between the union leader and the governor weakened the state's representation of taxpayers at the bargaining table. There were unsuccessful lawsuits to recover emails between the former lovebirds.

Even with all that baggage, the issue that really spelled disaster for Corzine was his "asset monetization plan," a desperate attempt to restructure the state's debt and get more money into New Jersey's treasury. Ignoring that Jim Florio nearly two decades earlier became a one-term governor, largely because he instituted the state's largest-ever tax hike, including taxing purchases of toilet paper, Corzine sought to increase road tolls by 800 percent over fourteen years. To drive the point home, he said in his State of the State message that pigs would fly over the State House before spending cuts or taxes alone would heal state finances.

Picking up on the theme, New Jersey 101.5 FM's highly popular afternoon talk show hosts Casey Bartholomew and Ray Rossi, known as "The Jersey Guys," began promoting a rally a few hundred feet from Corzine's office. After rousing speeches, the station released helium-filled pink balloons in the shape of pigs. The wind was just right and so over the State House's gold dome they went as reporters and photographers recorded the event. "Well, Jonny boy, they're in the air now," Rossi proclaimed to a cheering crowd of seven hundred reminiscent of the early 1990s when a similar though much larger rally saw protesters throw rolls of toilet paper at the State House.

Corzine hit the road with his plan, conducting thirteen town hall meetings in one month in January 2008—to his credit, all of them at night or on weekend afternoons, when angry toll-paying commuters could be there. It became a public flogging for the governor, each worse than the last. At one, Steve Lonegan—the once-and-future Republican gubernatorial hopeful, who'd remade himself into a conservative activist—got arrested and enjoyed a spike in publicity. Corzine eventually cut them off. This Vietnam vet was seemingly shell-shocked; he didn't do any more town halls for ten months, even though they'd been a staple of his first two years in office. When he cranked them up again, most were physically removed from people. Six were telephone town halls run by AARP. One was broadcast on gospel music and R&B sister stations. The final was an "Accessing Your Federal Government" event in the theater next to the State House.

In both the town hall meetings and political travel outside New Jersey, Corzine and Christie were alike—though Christie deployed both to much greater political effect. Corzine's out-of-state jaunts were mostly in support of quintessential Corzine types of things: a visit to Brown University for a

Holocaust conference; to New York to commemorate the Armenian geno-
cide, a friendship dinner with the Turkish Cultural Center, and National
Puerto Rican Day parades; to Washington for the National Darfur Rally
and to testify before a Senate committee on global warming; to Portugal
for an international climate change event. Corzine may have personally
believed in those issues, but such travel did little to overcome the mount-
ing problems in the Garden State or reverse the growing opinion that the
former farm boy had lost touch with average folks, or at least with the
priorities of a state executive.

In New Jersey the score sheet for his four years in office was mixed. His
administration revamped school aid, poured more money into a revised
school construction program—about $8 billion had been burned through
starting in the McGreevey administration with far too little to show for
it—expanded children's health insurance coverage, and instituted employee
benefit reforms.

He tried to get passed a bond proposal to further stem cell research,
which was defeated despite his spending $200,000 to support the ques-
tion. Voters hadn't rejected a public question in New Jersey in seventeen
years, and the vote—as well as a simultaneous one *against* dedicating sales
tax revenue to property tax relief—served as a kind of wake-up call to
where the voters stood on Corzine. He didn't push marriage equality hard
when the state Supreme Court invited him to, allowing the legislature to
settle for civil unions, which irked the traditionally Democratic gay, les-
bian, and transgender communities. He abolished the state's death penalty,
though that was never used anyway.

In the high-profile 2008 presidential race, he backed Hillary Clinton
in the Democratic primary—a nod in part to former president Bill Clinton, who had aided Corzine in earlier campaigns. His endorsement came
despite a political connection with Barack Obama that went back to Obama's
days as a state senator in Corzine's home state, Illinois, when Corzine ran
the Senate Democrats' national campaign effort. The thinking around the
State House was that if Clinton had won Corzine was on his way to being

treasury secretary, which would have been sweet revenge because the guy in the job during the Bush administration, Henry Paulson, had engineered Corzine's ouster at Goldman Sachs.

That talk resurfaced when Corzine became a high-profile economic surrogate for Obama in the fall campaign against John McCain. Corzine went to bat for Obama on NBC's *Meet the Press*, CNBC's *Squawk Box*, even Comedy Central's *The Daily Show with Jon Stewart*, a guy who grew up not too far from New Jersey's State House. What New Jerseyans were hearing from the governor about New Jersey on national TV made them wonder if Corzine were talking about the same state they lived in. "It's funny how he's become an expert on CNBC and we heard references made during the Democratic convention to good things that are happening in New Jersey, which certainly comes as a surprise to many New Jerseyans,"[10] said Patrick Murray, Monmouth University pollster.

Inside the Corzine tent, there was a different spin. Tom Shea, Corzine political adviser and former chief of staff, said whoever became president would follow Corzine's path. "Making tough decisions to clean up problems that have appeared over a long time is not necessarily a recipe for popularity."[11] It certainly wasn't for Corzine. At the time his job approval rating was around 40 percent.

Despite his sagging popularity and his relatively unsuccessful first term, the politically naive Corzine decided to run for reelection. Publicly he had the support of the high-profile political bosses who run New Jersey like a medieval fiefdom, but privately they were saying this was going to be a monumental, if not impossible, task. Even so, he had no substantial competition for the nomination—only political unknowns Roger Bacon, Jeff Boss, and Carl Bergmanson, the latter of whom had led a recall effort against the governor. That's because Corzine had something would-be contenders lacked—a huge bank account, even after all the money he spent on his earlier political conquests, gal pal Katz, and the divorce from Joanne. Tellingly, 23 percent of the people who voted in the Democratic primary cast protest votes for one of the unknown candidates, including

Boss, a guy who says he has proof the National Security Agency planned 9/11.

Although his job as U.S. attorney precluded Christie from attending political conventions or discussing personal ambitions publicly, he was the topic of discussion at every Republican gathering. Political scientist Murray knew Christie was running long before he left the federal post. "He pretty much made that clear when I saw him in '06, which may have been the first time I met him personally and actually talked to him. He came to Monmouth, we were doing a panel on ethics, I think, so he came to that. The poll had been going for about a year at the time, maybe, and he turned to [aide] Michele Brown and said, 'You've got to pay attention to this guy. We've got to make sure we stay on this guy's right side,' or something like that, jokingly, because of the polling issues. Clearly he was making a reference to life after the U.S. attorney's position."

At the 2008 GOP convention in Minneapolis, it was generally understood by most that if Christie wanted to run for governor, all he had to do was say it. His brother, Todd, and political alter ego, Bill Palatucci, made themselves conspicuous at the convention hotel. "I think there's an expectation that he's going to do it,"[12] James Harkness, executive director of the N.J. Senate Republicans, told Gannett reporter Greg Volpe.

"I very much wanted him to run," Palatucci said. "He's my former law partner, my good friend, a stellar tenure as U.S. attorney. During the time right after he left [federal office] we spent a lot of time together, sat down with a lot of key people to say here's what it would be like, here's what we have to do. There was a point with Mary Pat in particular of 'Do we really want to do this?' He had a number of high-level interviews with big New York law firms, who—hearing him tell it—made very substantial offers to attract him. I think there was at least one general counsel of a big firm."

In late 2008, two weeks after Obama had won the White House, Christie announced he would step down as U.S. attorney on December 1 after nearly seven years in that job. Six weeks later, he filed papers declaring his long-awaited candidacy. The official announcement was poorly handled. A "Dear Friend" email from campaign manager Bill Stepien was signed by Christie but not received by some media for two hours after other media got it. That set off frantic calls. Replies to the email referred people to Christie pals state Senators Bill Baroni or Joe Kyrillos, who couldn't respond because both were out of state. A Fairleigh Dickinson–PublicMind Poll showed if the election were held then, Corzine would beat Christie 40 percent to 33 percent. If it had been a poll of news media, Corzine would have won by a much bigger margin. The Christie launch could have been better handled by the Keystone Kops.

Mary Pat, brother Todd, Palatucci, and Jon Hanson, a longtime friend and founder of a private real estate investment firm called the Hampshire Companies with more than $2 billion in assets, were in charge of fund-raising. "My role in the campaign was . . . to be the unofficial observer of all that was going on and giving my two cents if he asked for it," Palatucci said.

You might think with a stellar record as New Jersey's leading federal prosecutor that Christie would be a household name, but he wasn't, according to Monmouth University's Murray, who runs the school's polling institute. "They didn't really know him, even while he was doing this. His name was not really well known until he ran for governor." That's not unusual. "People don't know who their U.S. senators are including those who have been here for three decades," said Murray, who recalled a poll he did asking people to name their U.S. senators and only 30 percent could name one of the two.

In the Garden State more people can name their mayor than their senator. In a poll taken when Jim McGreevey was governor, only 68 percent could name the state's chief executive. That ambiguity is no longer the case, Murray said: "If I asked people to name off the top of their heads who the governor is today, I guarantee you it's going to be higher than 68 percent who know who Chris Christie is.

"Every time there was a corruption bust Chris Christie's name was mentioned, within twenty-four hours people couldn't recall the name of Chris Christie even though they had seen it or were following the news," Murray said. "There was, however, building in the public consciousness the sense that there were a lot of corruption busts going on in New Jersey. Even if they couldn't recall each individual one, just the accumulation of those things allowing people to say, 'There's a lot of people being arrested.' When Chris Christie ran for governor, he didn't start out with good name recognition, but once the campaign started getting under way, they were able to connect him: 'Somebody was doing something, and it's him.'"

Unlike Corzine, Christie was not without well-known opposition in the race for his party's nomination. One was Lonegan, the former three-term Bogota mayor who had earned himself a conservative following in earlier statewide campaigns, one a losing—if colorful—2005 bid for the Republican nomination for governor, the other a successful drive to defeat Corzine's ballot question in 2007 that called for the state to borrow $450 million to pay for stem cell research grants. The second was Assemblyman Rick Merkt, who had been Christie's running mate in an ill-fated 1995 run for the state Assembly. He raised no money and didn't qualify for the TV debates, but he did join the other two for radio confrontations.

On New York's WOR, Merkt went after Christie for supporting a continuation of the state's popular property tax rebate program in its current form, including cutting off homeowners under sixty-five in the current year, although Christie hedged on the future of rebates. Under Corzine the sales tax had been raised in part to send homeowners rebate checks—which at their 2007 peak averaged $1,273 for seniors and $966 for homeowners under age sixty-five. They usually arrived in September, just about the time voters started paying attention to the November elections.

Merkt, a six-term assemblyman, called rebates a political stunt. "It's a feel-good political boondoggle that's out there so that people will vote for politicians, that's always what it's been, and it has been an excuse for not fixing property taxes."[13] Lonegan agreed: "This is just a scam to send checks to different people. . . . These checks go out to illegal aliens. They go out to tenants. They go out to people who own no homes at all. This is nothing but sending money out to buy votes."[14] Christie said rebates are not a gimmick and that he would not take money away from people struggling to pay their bills but that once he got property taxes under control, rebates were history. That set up a lively back-and-forth between Lonegan and Christie:

Lonegan: "So you're against rebates, but just not right now."

Christie: "No, that's not what I said, Steve. No, that's not what I said. Listen."

Lonegan: "You just said when you get property taxes under control, you'll get rid of rebates. Which is it?"

Christie: "Steve, that's not what I said. I know it's easy for you to be confused. But let's just listen and listen clearly, and you'll hear it. What I'm saying is that in the middle of a recession, I disagree with Steve and Rick. You cannot take relief away from people in the middle of a recession. And we will work over the next four years to bring property taxes under control in New Jersey."[15]

On radio the subject of the state's controversial left-leaning Supreme Court was debated. Lonegan and Merkt said they would replace all justices who came up for lifetime tenure—after seven years on the bench. Christie took a more diplomatic wait-and-see attitude. "If you legislate from the bench, you will not be reappointed. If in fact you're interpreting the constitution and interpreting the statutes, then you have an opportunity to be reappointed," Christie said.[16]

Lonegan pounced, saying no sitting justices would be renominated if he became governor and that he wanted voters to decide about lifetime tenure on the court. Then he sought to tie Christie to court activities Christie said he opposed. "The most liberal state Supreme Court chief justice is Stuart Rabner, and my opponent Chris Christie was the chief Republican fan, proponent, endorser and supporter of Stuart Rabner in the state of New Jersey."[17]

In fact, Christie was a big fan of Rabner, a lawyer who never had been a judge before becoming chief justice. Rabner worked for Christie in the U.S. attorney's office. He left that job to be chief counsel to Corzine at Christie's suggestion. From chief counsel Rabner was named state attorney general for a brief stint, then was nominated by Corzine to be chief justice.

"I'm wondering how you determined he's the most liberal chief justice in America," Christie shot back. "This is the type of foolish hyperbole we've come to expect from you."[18]

Conservatives appeared to split their loyalties between Christie and Lonegan, whose goal apparently was to make Christie a moderate at least, or a liberal like Corzine at most. He said Christie wouldn't sufficiently change Corzine policies. Moderate Republicans flocked to Christie. Having hard-core conservatives Lonegan and Merkt as opponents worked in Christie's favor among general election voters because they made him look moderate by comparison. (Fast-forward to 2012, when he occupied the same part of the spectrum compared with 2012 GOP presidential hopefuls.) New Jersey voters in the whole are a moderate bunch. Merkt argued Christie never took any stands and was vague.

Christie looked beyond the GOP skirmish, targeting Corzine, while Lonegan focused on the primary. Lonegan wanted to ditch the state's progressive income tax code for a single rate of 2.9 percent, eventually dropping to 2.1 percent. Christie ripped the plan, estimating it would cause as many as 70 percent of taxpayers at the lower end of the economic spectrum to have to pay more. Christie wanted to cut the corporate business tax, Lonegan wanted to eliminate it.[19]

Christie said all new employees would have a defined contribution plan like a 401(k) instead of a traditional pension. Lonegan said he'd save personnel costs by laying off ten thousand to fifteen thousand people in his first hundred days in office. Christie said he would consider power-generating windmills off the Jersey coast, Lonegan said they were a money-draining experiment. Christie and Lonegan differed on details of a school voucher program. Christie said they should enable students whose schools are failing to attend better schools in neighboring towns willing to accept them. Lonegan said they should be used to promote competition between public and private schools within cities.

When asked to name a Republican they admired, Lonegan chose South Carolina governor Mark Sanford, who later was forced to resign as chairman of the Republican Governors Association after it was disclosed he did not go hiking on the Appalachian Trail as he told his staff and family, but on Father's Day was in Argentina visiting a girlfriend. Christie chose Louisiana governor Bobby Jindal, at the time rehabbing his national political image after a widely mocked Republican response to President Obama's State of the Union address. (In 2011, Christie campaigned for Jindal's Republican Party before their midterm elections.)

Christie told voters he was the only option who could beat Corzine in the fall. Christie comfortably beat Lonegan, 55 percent to 42 percent, with Merkt trailing at 3 percent. He prepared to take on Corzine, which in reality he had been doing for months already, seemingly aware that he would cruise to victory in the primary. Everything had been trending Democratic, in the state and nation, and Corzine had the big bucks and the huge campaign staff. All Corzine had to do was hold on to his base. Christie knew the odds and faced it with customary confidence.

"The road ahead will not be easy. It will be filled with tough choices and sacrifice. But I know if we get back to the basics that have always made us great, then we can restore for people the hope and the faith and the trust that we want in our government," Christie told cheering supporters in Whippany.[20]

He said Corzine's economic policies sent business and jobs to neighboring states, that he was a good man and well intentioned but wrong for the job.

Lonegan, in East Brunswick, said he would work to elect Christie but told supporters, "This is just the beginning. America is an ongoing revolution."

Corzine celebrated his renomination at an arena named for Dick Codey, who had declined to run against him. The governor was joined by Vice President Joe Biden, who said, "Barack Obama and Joe Biden are committed to Jon Corzine's re-election." It was not a casual remark. Murray, the pollster, said independents in New Jersey liked Obama, "so look for Jon Corzine to attach himself to Barack Obama's hip."[21] The president would campaign with Corzine three times, including on the Sunday before the Tuesday election.

Corzine slammed President George W. Bush, saying Republicans delivered the longest, deepest economic recession in eighty years. He didn't mention Christie by name but made a jab at Christie's accepting campaign donations from a supporter whose law firm Christie had given a no-bid federal monitoring contract.

Gubernatorial candidates had to choose running mates for the first time in New Jersey's history. Prior to this race there hadn't been a lieutenant governor in the state. After two consecutive governors didn't finish their terms—Christie Whitman in 2001 when she went to Washington to head the Environmental Protection Agency for President Bush, and Mc-Greevey driven from office in 2004 after a sex scandal—leaving Senate presidents running the executive branch as well as the upper house of the legislative branch, voters approved a constitutional amendment to create the new office.

Throughout New Jersey's history the system had worked well when the governor was away a short while. But Codey ran the state for fourteen months even though he never won a statewide election. After Whitman left, Donald DiFrancesco was governor for eleven months.

The Christie campaign had spent six months vetting potential lieutenant governor candidates. In the end he chose Kim Guadagno, fifty, an Iowa native who was sheriff of populous and Republican-leaning Monmouth County. Guadagno, whose husband, Michael, was an assistant U.S. attorney under Christie before becoming a Superior Court judge, was poised, friendly, and politically savvy.

Corzine continued his stumble-out-of-the-stable routine that had been increasing since those pink pigs flew over the State House. It was hard to believe that a man who ran an international investment banking firm could have a campaign this inept. Democrats floated rumors that the governor was considering for his running mate Senator Loretta Weinberg, Senator Barbara Buono, and Randal Pinkett, Season 4 winner of NBC's *The Apprentice,* the show where Donald Trump "fires" people who lose at such tasks as selling lemonade in Times Square.

The Star-Ledger of Newark, long a supporter of Corzine, ran an editorial that included this:

> If this is a trial balloon, hold on while we load our BB gun.
> Randal Pinkett—the unabashed self-promoting winner of "The Apprentice"—is being mentioned as a possible running mate as lieutenant governor, with Gov, Jon Corzine.
> It raises this question: Governor, are you serious?
> And this one: What, no one from "Survivor" is available?[22]

Pinkett demonstrated he didn't know how things are done in Trenton by taking the unusual step of calling a news conference to express his desire to run with Corzine, who by now was having second thoughts. Democratic leaders, too, were worrying that Corzine might crash and burn and take the party with him.

Christie grabbed the moment to make a point about their differences. "I have almost a week of a head start campaigning with my running mate, which is nice, but more than that, what has transpired shows the people of New Jersey that I know how to make decisions, and it opens a window into how he makes decisions."[23]

That was a window reporters had looked through before. Corzine seemed to take forever to announce that Congressman Robert Menendez would replace him in the Senate when he left to run for governor. In the end, in a last-minute switch, Corzine chose Weinberg, seventy-four, one of the legislature's most liberal and reform-minded senators, as a running mate. Weinberg was a prime sponsor of a gay marriage bill that would characterize all unions as civil marriages and specified that no member of the clergy or any religion would be required to solemnize a marriage that violated their free exercise of religion. She also sponsored proposals to end the Jersey practice of allowing politicians to hold more than one public office at the same time.

She had been at odds with Democratic Party bosses running Bergen County's party machinery. When she got into a dispute with county boss Joseph Ferriero, whose eventual conviction on corruption allegations was overturned, was overturned, Corzine sided with her. Since Christie was known for his crime-busting activity, Weinberg seemed a perfect counterpart.

"Her integrity is beyond reproach, so that certainly would be a factor. And it's always fun to have someone who's willing to tweak the nose of the establishment. She certainly has that reputation,"[24] said Assemblyman John McKeon. As it turned out, even Weinberg couldn't save Corzine from himself.

CHAPTER SEVEN

I'm Fat But You're Ugly and
I Can Lose Weight

The Corzine campaign was snake-bit from the get-go. What should have been routine turned into disaster. Democrats dispatched Vice President Joe Biden to Corzine's primary election victory party so they could get photos of the duo for the general election campaign. If the idea were to save a sinking governor they might as well have tossed him an anvil. The state's largest public employee union chose this time to plan a protest outside the facility where Biden was to speak. The vice president, a big union backer, was not going to cross a picket line. The protest didn't occur, because Corzine forged a last-minute deal over long-negotiated salary givebacks and furloughs, on terms the union could accept.

It boomeranged on him.

The rally may have produced usable photos for Corzine ads but it created high-caliber ammunition for Christie: "People want leadership who is going to say what they mean and mean what they say. And the governor once again by doing this is showing if you push him, he'll give in."[1]

Biden made the news again later during a conference call with reporters. One of Corzine's highly touted projects had been in development for years but was being speeded up as a job-creating stimulus for construction trades. It also afforded the chance to get photos of Corzine with other Democrats holding shovels and turning soil, as work began on a new Hudson River rail tunnel between New Jersey and Manhattan. During the call, Biden, an avid Amtrak rider during his days in the Senate, mistakenly claimed the proposed tunnel was for car traffic.[2] That created a credibility gap longer than the tunnel, which would eventually be canceled by Christie.

Another Joe made state Democrats even more nervous. He was Joe Doria, longtime pol, former Bayonne mayor, Assembly speaker, state senator, and, most significantly for our story, Corzine's head of the Department of Community Affairs, the cookie jar agency that hands out grant money to municipalities. The FBI paid him an unannounced visit on July 23, 2009, the day of the big Bid Rig III operation. He wasn't arrested, but his home and office were raided. A red-faced Corzine forced Doria to resign. The issue burned Corzine in two directions. To the general public, a member of Corzine's cabinet appeared to be the focus of the FBI. To establishment Democrats, whose friendship with Doria stretched back decades longer than most had ever heard of Corzine, there was anger that the governor so quickly threw Doria overboard. During the next two years, Doria never was charged or even questioned. In a September 7, 2011, letter to Doria's attorney, John Azzarello, assistant U.S. attorney James Nobile said, "Based on the evidence of which we are currently aware, no charges will be brought by this office regarding the circumstances that led to the search."

And so the race was on. The three leading candidates were the Democratic governor, the Republican Christie, and independent Chris Daggett, who seemingly came out of nowhere. There were pundits then and now who think Daggett—a former state environmental protection commissioner under Governor Tom Kean and federal EPA official under President Ronald Reagan, who said he had soured on the Republican Party—was put in the race by one of the other two main candidates. It was noted by them that while he opposed both Corzine and Christie he spent a lot more time attacking Christie. In addition to that trio, there were nine other independent and third-party candidates—not unusual, but a little above average. None had a shot at winning and only five of 110 third-party and independent candidates for New Jersey governor since World War II had gotten even 1 percent of the vote. Libertarian candidate Murray Sabrin received 4.7 percent in his 1997 bid for the governor's job against Governor Christie Whitman, who won reelection, and Jim McGreevey, who would be elected later.[3]

Daggett earned a coveted spot in the campaign's three major televised debates for meeting the state's fund-raising benchmark—$340,000 in contributions, in installments of $3,400 or less. Doing so also earned him $2-for-$1 matching funds from the state, a post-Watergate campaign finance program that has been shredded in recent elections, much as it has on the national level. Only two independent or third-party candidates have ever qualified in New Jersey—Sabrin and Daggett. In 1997, Sabrin drew financial support from Libertarians from other states looking to make a splash in a year with few other races of note; roughly 40 percent of his publicly identified campaign contributions came from outside New Jersey, twice as much as for the other candidates. Republicans, who felt Sabrin nearly cost Whitman reelection, also stewed because identities for donors who wrote checks for less than $400 didn't have to be reported but were eligible for public matching funds. In 2000 they pushed a bill through the Senate that would have deemed out-of-state contributions and small donations ineligible to be matched, but the gambit died in an Assembly committee. (They're probably thankful that the bill died now, considering how extensively Christie tapped his national fan base for his 2013 reelection with fund-raisers in California, Virginia, Massachusetts, Florida, Wisconsin, Minnesota, and elsewhere.)

Daggett raised his funds through more traditional routes such as family, friends, and work acquaintances but without an out-of-state, third-party political network to gin up cash. He raised more than $685,000, 80 percent of it from within New Jersey. His first donation came from Saul Cooperman, who was New Jersey's education commissioner under Republican governor Tom Kean, Christie's mentor. Anne Evans Estabrook, a real estate developer who was briefly the GOP establishment's first choice to run for U.S. Senate in 2008 before she suffered a mini-stroke, donated $2,500 to Daggett's campaign. Daggett got $2,000 from William Simon Jr., a New Jersey native and son of William E. Simon Sr., who was treasury secretary under Richard Nixon and Gerald Ford. Simon Jr., an assistant U.S. attorney under Rudolph Giuliani, made an unsuccessful bid to be

California's governor in 2002 and had hired Daggett years earlier to bring his environmental experience to his global merchant bank. Roy Vagelos, the former president and chief executive officer at Merck, gave $1,000. Only two elected officials endorsed or donated money to Daggett, both of them Democrats.

Corzine's political standing was so shaky by end of July that there was discussion about whether he should drop out of the race. Instead, the Obama political team sent in reinforcements and demanded changes. Corzine wasn't a commanding public speaker, was sometimes tone-deaf politically, and faced a worsening recession. But those problems could have been offset if not for a campaign staff State House regulars called the Kiddie Corps, people so amateurish, arrogant, or inexperienced that they put their personal feelings above the best interests of their candidate. The campaign hierarchy included aides from his gubernatorial office, such as Maggie Moran and Tom Shea, who had kept Corzine isolated and didn't win him any friends, even among fellow Democrats, some of whom wanted to warn him he was in deep trouble with voters.

"Well, he wouldn't talk [to me]—listen, they kept me away from him," said Senator Steve Sweeney. "Maggie Moran used to tell people I was going to primary him. Seriously, I'd walk through here, I'm the majority leader of the Senate, she'd see me walking through the hallway and walk the other way. I had zero communications with a lot of these guys, because I was viewed as the enemy. Even though we worked together on paid family leave, we would do things that I thought was good, I was the one that, God forbid, took on the public sector workforce to try to bring balance to the damn place. It wasn't an attack, it was just a matter of bringing balance. But [the unions] all ran to him, 'You've got to do something about Sweeney,' and he couldn't do anything about me.

"Tom [Shea] was an odd guy. He really was. I don't know where he came from, and all of a sudden he was this political genius. And everything went into a dark hole. I never got to know Tom that well," Sweeney said. Shea had worked for Corzine in the U.S. Senate, moved to Florida, then returned to his native New Jersey to be Corzine's chief of staff in Trenton. Sweeney was the Democratic majority leader but said Shea almost never discussed Corzine's legislative agenda with him. "Extremely rare. And when we did, nothing ever got followed up on. Nothing."

Corzine's problems extended to the legislature, which undermined him in the media rather than guarding his back. Sweeney recalled a meeting after Corzine's toll road proposal collapsed in which he didn't have an answer to a question asked by Senate president Dick Codey about a new debt reduction plan. As the meeting let out, a reporter asked Corzine the exact same question—as if someone texted or emailed him the question because it would make Corzine look bad.

"He had people around him that didn't want him to be successful," said Sweeney. "Codey wasn't wrong to be frustrated. And maybe he should have gone and tried it anyway, to see if Corzine backed off. But Jon had people within our own party that were constantly undermining him, constantly. I'll put it this way: There wasn't a whole lot of people pulling to help, as there should have been. You look at the Republicans in the legislature, they're with their governor."

With that political backdrop and subpar poll numbers, Corzine's road to reelection would be a scorched-earth one. He had the money to batter Christie and the willingness to go negative, as evidenced by his campaigns in 2000 and 2005.

Corzine's first run for governor was waged in the aftermath of Jim McGreevey's resignation. Reporters had heard rumors for years about McGreevey's sexual orientation, dating to before his 1997 bid for governor. Inquiries into the veracity of those stories never proved anything that could be printed—which was regrettable come 2004, when he quit, citing an affair with a male staffer and the prospects that he could be blackmailed.

In 2005, there were rumors being pushed by Republicans about Corzine's relationship with an aide, including the detail that she had been whisked off to Ohio to quietly abort a pregnancy. Most years, it's the sort of wild, hurtful whisper campaign that might go unchecked. In the wake of the McGreevey experience, though, Gannett sent reporter

Tom Baldwin—a fearless rabble-rouser who would ask anyone about anything—to pull Corzine aside after an event and ask about the rumor. Corzine denied it, vehemently. No story was ever printed about the specifics of the rumor, except a reference to Corzine saying an attack in a whisper campaign was inaccurate "garbage."[4] Democrats, though, apparently expected a story from Baldwin and struck back hard, planting a piece the next morning in the *New York Daily News* gossip column about a cozy relationship Corzine's opponent, Doug Forrester, had struck up with a former Miss New Jersey in his 2002 run for U.S. Senate.[5]

Moral of the immoral story: Corzine had zero problem going negative.

So he hired Jeff Whelan, a reporter who covered Christie's U.S. attorney's office for the Newark *Star-Ledger*, to do what's euphemistically called opposition research, more commonly referred to as "digging up the dirt." Politicians had often hired former reporters to their public relations as governor, either in a department or a governor's office, but Whelan's employment by the campaign raised eyebrows for some members of the journalism community because he left a supposedly neutral profession not just for a job advocating for an agency or elected official but for a partisan job focused on undermining a once-trusting subject and source. Incidentally, as governor, Christie later hired the three daily newspaper reporters who most closely covered him in his Morris County freeholder days—Brian Murray, Lawrence Ragonese, and Fred Snowflack—as spokesmen for various departments in state government. Maybe he has a long memory and a soft spot for familiar faces—or maybe he learned to lock up former reporters who are familiar with history but now looking for work as newspapers downsize.

Among the campaign news that came out of the U.S. attorney's office was that Michele Brown, a neighbor and friend of the Christies who worked as a federal prosecutor for eighteen years, starting eleven years before Christie ran the place, had received a $46,000 loan in 2007 from Christie, which she and her husband were paying back at $500 a month for ten years. Brown and her husband, Michael Allen, had run into financial trouble with credit card debt piling up after Allen lost his job, Christie said.

Democrats questioned whether that loan was evidence of a continuing professional relationship between Christie and the federal prosecutor's office—particularly because Brown was in charge of the office's handling of the Democrats' request for public records about Christie's tenure, documents that were long overdue. Corzine running mate Loretta Weinberg said for Brown to be involved in retrieving records was a conflict of interest and asked that she be removed. Less than two weeks after news of the loan broke, the Justice Department told Christie's interim replacement, Ralph Marra Jr., to remove Brown as coordinator of the Freedom of Information Act requests and Brown resigned the same day, *The New York Times* reported, quoting a federal official who said he was briefed on the communications.[6]

Marra defended the handling of the requests, saying Brown only supplied records relating to herself. After she left, volumes of records were turned over to Corzine, whose campaign wasted no time in doling portions out to reporters. Marra would later be the subject of a Justice Department inquiry after his comments during the announcement of the July Bid Rig raid veered into what sounded like a political endorsement of Christie; he has since been appointed by Christie as the top lawyer at the New Jersey Sports & Exposition Authority.

There was a second issue. Christie didn't disclose the loan to Brown on state and federal ethics forms and didn't pay $420 in federal taxes on the interest income in 2007, which he said was an oversight. Christie called the issue "fake hysteria" and "fake outrage" during a teleconference with reporters, saying it was a ploy to distract from Corzine's poor fiscal record, including high taxes and higher unemployment than neighboring states.

Christie pointed out that Brown worked under Democratic and Republican administrations. His running mate, Kim Guadagno, said Corzine should be ashamed for smearing a veteran public servant. Christie noted Corzine had his own issues with a personal loan and for a much larger amount—a $470,000 mortgage loan to ex-girlfriend and state public employee union official Carla Katz, which Corzine later forgave. That wasn't the only money exchange in what was looking like a classic example of the pot calling the kettle black: *The New York Times* reported that when Corzine and Katz broke up, Corzine paid Katz more than $6 million.[7] And while Katz didn't work for Corzine, he did have to negotiate state employee contracts worth millions with her. In 2007, Corzine caved during negotiations on something Katz wanted in union contracts. After saying state employee retirees would have to start paying for part of their health benefits, Corzine backtracked, sticking New Jersey taxpayers with the bills.

Brown resigned because, she said, she didn't want the issue to interfere with the work the U.S. attorney's office did. Marra, who had promoted Brown to the number two position in the office after he became acting U.S. attorney when Christie left in December, said he accepted the resignation "with great regret."[8] Brown took a job with a law firm that represented one of five companies identified as targets in the Christie investigation of the hip and knee replacement manufacturers. While in Christie's office, Brown had led the case and helped her boss negotiate the settlement.[9] Among the partners at the firm where Brown landed was Walter Timpone, who'd nearly been hired as Christie's top lieutenant seven years earlier and but remained a Christie ally.

Christie called the loan incident the low point of the campaign for him—actually, the whole month of August was brutal, as the campaign heated up.

The Christie loan wasn't the only time Michele Brown made campaign news. While a federal prosecutor, she attended a campaign strategy session on her own time. *The New York Times* reported that she had pushed for the huge takedown known as the "Gang of 44" arrests to be made before Christie successor Fishman's team took the reins. She had been among the aides who'd traveled with Christie to expensive hotels (and in AP coverage, the only one mentioned). She was also among those in the car when Christie was ticketed in Lambertville in 2005 for speeding, 58 mph in a 40 mph zone, and driving an unregistered, uninsured vehicle, his wife's. He was allowed to drive away, because his kids were in the car, he said, and pleaded guilty to reduced charges and fined $250. The registration on Mary Pat's car was expired but it was insured at the time of the stop.

Christie's campaign tried to respond with humor. Spokeswoman Maria Comella said, "Before the Corzine campaign wastes any more of the governor's Wall Street millions on opposition research, we're going to let them know that Kim [Guadagno] received a ticket in 2007 for driving while on a cell phone and Chris got detention in the ninth grade for too much talking in class."[10]

She said the day of the traffic stop the candidate was with his family and Brown. But that wasn't the way Christie's opponents sought to spin it. In a whisper campaign, some news organizations were led to believe that Christie and Brown were the only ones in the car, an obvious attempt to smear Christie. Seeing it for what it was, most news organizations didn't take the bait.

"Listen, that's the kind of extraneous stuff you have to put up with in a campaign," Bill Palatucci said. "You're trying to talk about issues and qualifications and you're talking about traffic tickets in Lambertville." Palatucci said he spoke to students at Rutgers University at a campaign season event after Steve DiMicco, Corzine's consultant, had been there for an hour. "And they will tell you, the students who were there, that it was kind of day and night. Steve talked about how it was going to be an attack on character. He was saying that this is a person you don't want for governor, it was going to be focused on that," he said. "So that was a strategy of theirs. They couldn't talk about Jon Corzine's record and why he was so unpopular."

On New Jersey 101.5's popular Jersey Guys show, afternoon hosts Casey Bartholomew and Ray Rossi zinged Christie at length about the matter and mused about the actual occupants of the car. Todd Christie, the candidate's brother, then made what he called "probably my biggest mistake of the campaign"—he called the station, to get on the air and stand up for his brother's integrity.

"There were some insinuations that were really out of line. And I left headquarters that afternoon and was just beside myself because I knew the story—I knew who was in the truck and who wasn't in the truck," Todd said. "And I called into the show, and at the last second was like, 'Holy shit, what am I doing?' Like he's going to kill me. What's it going to prove? I'm his brother, and I'm defending him."

The campaign had been working to keep Todd disciplined, after he had openly sparred with Steve Lonegan's campaign manager in the primary.

And now he was about to pour gasoline on a story the team just wanted to end as quickly as possible. So he hung up the phone—which then got talked about on the radio, in conspiratorial tones.

"It just kind of fueled his fire," Todd lamented. "Then within fifteen minutes, Bill Stepien [the campaign manager] called me and said, 'Did you really call in?' At first I was like, 'No, no, no. Who would call in?' And then less than a minute later, the big guy called and I was like, 'Yeah, I did.' It was not a pleasant moment for me."

Christie's driving returned to the campaign regarding a July 26, 2002, accident in which a motorcyclist involved in a collision with Christie in Elizabeth went to the hospital. Driving a leased BMW sedan, Christie apparently became confused and tried to turn right onto a street that was one-way in the other direction. Andre Mendonca's bike was headed toward the sedan and both drivers applied the brakes, according to the police report, which said Christie's car came to a stop and the motorcycle "fell on its side and slid into his vehicle." Police said Christie identified himself as the U.S. attorney and was not ticketed. Police director James Cosgrove said Mendonca was put in a neck brace and driven by emergency responders to University Hospital in Newark. Court records indicate Mendonca filed a civil suit in 2004 that later was dismissed. Seven years later during the campaign, Christie said he wasn't aware there was a lawsuit and that he didn't know how it was resolved, but he never paid the motorcyclist a settlement and never had any other contact with him. Stanley Marcus, Mendonca's lawyer, told the Associated Press he didn't remember the accident or how it was settled. Comella said her boss "knows he can always be a better driver."[11] State Democratic Party chief Joseph Cryan said Christie's not being able to recall all the details of the 2002 accident was not credible.[12]

That incident led James Ahearn, columnist for *The Record*, to take a look at Christie's driving record over twenty-four years. "Since 1985, the man who is now the Republican candidate for governor, has been cited 13 times for moving violations. He was involved in six accidents, two of them since 2002, when he became the top federal prosecutor in the state. The best thing to be said about his driving record is that if elected in November, which seems increasingly possible, he won't be doing much driving. A State Police officer will be driving for him."[13]

Christie's difficult month of August ended with him looking to reset the terms of the conversation in what his campaign dubbed a major post–Labor Day speech at the Paramus Elks lodge—which, in quintessential Jersey style, sits in the parking lot of a highway shopping plaza, behind a Raymour and Flanigan furniture store. He broke no new ground, though, offering familiar generalities in promising to focus on property taxes.

The candidates' first debate was about finances and how each would deal with the poor economic climate. Daggett had a plan to extend the sales tax to things that were tax-exempt and cut property taxes by the same amount, while also trimming income and corporate taxes. Corzine refused to take a no-tax-hike pledge, saying to do so was irresponsible to balance the budget. Christie spent his time talking about the other two, saying both would raise taxes but that he wouldn't. *The Wall Street Journal* editorial page was unimpressed by Christie's campaign and debate performances, saying he was running an "empty campaign" and risked blowing a prime opportunity to topple the Democrats. "Even if Mr. Christie ekes out a win because Mr. Corzine is so unpopular, the Republican will arrive in Trenton with a mandate to do what he campaigned on—nothing."[14]

Christie had his first conversation with Senator Steve Sweeney just as the debate wrapped up.

"Sweeney told me the night of the first debate at NJN [New Jersey Network, then the state's public TV station]. I got done with the debate and I went up to say hello to my wife and my brother, and they were sitting right across the aisle from Steve," Christie said. "I had met Steve maybe once at [a New Jersey Association of Counties] convention. I didn't know him. I knew who he was obviously, and I knew what he looked like and who he was. And when I got up there, he got up and got in between me and Mary Pat beforehand and put his hand out and shook my hand, and he said to me, 'I look forward to working with you.' That night he told me we're going to be working together."

Sweeney says he'd known for two years that Corzine would lose. "I go to the gym at 5:30 in the morning. I'm working out with people who I absolutely know are staunch, dyed-in-the-wool Democrats, I mean Roosevelt Democrats, that were telling me they wouldn't vote for him."

Sweeney said people gave up on Corzine because they felt "that he didn't do anything. That nothing was getting done. The biggest complaint that I would hear from people is that it's only gotten worse. That things didn't get better. And Jon came along with this expectation as this is a guy who knows how to make things happen. This is a guy that's going to fix things, because you can't be the CEO of Goldman Sachs and not be a go-getter and all those things. They raised the bar so high that it was hard to clear. He raised it.

"When the campaign started, once there was a Chris Christie and a Jon Corzine, the big thing for us was, 'You can't vote for this other guy. . . . This guy is polar opposite what we believe in.' 'Yeah, you know, I haven't worked in such a period of time.' The problems with the national economy, he got saddled with it."

"I think," said former governor Jim Florio, until Corzine the only incumbent New Jersey governor to lose a general election, "and I say this from personal experience, that it's better to be the governor coming out of the recession than the governor going in."[15]

Despite all that, Corzine had been rising in the polls and by now was in a dead heat with Christie. The surprise was Daggett, who earlier had been considered insignificant in the race. He steadily gained steam since the first debate, which came on the heels of the announcement of his tax plan. By now, however, Christie had begun taking aim at Daggett to stem his rise in the polls. In the second debate he framed Daggett's plan as a $4 billion sales tax increase, ignoring the corresponding cuts to business, income, and property taxes. With Christie's words amplified by TV ads purchased by the Republican Governors Association—which, not coincidentally, received large soft-money contributions from Christie's brother, Todd—the tide eventually turned on the independent and his $1.5 million campaign war chest, roughly one-tenth of what Christie would spend. Daggett peaked at 20 percent in one poll; if accurate at the time, it means two-thirds of his backers later abandoned him.

There was another debate of sorts, the traditional joint editorial board meeting for statewide candidates held by the six Gannett-owned newspapers in New Jersey. It had become such a staple of the campaign season that in 2006, Democratic U.S. senator Robert Menendez—who had some of the same political consultants as Corzine—publicly announced he'd attend the meeting before an invitation had even been discussed by the newspapers.

Christie and Daggett came and responded to the editors' twenty recommendations for getting the state's house in order, agreeing with each other on eighteen and concurring with the editors on twelve. Corzine didn't show, the first candidate not to do so in the history of the joint editorial boards, which are covered in print and webcast. In fact, he never responded to several requests made through Sean Darcy, a hanger-on from the McGreevey administration who longed to be higher in the official Corzine pecking order. If the governor thought he'd gotten good advice, that notion melted as soon as he saw the photo on the front pages of Gannett's papers the next day. Between Christie and Daggett was an empty chair with Corzine's name on a placard. Where was Corzine? Less than a half-hour away in Union Township at the opening of the Elizabethtown Gas Co. customer care center. The media picked up the story and Corzine had enough egg on his face to make breakfast for him and his entire Kiddie Corps.

Corzine also refused to take part in the gubernatorial debates hosted by a major New Jersey radio network, which, like the Gannett editorial board, was a traditional part of the landscape for campaigns for governor and U.S. Senate.

None of these decisions was made without Corzine's approval. He was accustomed to paying subordinates to tell him what he wanted to hear. "Even friends of Corzine say his management style is erratic at best. For all his affability, he consults with almost no one except a small coterie of advisers, and often makes decisions based purely on gut instinct,"[16] *The Daily Beast* Web site wrote. Corzine was like the emperor without any clothes.

Christie's campaign was more a disciplined, focused effort. His chief paid adviser was Mike DuHaime, a New Jersey native and political lifer whose dad had once sought the GOP nomination for U.S. Senate. In 1997,

DuHaime tasted his first political professional success as the campaign manager for a Republican challenger, Anthony Bucco, who toppled an incumbent Democratic senator, Gordon MacInnes, in Morris County. Recall that Christie tried to take out Bucco in an ill-advised power play in 1995. And 1997 was the year Christie got his comeuppance in the freeholder primary—meaning DuHaime witnessed the fall.

The 2009 campaign was an important one for DuHaime, who in 2008 had piloted former New York mayor Rudolph Giuliani's presidential campaign—the one that ran aground in Florida after intentionally skipping the contests in Iowa and New Hampshire. After Christie's primary victory, DuHaime added Maria Comella, the deputy communications director from the Giuliani campaign, who later spent part of 2008 with vice presidential nominee Sarah Palin, to run the press operation. She became Christie's deputy chief of staff for communications in Trenton. Christie's campaign manager, the guy on the ground each day, was Bill Stepien, a DuHaime disciple who worked for Giuliani's presidential bid and later became another of Christie's deputy chiefs of staff, for legislative and intergovernmental affairs.

Corzine's Kiddie Corps sure knew how to make themselves look stupid. Not only did they thumb Corzine's nose at the millions of readers of Gannett papers and radio listeners, but they launched political ads that went where few ads had gone before—and for good reason. In what *The New York Times* called "about as subtle as a playground taunt"[17] Corzine ran ads showing Christie stepping from an SUV in slow motion, his girth moving in several directions at once under his shirt. And just to drive the point home, a voice-over said that Christie "threw his weight around" in trying to avoid traffic tickets.

In case viewers missed the point, for contrast Corzine was running foot races every weekend, once with Mayor Cory Booker through the streets of Newark. When asked about the ads, Corzine said smugly, "There isn't a candidate in the world that likes how they're depicted in their opponents' ads."[18] He added that some of Christie's ads had shown the governor's bald head.

In his ads, Corzine appeared to be trying to send a subtle message that Christie was reckless with his health and maybe so in other ways. "As much as they might dislike the incumbent, they have to feel that the challenger is somewhat of a safe choice," said Patrick Murray, director of the Monmouth University Polling Institute.[19] Kerwin Swint, a political science professor at Kennesaw State University in Georgia who wrote a book on the twenty-five dirtiest political campaigns of all time, said unflattering photos in campaign ads are not uncommon. But it is rare for politicians to directly criticize their opponents' looks because that can make them appear mean-spirited.[20]

Christie handled it with humor sometimes: "I'm slightly overweight. Apparently this has become a great cause of discussion in the State of New Jersey. I don't know what that has to do with being governor."[21] He said the weight issue never came up on the campaign trail except when he was told he looked thinner in person than on TV. "Then I say, 'Those are the governor's commercials, not mine.'"[22] During a campaign stop at a senior citizens complex someone asked, "How's your diet?" Christie responded, "Not as good as it should be . . . I'm a work in progress." There was a pause, he smiled at the questioner, then added, "Thanks for piling on."[23]

For Christie, his weight had been a lifelong struggle, starting when he was a chubby kid being teased by his peers. He slimmed down while playing high school sports but never shook the feeling. "I was thin, but I felt fat," he told Oprah Winfrey in a 2012 interview, acknowledging "there is a certain compulsiveness at times to my eating." He developed a shell about the barbs and jokes but would make repeated efforts to lose weight, if only for his children. Losses were often followed by gains, and losing weight would prove to be a struggle, even after as governor he began to see a dietitian, hooked up with a personal trainer, and worked out four days a week. "I weigh too much because I eat too much. And I eat some bad things, too."[24]

New York–based radio talker Don Imus, who hated Corzine, asked Christie's opinion of the ads and got this: "My reaction was it's just silly. You know, it's beneath the office he holds. If you're going to do it, at least man up and say I'm fat. You know, then afterwards he wusses out and says 'Oh, no no, I didn't mean that.' Man up, if you say I'm fat, I'm fat. Let's go. Let's talk about it."

Imus replied, "Well, you know, here's the thing we found interesting, is that most of the people who are going to vote in New Jersey are fat, like most of the people in the country are fat."

"That's why I'm feeling good," Christie said.

But, Imus asked, shouldn't you be setting some kind of example?

"Well, I think I am, Don. We've got to spur our economy, Don. Dunkin' Donuts, International House of Pancakes, those people need work too."

Other times, he responded to questions about his weight with serious straightforwardness: "It's one of the more difficult things I've had to deal with in my life. . . . I was a really good U.S. attorney, and I was struggling with it for those seven years. It's just part of who I am, unfortunately."[25]

He had, in fact, endured references to his girth throughout his political career. In 1996, Christie and fellow Morris County freeholder John Fox made a friendly wager about which of them could lose the most weight by the November election. "We'll have to take them up to the county trash transfer station for the weigh-in," quipped freeholder director John Eckert, suggesting a scale that registers tonnage would be more appropriate than a bathroom scale. Each vowed to lose forty pounds. The one losing the least would have to donate $500 to charity. Neither would say what they weighed. "We'll have a weigh-in, probably tomorrow and no, it will not be public. We will not be disclosing that data," said Christie, who still doesn't answer questions about how much he weighs.[26]

It also came up in the lieutenant governor debate. One of the moderators, Eric Scott, asked Senator Loretta Weinberg whether she thought Christie was fat and whether the ads run by the Democrats' campaign were fair. Weinberg said there had been negative campaigning, then wandered around the ballpark for a while with her answer before opining it shouldn't be a topic of conversation because no candidates were Hollywood perfect: "I don't think there are too many of us in this race who can make it into the finalists of 'The Bachelor' or 'The Bachelorette' programs."[27]

Weinberg spent much of the debate blaming former president George W. Bush for the economic problems the Corzine administration faced. The Christie campaign expected it—so much so, in fact, that it became a running joke in the debate rehearsals, where Senator Bill Baroni played Corzine.

"Every answer he gave, he found a way to work George W. Bush in, in a way that only Baroni could, and try to get under my skin, and work it in, and work it in," Christie said. "And finally, we got to closing statements. And we knew what the order was going to be already, Corzine was going first with his closing statement. Baroni starts his closing statement, he said, 'I want to thank the sponsors of tonight's debate. I want to thank the panel of questioners for great questions. I want to thank Mr. Daggett for a spirited debate. And I would like to thank George W. Bush's U.S. attorney, Chris Christie.' And we all just absolutely broke up."

Debate prep is as much about making sure a candidate keeps his or her cool as it is about getting their points across. On the Democratic side of the campaign, the burly Senator Steve Sweeney played Christie in debate prep and succeeded in rattling Corzine with lines about the pension and health care reform.

"I drove him nuts. I called him Norma Rae. I know it bothered him, because every time—and I liked Jon, but every time he'd say, 'You gonna call me Norma Rae again?' I knew I got under his skin," said Sweeney, who said you could get Corzine upset by challenging his word.

At that lieutenant governor debate, Weinberg also steered conversation back to a wedge issue Democrats used to turn off female voters to Christie, a theme that followed him into the governor's office, when he reduced funding to family planning centers.

The campaign push centered on a state requirement that all health care insurers pay for forty-five mandated medical tests. Christie proposed allowing less expensive "mandate-free" policies to be sold that wouldn't cover all forty-five, as a way to entice some of New Jersey's 1.4 million residents without insurance, especially younger adults, to buy coverage. In order to offer the bare-bones policies, companies would have to offer a full-mandate coverage plan as well. But Corzine & Co. never mentioned that part.

"I wouldn't cut from the mandated coverage. What I'm saying is that right now, we have 550,000 women . . . who have no insurance at all. And what I propose is to say that for those people, individuals who are currently uninsured, we should get them some insurance they can afford,"[28] Christie said when his proposal was unveiled.

Democrats jumped at the chance to accuse Christie of wanting to do away with mandates, especially focusing on issues important to women—mammograms to detect breast cancer and forty-eight-hour maternity stays after a baby is born. That was used more in Corzine TV ads than any other issue. Christie called Corzine deceitful and the ads shameful: "I would not have a plan that would ever prevent any woman who needed a mammogram to get one," said Christie, whose beloved mother's breast cancer was discovered in a mammogram, enabling Sandy to seek early treatment that kept her alive for another two decades.[29]

Christie's father, Bill, was getting upset by the campaign's tenor. "He worked South Jersey really hard during the campaign, took everything personal," Todd Christie said. "Chris tries to let the personal things roll off his back. My father would call me and text me just beside himself when the commercials were running and just some of the bad stuff was going on. I think he's kind of toned down a little bit the last couple of years, although we've got him now disciplined not to call Chris, just to call me and blow off steam to me because Chris doesn't need it."

Democrats also sought to undermine Christie by going after his brother. Corzine ran an ad that insinuated Todd Christie was not indicted in a securities case because his brother, at the time the U.S. attorney for New Jersey, intervened on his behalf with the U.S. attorney for the Southern District of New York.

Todd Christie was chief executive officer for Spear, Leeds & Kellogg, a Wall Street trading firm found by the U.S. Securities and Exchange Commission to have engaged in illegal trading practices between 1999 and 2003—for what was called "naked short selling," in which a stock's price is driven down by individuals selling shares that aren't ever delivered. Twenty traders from a number of firms, including Todd, a specialist who handled trades on the stock market floor of IBM and, most importantly for this saga, America Online, were cited in the SEC's civil complaint. Fifteen were indicted. Todd wasn't among them, though through hundreds of questionable trades he had earned his firm the fourth biggest profits at customers' expense among the twenty traders.

Todd Christie had become very wealthy when he made more than $60 million as Goldman Sachs bought Spear Leeds for $6.3 billion in 2000. He put some proceeds into a family foundation, through which, according to his Uncle Joe Grasso, he has given $1.25 million to St. Barnabas Medical Center, grateful for the care it provided his mother after her 1996 aneurism and his first wife when they were struggling to conceive a baby.

But Todd left the company in 2003 around the time that word of the investigation surfaced, and in 2008 he acknowledged violating federal and New York Stock Exchange rules. The U.S. attorney on the case, David Kelley, whose office had secured corporate fraud convictions of Bernie Ebbers and Martha Stewart among others, left public life in 2005. Two years later, then a partner at Cahill Gordon & Reindel, Kelley received a no-bid contract from Christie's U.S. attorney's office through a deferred prosecution agreement in which Christie agreed not to charge Biomet Orthopedics, one of five medical supply companies Christie's office accused of bribing surgeons with kickbacks for using their products. Biomet paid nearly $27 million to settle the investigation and agreed to be monitored for eighteen months.

Chris Christie was asked about the Kelley matter when he testified before Congress by Representative Brad Sherman, D-Calif., who asked if it created the perception of a quid pro quo. Christie said, "No, sir, because my brother committed no wrongdoing and was found not to have committed any wrongdoing, both by the southern district of New York and the SEC."

After Corzine's ad hit the airwaves, Todd Christie, wife Andrea, and his daughter from his first marriage, Gabrielle, then around eight years old, were eating at a restaurant in Mendham, something they did every other week to talk, catch up, and have fun. That particular meal wasn't as fun as usual.

"I can see Gabrielle's just not herself," Todd recalled. "She's very much like me, very outgoing, very funny. I kept asking her what was wrong. She finally came over and sat on my lap and starting crying. I'm like, 'You've got to tell daddy, what's the matter.' She said that a couple of friends at school had said that now they know why your daddy has so much money, it's because he stole it. And she was crying and said, 'Did you steal money, dad?'" Todd said. "After we left the restaurant I called Chris and said, 'It can't get any worse than this. We've got to beat the daylights out of that guy.' When your daughter's crying, asking if you stole money, I don't know how it gets worse than that."

None of the criminal accusations stuck against any of the fifteen specialists charged. Three were acquitted by juries. Two were convicted by juries but their convictions were later reversed. Two others pleaded guilty, but those pleas were later vacated. Charges against the other eight were dropped by prosecutors. Todd thought federal prosecutors had flawed numbers and a flawed theory but kept pushing it because they were embarrassed that New York attorney general Eliot Spitzer was going after Wall Street while they weren't.

Prosecutors accused traders of rigging the order in which trades of stock were executed by flagging any instance in which it took more than fifteen seconds to execute an order. Todd said the New York Stock Exchange's window was two minutes. Additionally, he says, the massive volume of trades of AOL stock at that time often overwhelmed the NYSE's computers, rendering trade orders inaccessible as they backed up in a queue.

"We never wanted it let out at the time that their system couldn't keep up with it," Todd said. "They were in this PR war with NASDAQ. NASDAQ was saying they were the stock exchange of the future. Remember all those commercials? They were high-tech, all this jazz. So the last thing the Stock Exchange wanted to let out is that their system isn't capable of handling 18 million shares a day.

"The whole thing was a joke," Todd said of the investigation. "There are a lot of plusses to being Chris's brother, a lot. I don't mean in terms of him being governor, because if anything I do less [with him] now as governor than before he won. I meant in terms of him as a person and some of the great people I've met because he's governor. But there's plenty of downsides to being Chris's brother, and that's one of them."

Dawn Christie, who at times expressed disappointment the public didn't know the governor has a sister, took a different view after the ads. "I remember when the first ads came out about Todd," Chris said. "She called me and she was like, 'It's so great being the anonymous sibling.' So I think there were moments when Dawn has definitely used it to her advantage."

Todd said that following the campaign, Maggie Moran of the Corzine camp sought him out to deliver an apology. They've met a few times for what he found to be surprisingly cordial conversations. He says that as difficult as the campaign slings were for him personally, they affirmed his opinion of his brother.

"Listen, if that's all they can get on Chris, which obviously they spent a ton of dough researching him and trying to dig up stuff, if that's the best they can do, that is pretty good," Todd said. "That kind of reinforced for me what I thought about him, which is that he lived one of the cleanest lives I've ever seen. I can count on one hand the number of times I've seen him intoxicated. He's just—that's just what he is."

Christie had weathered the opposition research and advertising deluge in decent shape, though he'd fallen behind slightly in public polls. His campaign had more limited funding and needed to husband resources for the stretch drive. The lead-up could have been worse, Republicans felt. Palatucci said his days behind his father's bar made him think for the average guy the Corzine ads were just a tone off. "Even the stuff on Todd, as rough as it was, I just remember looking at their TV commercials and thinking they just didn't quite have it right. They bought $2 million of TV this week. So you put the TV on that night. You kind of sit there cringing, looking at it, then you go, 'Oh. It's nasty and bad, but does that one work?'"

The Corzine campaign may have been overconfident because Obama's pollster, Joel Benenson, who lived in New Jersey, told them they would win by 6 points. "I'm sure he is a marvelous national pollster, but doing targeted turnout projections in an '09 race in New Jersey versus '08—that's day and night," said Palatucci.

As the candidates raced toward Election Day, and when it seemed Corzine had no other places to wound himself, he miraculously found one—and, incredibly, it harked back to those pink flying pigs. He said his administration was looking at "ideas for additional resources" from the New Jersey Turnpike. Even though he said an 800 percent toll hike wouldn't be a part of a second term, he told *The New York Times* he might reconsider his plan to lease the turnpike, an idea that was thoroughly trashed by a public that loved the turnpike in much the same way Coca-Coca drinkers loved the classic beverage, and rejected the company's New Coke. "The idea worked. So maybe we just need to scale it back," Corzine said.[30]

"Let's face it, he has been caught," Christie said. "When Jon Corzine doesn't have to face the voters for four more years, he's going to sell the Turnpike, sell the Parkway and raise the tolls 800 percent."

Toward the end of the campaign Corzine closed his checkbook, whether from overconfidence or from feeling he was being misled by those around him—or some of both, we may never know for sure. In the final week of the race, culminating with Election Day, Corzine didn't put a dollar into his campaign. Four years earlier, he dropped more than $3.8 million in the race's final week. In his 2000 race for Senate, he added more than $3.6 million in the last-week stretch.

Over a dozen years, he'd spent more than $144 million on his political career, including $60 million to win his Senate seat, $43 million to win the governor's mansion, and $28.5 million to run for reelection, plus donations to other candidates and committees. That doesn't even include donations by his charity that sometime had a political benefit. After all that, though, he shut the spigot at the height of his final and toughest campaign. In one of his earlier races he fed volunteers prime rib on election night. Reporters pulled rank to be at his headquarters this time, only to discover the meal was hot dogs.

Two days before the election, Obama visited to rally supporters for Corzine. Sweeney said people were excited—that the president was going to save the election, that the polling affirmed their optimism. Sweeney told them they were wrong.

"I said, 'I don't care about the polling. I'm telling you guys, this is not going in the direction we want it to go,'" Sweeney said. "And that night, Jon Corzine called me at home. Now, realize, I put a lot of work into helping him. I was traveling two, three times a week up to Newark to do this debate prep and to really piss him off on a regular basis. I think I got to know Jon a lot better. I would never change the way I was before, but if I had had the relationship with him as we were working through, it would have been much better earlier on. But he called me up and said, 'Why do you keep saying we're going to lose? I poll, I'm up. I'm up.' I said, 'Jon, I'm spending way too much time convincing your base to vote for you.' And he said, 'Well, that's down by you, the numbers are worse down by you. They're better up here.' And I said, 'Listen, you can tell me that, but I'm telling you.' When I told him, he just could not believe it."

Obama's aggressive support and his pollster's sunny predictions notwithstanding, voters dropped the hammer on Corzine. Christie finished 86,700 votes ahead of him, winning by a margin of 48.5 percent to 44.9 percent, the first time in twelve years Republicans had won a statewide race in New Jersey. Independent Daggett got 5.8 percent—a distant third, but still the most since 1913 for anyone outside the two major parties. The other nine candidates, in keeping with New Jersey history, shared 1 percent.

Exit polling showed Corzine had trouble with the Democratic base. Among voters who say they voted for Corzine in '05, the governor held on to 76 percent but 15 percent deserted him for Christie. Among those who voted in '05 for Doug Forrester, 96 percent stayed with Christie, 3 percent went for Corzine. Christie won nearly 60 percent of independents, compared with Corzine's 33 percent. Among those who did not vote in the last gubernatorial election, Christie took 50 percent to 41 percent for Corzine, who didn't get the congeniality prize, either. Three out of four (76 percent) said the governor unfairly attacked Christie, while 66 percent thought Christie played dirty.[31]

"New Jersey voters have grown accustomed to negative campaigns," said Monmouth University pollster Patrick Murray. "But this certainly ranks among the worst. It's rare that with so much at stake for voters, the candidates avoided any real policy debate and decided to take this campaign so deep in the mud."

We will never know the true effect of the ugly ads—only 29 percent said ad content was an important factor in their decision—but the exit polling gave a clearer view of Daggett's impact. Were he not in the race, 33 percent of his supporters said they would have voted for Corzine, while 20 percent said they would have voted for Christie and 43 percent said they wouldn't have voted.[32] Recall that political observers noted Daggett spent a lot more time during the campaign attacking Christie.

"There seems to be little question that Daggett's presence in this campaign gave disgruntled voters another option. Most pre-election polls showing him in the double digits indicated that he could hurt Christie. It turns out with a much lower performance; the opposite may have been true," Murray said.

Christie's election marked the continuation of a few long-term trends in elections that favored Republicans in 2009. Not since 1985 had New Jersey voters elected a governor from the same party as the president and not since the 1960s had they gone with candidates from the same party in three straight gubernatorial races. In a sense, the Republicans were due—even without the economic troubles, flying pigs, or the amateurish moves by Corzine and his self-absorbed Kiddie Corps.

In South Jersey, generally considered that area below Route 195 which runs from Trenton to the Jersey Shore, Christie surged. He also won in Middlesex County, which hadn't voted for a Republican since 1985. There was a heavy voter turnout in Monmouth and Ocean counties that gave Christie 58,500 more votes than Republican Doug Forrester got in 2005. Former state Senate president John Russo, an Ocean County Democrat, said Corzine ignored the Shore and that his campaign staff didn't even call him when he and other Democratic veterans offered help. "I don't think it was anything the Republicans did. It was a woefully inept campaign," Russo said.[33]

On the other side, Corzine's victory margins from four years prior fell in heavily Democratic areas of the state—by 10,400 in Hudson County, 11,000 in Camden County, 13,000 in Essex County, and almost 16,000 in Union County. But while unhelpful, that's hardly why Corzine lost. Turnout increased in every New Jersey county, compared with four years earlier—but the eight counties with the biggest increases, all of them more than 11 percent, were GOP bastions. Republicans smelled blood in the water and, with the help of a voter turnout machine like one never seen before in New Jersey for their party, pounced.[34]

Cynics thought Christie cut a deal with South Jersey Democratic boss George Norcross to put the damper on the get-out-the-vote effort. Sweeney, an ally of Norcross and a South Jersey resident, disagreed, and the numbers seem to support him. Turnout in Camden was the same in 2009 as in 2005, 24 percent—dreadful, to be sure, but the same. In other cities, it fell from 37 percent to 33 percent in Trenton and from 38 percent to 30 percent in Newark.

"We put the effort in," Sweeney recalled. "The excitement wasn't there. You can feel it. You can feel the excitement in some elections. When I ran against Ray Zane in 2001, when McGreevey ran for governor, we were at the Cherry Hill Racetrack, Ted Kennedy was there. You could feel the excitement in the air. Corzine was there. It was an exciting day. In fact, I still have the pictures of Kennedy with my kids. That excitement was real. The energy was real. People were willing to knock buildings down for Jim McGreevey and, honestly, me. There was a big labor presence. There were thousands of people there," Sweeney said. "The dynamics changed over the years. We never paid people to do get-out-the-vote. We never did. We don't. I do not write checks for people to knock on doors Election Day. We always had volunteers, and it's always been in their best interests to support us, to be honest with you. Jon Corzine comes along, and we're paying volunteers. That's not volunteers. When you have the same people that now you're writing checks to do it.

"The energy, it was just not in the air, to be honest with you, it was just not there."

One of the surprising aspects was how quickly it came down. Coauthor Bob Ingle joined Eric Scott, 101.5 FM's news director, for on-air election coverage across the station's network, as had been the case in statewide elections for a decade. Since 7 p.m. they had joked about still being on the air the next day at 6 a.m. when morning man Jim Gearhart came to work. Before the broadcast Scott and Ingle had discussed that for Corzine to win he had to do well in heavily Democratic counties Essex, Camden, and Hudson. Christie had to do well in Republican counties Monmouth and Ocean. At 10:16 p.m. the Associated Press declared Christie the winner.

Asbury Park Press photographer Tom Costello, who was running a live video feed from the studio for the Web, noticed it first and pointed it out to Ingle, who motioned for him to show Scott, who had been giving returns from other races across the studio.

Scott paused, looked up at Ingle and said, "You know, Bob, I am a little reluctant to say this, this early."

"Let's tell the people what we know, Eric."

Scott quickly checked the heavily Democratic counties and then the heavily Republican counties. Corzine was under par for the counties he needed, Christie was over in the ones he had to have.

It was still hard to believe it was over this quickly, but Scott shook his head left to right, took a deep breath, and announced, "Chris Christie is our new governor."

Kevin McArdle, 101.5 FM's State House reporter, was called at the Corzine headquarters and asked to get certain interviews. Other reporters, including some who were broadcasting returns on TV, overheard McArdle's end of the conversation and found out it was all over but the concession and victory speeches. Later, on the air, when McArdle was asked what the mood was like at the Corzine campaign headquarters, he quipped Corzine's defeat "sent more people home than Babe Ruth. When I got here there were two escalators, one going up and one going down. Now there are two going down."

Christie had woken up on Election Day unsure how things would turn out. Democrats, particularly in the urban counties, were good at get-out-the-vote efforts, and Corzine had always funded a particularly thorough operation. In New Jersey, those GOTV efforts aren't necessarily driven by enthused volunteers but are fueled by "street money," Election Day payments ostensibly for helping get people to polls, monitoring polling places, and so forth. Such cash being thrown around on Election Day might raise worries about bribery in other states. In New Jersey it's considered progress. Until Governor Woodrow Wilson signed a law in 1911 outlawing the practice, up to one-third of the electorate routinely accepted money for their votes.[35]

"We did not have the mind-set going in that we were going to win, although I thought we had a chance," Christie said. "I assumed it was going to be very close, and I was always worried that at the end we'd get nipped out by a half a point or a point and that there'd be wild numbers out of Hudson and Essex and those areas. I remember kind of in the last couple of days of that last full week, we got some public polls that came back that were good. And our private polls were always good. But I didn't quite want to believe it. Our sense was that this was going to be a long night and might not go our way."

That morning he and Mary Pat voted, took their children to school, then climbed aboard the campaign bus for one last day on the hustings. From the road, Christie called his pollster, Adam Geller, for a prediction.

"What's going to happen?" Christie recalls asking.

"I hate when clients ask this question on Election Day," Geller said.

"Dude, the check cleared, what do you care?" Christie cracked. "If I win, I'm going to be governor. And if I lose, I'm not, and either way you're going to be fine. So what do you care? Tell me."

"All right," Geller said. "If we have the normal kind of gubernatorial year turnout, which I think we will, then you're going to win tonight by about 4 points. Anywhere between 4 and 5."

"Really?"

"Yup," Geller said, ending the call.

Mary Pat had been listening to her husband's end of the conversation and wanted the full update.

"What did he say?" she asked.

"He said we're going to win by between 4 and 5 points."

"He's crazy," Mary Pat said.

"Yeah, I know," he agreed.

Good vibes intensified by mid-afternoon and flooded in shortly after the polls closed.

Christie's final campaign stop was at the Golden Dawn Diner in Hamilton, a big, sprawling suburb that now dwarfed the city it neighbors, Trenton. That was the site of Christie's first retail campaign stop after launching his campaign back in February with a formal announcement speech in Newark, where he was born, and he liked the symmetry of ending there. Hamilton was also his campaign's number one targeted town. (He wound up winning it by pretty much the same margin he won the state.)

Stephen Taylor, a former federal prosecutor then in private practice, that day was in charge of his former boss's poll watchers keeping tabs on Trenton. (He would later head Christie's Division of Criminal Justice.) Christie was shaking hands and chatting up diner patrons in Hamilton when he noticed Taylor there—obviously not his assigned post.

"I need to talk to you alone for a second, boss," Taylor said.

The two walked back into the men's bathroom for some privacy.

"No one's voting in Trenton," Taylor said.

"What do you mean no one's voting in Trenton?"

"The numbers are way down," Taylor said. "In all the targeted precincts that were heavy Democratic precincts, there's no one voting. I'm telling you, it's eerie. I'm going to go back there, but I knew you were going to be here, and I just figured you needed to know."

Taylor left, and suddenly Christie's pollster didn't seem quite so unhinged. "That was the first time that day that I started thinking to myself, 'Hold on. If nobody's voting in Trenton, we might have a shot here.'

"I rode the bus home by myself. Mary Pat had gotten off the bus by that time. There was me and a trooper, and that was it on this huge bus. I was riding back up to Parsippany, and so I had about an hour or so by myself on the bus, and that's the first time I really started to think seriously about it, like I might win this thing," Christie said. "I think in the end, it kind of was good that way. Good that I wasn't sitting there all weekend and into Tuesday thinking I was going to win for sure. I think it was much better for me, at least, psychologically. I had plenty of time to get ready. I had a whole transition to get ready. And I think it kept me really hungry and edgy and not letting up."

Polls closed at eight o'clock that night, and the conclusion was surprisingly near. Palatucci's experience told him things were going Christie's way early on when he was invited into a room—off-limits to Christie—where the candidate's lawyers were preparing for a recount. There was a standard conference call after the polls closed with representatives of all three campaigns and the state Division of Elections in Trenton, which wanted to know what problems from the field needed to be addressed. A year before, when Obama won, it was chaos with requests for provisional ballots and extended polling hours. Not in 2009. "Crickets," Palatucci said. "I almost fell on the floor. I'm expecting 'There are lines in Camden, we need to keep the polls open. There are lines in Newark. We've run out of provisional ballots in Asbury Park.' It was silence. I swear to God nobody from the Corzine campaign said a thing. A statewide campaign in New Jersey with Jon Corzine's checkbook and the Corzine campaign doesn't have any request to keep any poll open? I went running upstairs as fast as I could, like 'Holy shit!'"

Christie realized he had won at 8:45 p.m., when he got a phone call from Jeff Michaels, who had been chief of staff under Republican governor Donald DiFrancesco, then became a lobbyist and eventually formed a lobbying firm with Phillip Norcross, brother of Camden County Democratic Party boss George Norcross. Michaels had just gotten a call from Woodbridge mayor John McCormac, a Democrat who served as state treasurer under Jim McGreevey, who wanted to tell Michaels that Christie won in Woodbridge.

This was huge news. Woodbridge had become a staunchly Democratic suburb, in staunchly Democratic Middlesex County, not to mention being one of the state's largest municipalities. After winning Woodbridge by 15 points in 2005, Corzine had now lost it by 8 points. Michaels knew the significance; he stopped scouring the political landscape for clues and headed to the hotel for the celebration.

Christie knew, as well. He was awaiting the returns in a hotel suite with family members and Republican bigwigs, such as Governor Tom Kean, Governor Christie Whitman, and Richard Bond, a former Republican National Committee chairman. He motioned to Mary Pat from across the room, asking her to come over, then brought her into the suite's bedroom and closed the door so they could have a private talk.

"We won Woodbridge," he revealed.

"Oh, good," said Mary Pat.

"No, no, no. You don't get it. I'm going to be the governor."

"What?"

"It's over. If I won Woodbridge, it's over. This is over. It's over now, so here's what you need to do," he said. "You need to start getting your head around the fact that in an hour or two, we're going to be downstairs and our lives are changing forever. So get ready."

Christie had only started to come to terms with the prospect of winning a few hours earlier. Mary Pat hadn't even begun. "I knew that neither one of us before that moment were really ready—I mean, really had internalized that we were going to win," he said. "We did not have that level of confidence."

He asked her to keep their news quiet, for now, from the others in the suite. "When we go back out there, don't let them know we know, because I don't want things to get crazy right away. Let's just wait to hear it."

The Christies hadn't spent a lot of time with the kids explaining how their lives were about to change. The only conversation took place just before the family was to take to the stage for the victory speech when the kids and Mary Pat huddled with Christie. The governor-elect told them, "When we walk out on that stage tonight together, our lives are going to change. But the most important people in our lives are here in this circle right now."[36]

A little past 9 P.M., more affirmations came in, and realization spread.

Palatucci, who had been peppering anyone he could think of with messages asking what they'd heard, got an email on his BlackBerry from George Norcross, the Democratic boss in South Jersey: "It's Governor-elect Christie for sure."

"It was the first time that evening I saw Palatucci smile," said Christie, who hadn't told his friend about Woodbridge.

Right after that, campaign strategist Mike DuHaime, campaign manager Bill Stepien, and communications director Maria Comella walked into the suite asking to talk to their candidate. Back into the bedroom for another chat.

"You won. It's over," they told him. "There is no chance he can come back from this. I don't care how many votes he gets out of Hudson and Essex, there's not going to be enough."

"And they then told Palatucci that, and Palatucci and David Samson got completely paranoid and said, 'They're going to try to steal it now,'" Christie said.

Samson went back downstairs to the legal war room; he and Palatucci emailed the lawyers the campaign had assigned to each county courthouse to get on a conference call in five minutes. He hopped from county to county asking: "What's going on? How many Democrats are there? Are people locked in a room?" Nothing was happening, at any courthouse.

"David came upstairs," Christie said. "He literally had in his briefcase that night the application for a recount. He had already written it. It was already done and ready to be served, and I said, 'What are you going to do with that now?' And he said to me, 'I guess change the caption.'"

Christie, Mary Pat, and his closest advisers knew he had won but not the others gathered elsewhere in the suite. That ended with a scream.

"I heard Christie Whitman let out a scream. She was in the suite; we were in the bedroom and I said, 'What the hell?'" His victory had just been projected on Fox News. "I had already kind of internalized that I had won, but what I realized was they didn't know. None of them out there— Kean, Whitman, other family members out there—knew. So we got up, and I walked out there, and Whitman came half-jogging over to me and she grabbed me by both shoulders and she was like, 'You did it! You did it!' and she gave me this big hug."

Todd Christie hugged and then picked up his father, who wrapped his legs around his son while they whooped in celebration. "I think he was prouder and happier than Chris was when Chris won," Todd said.

In his pocket, Bill Christie had with him a little memento from his father, James—an 18-karat gold stick pin with a little diamond in the center. He had admired the pin as a child though never knew how his father got it, presuming it was a gift—or perhaps had been his grandfather's. These days, Bill brings it to special events such as an address to the legislature. "I had Dad in there," Bill said, pointing to his pocket, "and I was thinking to myself Dad is saying, 'I know his name is Christopher Christie, but it can't be my grandson. We came up from nothing.'"

The governor-elect was approached by Kean, who thirty-two years earlier had opened his front door, and a world of possibilities, to an inspired fourteen-year-old named Chris Christie. He put his arm around the state's next chief executive, pulled him in close and whispered:

"Life's amazing, isn't it?"

CHAPTER EIGHT

Gearing Up for the Third Battle of Trenton

Jon Corzine was impressive in small groups and in one-on-one conversations, where he could talk intelligently about a wide range of subjects. In a formal speech, however, his soft, rambling sentences rarely commanded the room, like a high school student struggling to get through an oral book report. In public he had trouble articulating his visions, or connecting to his audience. Such was the case with his final State of the State address, delivered one week before he left office, in which he offered a glimpse of what could have been had the economy been better.

He had lost the election to Christie about two months before and he was close to cleaning out the desk and departing, but, incredibly, Corzine made it seem as if he himself only recently learned of his administration's accomplishments. He said he had gone to the state-run television operation, New Jersey Network, to tape an interview with veteran journalist Michael Aron, known for doing his homework and using his vast institutional knowledge in interviews. Aron arrived in New Jersey first to work at a magazine, after being fired from *Rolling Stone*. He recalled, "New Jersey appealed to me. And it's proved true. New Jersey never lets you down. If you're a journalist, the politics are for real, a microcosm of everything going on in America, and it's been a privilege and an honor to work for the state's television for 28 years."[1]

In his speech to lawmakers, Corzine said, "Michael Aron, our distinguished dean of the State House press corps, began the interview by reading a lengthy list of my administration's accomplishments." He added a few lines later, "When Michael finished reading his list, something really clicked . . . we had accomplished a great deal together."

Do you suppose Corzine asked himself why such a list was not produced internally for his use? State House journalists chuckled at Corzine's admission he had an epiphany under the klieg lights about his past four years in office. They weren't the only ones who noticed.

After Christie was elected, but before he took office, he held numerous press conferences to announce staff and policy. The day after Corzine's State of the State, the governor-elect called reporters to a small conference room on the second floor of the State House. The first question was from NJN's Aron. He began, "The new school funding formula is often presented as Governor Corzine's crowning achievement—"

"By you, I think, actually, Dean Aron," Christie shot back. Reporters broke up in laughter. The quick retort was quintessentially Christie before the cameras—where he can talk on any subject, usually without notes because he's comfortable with himself in a way Corzine never was when meeting the press. There was a tone to it that communicated this wasn't the last Aron, the TV operation's news director, would hear from Christie.[2] A little over two months later, Christie announced his intention to eliminate all state funding for New Jersey's public broadcaster.

Once a year since the 1890s the New Jersey Legislative Correspondents' Club, made up of the Trenton-based reporters who cover state government, puts on a show with song parodies and jokes making fun of politicians and government hanky panky—in New Jersey, there never was a shortage of material. Governors, and former governors, then give it back in roastlike speeches. In his first appearance at the event as governor, Christie zeroed in on the state-owned TV network:

"NJN used to be known as New Jersey Network. Guess what guys: Now it means No Jersey Network. I know, I know, you all feel bad for them. But those are not the folks you should feel bad for. I ask you tonight to think about all those insomniacs across the state of New Jersey who have counted on listening to Michael Aron to lull them to sleep each and every night. These are the people you should feel sorry for."

Christie wasn't done batting around NJN that night. He returned to the network as the final target in a rapid-fire, thirty-eight-minute stand-up routine that would have made comedian Don Rickles proud, ending with a long riff about watching a DVD of NJN's election night coverage—provided to him by Aron as a sign of friendship, he deadpanned, because the Parsippany Hilton, where Christie was election night, didn't have NJN. (He wound up getting election returns that night through media consultant Russ Schriefer's Apple computer, by pointing the mouse over the counties on a New Jersey map on the *New York Times* Web site.)

Christie said Aron reported the election returns in "funereal tones," waiting for Corzine to rally to victory. Finally, Christie said, long after the Associated Press had called the race, Aron joined in: "With 95 percent of the vote in, NJN is finally ready to concede, I mean call this race for Chris Christie." He said Aron turned to the assembled political analysts for reaction by starting, "Let me go to a fellow Democrat—a Democrat . . ."

"When you're getting that kind of coverage day in and day out, how could you ever let it go?" Christie concluded. "So this whole budget thing, Michael, a little head fake. A little Christie shoulder fake for you. I mean, why the hell would I want to give that up? So all of you who are worried about NJN, don't worry. They'll be fine—over my dead body."

When he was finished there was guarded laughter from the audience and at the NJN table some were near tears. Later that evening they were in tears literally.

Two months before the hard-elbowed jokes at NJN's expense, Christie had proposed ending state funding for the state's TV and radio operation. Philosophically, he didn't think the state should be in the news business and with a $10 billion deficit, the state had to trim anywhere it could. About 130 NJN workers were on the state payroll with hefty state benefits. That included many holidays off—not just ones not enjoyed in the private sector, but also some not enjoyed by employees of other state governments. Until recently—abolished under Corzine, actually—state workers got both Presidents Day and Lincoln's Birthday. And when one of the state holidays rolled around there was no NJN News broadcast. Christie once remarked there was news on Thanksgiving but no news presented by NJN that day. Aron countered there had been news on holidays until the state funding was cut so much they couldn't afford the holiday pay. Christie wasn't the first to object. Governor Christie Whitman, also a Republican, compared NJN to Pravda, the Soviet Union–controlled propaganda machine. Even Democrats, such as Corzine, had floated the idea of privatizing NJN.

At least part of the image had to do with developments after Governor Jim Florio, a Democrat, lost his reelection bid to Whitman in 1993. Aron said he was approached by George Norcross, Democratic Party boss of South Jersey, and John Lynch, then a state senator, now a felon (due to prosecution by Christie's U.S. Attorney's Office), who was boss of the middle part of the state. They asked Aron if he would be executive director of the Democratic State Committee. Aron was taken off the air while he made up his mind. He decided he would rather be a newsman. "It didn't feel right to give up journalism. But it took a year or two for Republicans to stop talking about it. By 1996, I thought I had outlived that tag, that mantle, that aroma."[3]

Fast-forward to 2011, when Christie finally pulled the plug on NJN. After considering several proposals, his administration settled on a plan to sell NJN's nine small radio stations for about $4.3 million (less than half of it in cash, and for less than the stations' appraised value) but hold on to the TV licenses and cut a deal with WNET, a New York–based public broadcaster considered the nation's flagship PBS station, to run the New Jersey operation, which was renamed NJTV. As part of that plan, WNET contracted with Caucus Educational Corp., a not-for-profit production company run by Steve Adubato Jr., who hosted the public affairs programs his company produced with corporate donations, most of which included his name: *Caucus New Jersey with Steve Adubato*, *One on One with Steve Adubato*. His salary was $341,000 in 2009. He also is a columnist, corporate communications consultant, and author of books on career improvement, a former state legislator and the son of a Newark-based Democratic political boss, Steve "Big Steve" Adubato Sr., whose proudest accomplishment is an award-winning charter school, the Robert Treat Academy.[4] The day after he won election, the school was the first stop on raspy-voiced, sleep-deprived Christie's victory tour, with Adubato hugging Christie around the shoulders and neck from the seat behind him as the Assembly began.[5]

NJN fans, and Christie critics, said the privatization was about currying favor with conservatives across the nation who hate public broadcasting they see as too progressive in tone, that the administration could have done better with other proposals, and that the state's holding the license over the heads of WNET amounted to political control still—not to mention that hiring the former Assembly member and son of a political boss to do production was tantamount to injecting more politics into the TV operation. Before the Assembly Budget Committee looked at the proposal, Dudley Burdge of the Communications Workers of America, which represented NJN employees, said, "Last September Steve Adubato Jr. confidentially told several of our NJN members that he and WNET would be taking over NJN. Through a process with marked lack of transparency, that's exactly what happened."

Some wondered if Christie was getting even for what he called the lowest point of the 2009 campaign. The story about his loan to Michele Brown was first reported by NJN's Zachary Fink.

Others saw an even darker motive, a Republican governor currying favor with a sympathetic Democratic Party boss whose help Christie would need to get his program through by giving his son a larger stage. Adubato Jr. said in a State House news conference he had never discussed the prospect of taking over NJN with his father, which had the Trenton-based press snickering all the way back to their second-floor offices. Adubato Sr. said, "I have not spoken to any lawmakers, the governor or even my son about WNET's proposal to take over the operations of NJN."[6]

Christie also said he had no discussions about it with Adubato Sr. He said—while being interviewed on Adubato Jr.'s televised call-in show—it was just another "typical conspiracy theory."

Jeff Tittel, New Jersey director of the Sierra Club and an evergreen presence on Press Row in Trenton, found an environmental reason to oppose pulling the plug. He said the wealthy businessman David Koch, whose political goals include fighting climate change regulations, is on the

WNET board and had recently funded, through his foundation, a *NOVA* show about new energy sources that featured the types of industries in which Koch Industries operates. Tittel said NJN will lose its independence and that protesters will lose their voice. "No matter how you look at it, the governor's pulling the plug on NJN, it will hurt governmental oversight in New Jersey. It will hurt the ability of activist groups and citizen groups to have an impact on their government and to effect change in the State of New Jersey. I think that's part of why this is happening," he said.

A last-minute attempt to kill the deal overwhelmingly passed the Assembly, even though state treasurer Andrew Sidamon-Eristoff claimed that the station would go dark if the deal died. It failed by one vote in the Senate. The resolution's primary sponsor, Senator Loretta Weinberg, said the state would be on the hook for millions of dollars annually to support the new operation, spending at least $4.7 million a year. "So while we hand the network off to a New York operator, we are not saving that much money."[7]

Democratic boss Adubato Sr.'s protégé was Essex County executive Joseph DiVincenzo Jr., a power broker in his own right, friend of Christie's, and in a position to control matters all over the state from his Newark office because one of his county employees was Sheila Oliver, the speaker of the state Assembly. She got the leadership post, becoming the first black woman to achieve that position in New Jersey, in a deal worked out among party bosses—including a meeting at the 2008 U.S. Open tennis tournament between DiVincenzo and Norcross[8]—that sent Speaker Joe Roberts of South Jersey into retirement so that Steve Sweeney could become Senate president. Roberts and Sweeney, an ironworkers union official and former Gloucester County officeholder, were both part of the Norcross machine in South Jersey—not even in the Soprano State could you have the leaders of the Assembly and Senate from the same area. Roberts, whose political career was owed to Norcross, denied that's why he left, but no one took him seriously. Sweeney booted Dick Codey from the Senate president's job, one Codey held for ten years.

NJN ended its forty-year run on June 30, 2011. Its farewell newscast featured emotional good-byes and footage from years of broadcasts—

including radio hosts Casey Bartholomew and Ray Rossi's flying pigs rally—and aired at the same time Christie was announcing more than $900 million in line-item vetoes that slashed the Democrats' spending plan. It was one of the bigger news events of the year. Someone from WNET in New York called to find out if NJN was covering it. A TV staffer told them no, everyone had lost their jobs.

The NJN episode is an example of how Christie uses humor as a hammer when focused on a situation that irks him. He never forgets, either. NJTV eventually hired Aron as its vice president of news and public affairs, and he appeared on the station's midterm election coverage in 2011. The next day, before heading to New Hampshire to campaign for Mitt Romney, Christie held a news conference with Aron in attendance and said he'd watched the election broadcast.

"Looked good last night, Michael, by the way," the governor said when Aron asked a question. "The makeup was excellent. Someone said 'Look at Michael, he looks younger.' I said, 'Hey, he's been on vacation a lot.'"

Later, when Aron's NJTV colleague Laura Jones asked in jest if she didn't look good on the election broadcast, the governor responded, "Listen, Laura, no one's surprised when you look good. But you know, Aron really looked good last night. I'm not kidding you, Michael. We had a bunch of people at Drumthwacket last night, and independently, three or four people said, 'You know, Michael really looks good tonight.'"

Nobody ever said Christie was a softie. When he has you in his sights, you'd better be prepared for the worst.

One of his first targets in the legislature after winning the election was Assemblyman John McKeon. The Democrat from Essex County proposed a law after Christie's election, but while Corzine was still in charge, changing how U.S. Senate vacancies are filled to require that someone in the same party as the departing lawmaker is selected. Both of New Jersey's senators were Democrats, including Frank Lautenberg, at the time closing in on his eighty-sixth birthday. McKeon framed it as a favor to Christie, taking the political pressure off him that would follow if one of those Senate seats opened up, plus a way to avoid a $10 million special election. Christie lit into the idea, and its sponsor. "This is garbage. It's garbage. It's political lying, is what it is. You really think that's John McKeon's intent on this?" he said. "This is the kind of garbage I got sent here to fix. There's no niceties to be put around this. This is a political power play by the party who is losing power, and it's wrong."[9]

Christie made clear throughout his transition that he intended to deploy every power afforded to the governor's office—and there are said to be more of them in New Jersey than any other state.

"I am going to use every tool at my disposal to force change," Christie told municipal officials at an Atlantic City convention. "I am not here to wait one or two or four or eight years for change to come. Change is going to come, and it's going to come now."[10]

"I am told that the governorship of New Jersey is among the most powerful in the nation, so we will see, I think, any number of times over the next four years tests of the limits of that power," he said.[11]

Christie had been an aggressive U.S. attorney, surrounded by nononsense people he trusted. It was a winning formula he wanted to replicate. During a State House news conference as a candidate, he said Trenton wouldn't be the same after he brought his friends down from the U.S. attorney's office and let them loose on cleaning up the state's bureaucracy. And right off the bat, Christie's senior staff looked a lot like his team in the federal post. "I have a great association with the people in that office, and they helped me to develop the record that laid the foundation for the people of the State of New Jersey to entrust me with the governorship," Christie said.[12]

Among the former staff to join Christie in Trenton:

Jeff Chiesa became the governor's chief counsel. It was the third time Christie hired Chiesa. First he was brought into the law firm Dughi & Hewit, then the U.S. attorney's office, where as head of the public protection unit he oversaw prosecution of politicians. When he joined the governor's staff he had worked with Christie for about sixteen years. After two years as the governor's chief counsel, he became Christie's attorney general. He was replaced by Charles McKenna, another former federal prosecutor whose eighteen years at the U.S. attorney's office included the investigation into the kidnapping and murder of *Wall Street Journal* bureau chief Daniel Pearl. McKenna was executive assistant U.S. attorney during Christie's seven years there, with executive oversight for all investigations.

He started in the Christie administration in Trenton as his director of homeland security and preparedness.

Kevin O'Dowd was a federal prosecutor, too, a seven-year stint that included time as chief of the Securities and Healthcare fraud unit; he was hired as Chiesa's deputy chief counsel and served as liaison to the legislature. He earlier worked in the Trenton administrations of Governors Christie Whitman and Donald DiFrancesco. When Chiesa left to head the Department of Law and Public Safety, O'Dowd was expected to become chief counsel—but instead became chief of staff beginning on January 31, 2012. His wife, Mary, was named Christie's health and senior services commissioner in 2011. When O'Dowd moved up, he was replaced as deputy chief counsel by another one of Christie's former prosecutors—Paul Matey, who'd first come to Trenton as Christie's senior counsel and chief ethics officer.

Michele Brown, reluctant star of various story arcs in the 2009 campaign, who resigned from the U.S. attorney's office after the NJN report on the loan Christie gave her and her husband, after questions about the loan from Christie and her role handling requests for public records.

Deborah Gramiccioni, another former prosecutor, was named head of Christie's authorities unit, the portion of a governor's counsel's office that keeps an eye on what the independent and historically wasteful entities are doing. She was already working for the state during the Corzine administration, at the attorney general's office, and was one of the few high-ranking officials kept on. The state's authorities, dozens and dozens of bureaucratic boondoggles and burying grounds for deadwood and unemployed friends and relatives, have been a focus of the governor's wrath. Gramiccioni flagged the spending, and Christie flogged. He started vetoing actions taken by the boards in his first weeks in office; the savings weren't always large, but Christie's message was unmistakable. Gramiccioni met her husband Christopher when they both worked for Christie at the U.S. attorney's office; he went on to be second in command in the Monmouth County prosecutor's office, a post that opened because Christie bounced the former county prosecutor rather than reappoint him. During the staff reshuffling at the start of 2012, she became Christie's deputy chief of staff for policy.

By the end of his second year in office, Christie had appointed more than two dozen former federal prosecutors, around twenty of whom worked for him, to jobs in his administration or as state Superior Court judges, including four cabinet posts. He also brought a number of former staffers to Trenton with him, such as press secretary Michael Drewniak, a former *Star-Ledger* State House reporter.

The other major recruiting pool has been New York, both the city and the state:

State Treasurer Andrew Sidamon-Eristoff is a descendant of a noble family in Georgia who fled after the Soviets invaded; his great-grandfather was a partner of Andrew Carnegie. Sidamon-Eristoff used to represent Manhattan's East Side on New York's City Council, then was New York state's tax and finance commissioner.

James Simpson heads the state Transportation Department; he's a former New York Metropolitan Transportation Authority commissioner who later headed the Federal Transit Administration—and, in that latter job, praised Corzine's ill-fated toll road plan.

Christie's corrections commissioner, Gary Lanigan, and Motor Vehicle Commission chairman Raymond Martinez also used to work in New York.

Two other former Christie subordinates preceded him to Trenton, Matt Boxer and Stuart Rabner. When word circulated that Corzine was recruiting at least one more trusted Christie employee for his administration, an irritated Christie got on the phone to the governor.

"I called him. I remember we were on a ski vacation in Vermont. He had already taken Rabner and Boxer, and I understood on good authority that he was sniffing around [Marc] Larkins," said Christie. "I called him and he called me back. And I said to him, 'Listen, Governor, you, when you were senator, emphasized to me how disturbed you were about the lack of diversity in the U.S. attorney's office. And so I worked really hard to bring in some good young African Americans and Asians and Hispanics. And now you're trying to take all of them to be in state government. I've given you Boxer, and I've given you Rabner. And you're not taking Larkins, so you really need to knock it off.' And he said to me, 'Well, what if they want to come?' And I said, 'No, they don't want to come. You're trying to coerce them into coming, and I want you to stop.' And he paused, and he said, 'Okay.' And that was that."

Larkins, who is black, stayed in Newark with Christie but came to Trenton with him to run the state's school construction program, which under previous governors had raced through billions with little to show for it.

Boxer was hired by Corzine to keep an eye on the state's numerous independent authorities that had morphed into monuments of patronage and corruption, then moved to comptroller when that office was created. His six-year term as comptroller ends in 2014, just days before Christie's four-year term ends.

Rabner is a Harvard-trained lawyer whose Holocaust survivor parents came to the United States broke in 1950. A straight-arrow known for his integrity and sincere thoughtfulness, Rabner went from Christie's office in Newark to Corzine's chief counsel, his attorney general, and then chief justice of the state Supreme Court at a pace that would make NASCAR proud. How did Rabner go so far so quickly? You might say he was doing the right thing at the right time for the right reason.

"My wife and I have a tradition of starting the day with our children at a soup kitchen," the chief justice said. "We've always thought it was an important way to show the kids up close how fortunate they are and instill in them the importance of helping others.

"That Thanksgiving Day, while we were at the soup kitchen, then Senator Corzine arrived to help serve food, without any press or visible staff. My kids and wife were assisting with the tables, and I was already on the serving line. I ended up standing beside the senator for about twenty minutes, and we chatted while serving.

"Fast-forward four years to the transition period for Governor-elect Corzine. One Friday afternoon, my boss at the time, U.S. Attorney Chris Christie, called me to his office and said he had just been on the phone with Corzine. [Christie] told me that he had mentioned my name to Corzine as someone to consider for the incoming administration. In response, Christie told me that Corzine said he remembered meeting me at a soup kitchen years before.

"I've since shared this story with many students when they ask, 'How do you become AG or Chief Justice?' I tell them that, as corny as it may sound, they should work hard and do what they believe is important in life—and not simply check off items on a list."

Rabner's quiet manner belies the strength of his character. He's living proof nice guys can finish first. He grew up in a middle-class household. His father, who survived a Soviet slave labor camp in World War II, worked in a garment factory in New York, later ran a newspaper and a candy shop. In the summer, Rabner worked long hours in the candy shop and as a federal prosecutor he often worked seventy hours a week when preparing a case.

One of those cases was the corruption prosecution of Nicholas Bissell Jr., a Somerset County prosecutor who had people shaking in their boots. But not a thin, bespectacled prosecutor named Rabner. "There was no yelling. No theatrics. It was just one fact after another. You watched Bissell's demeanor just droop, his expression change from confident to crestfallen," said attorney Henry Klingeman.[13] Bissell was convicted but fled justice and committed suicide in Nevada as U.S. marshals moved in to arrest him. "He [Rabner] was deeply affected by [the suicide]. He is a tremendous humanist and had tremendous judgments on decisions affecting people's lives," said Perry Carbone, who worked on the Bissell case with Rabner.[14]

In high school Rabner performed in musicals, playing Curly in *Oklahoma!* and still sings in his Conservative synagogue. The loss of many family members in the World War II death camps gave him a deep appreciation for the opportunity the United States represents. "This country has been so incredibly good to my family." By choosing public service, he said, he is in part repaying a debt of gratitude.[15]

A chief of staff needs to know the secrets of how government works, difficult for anyone who hasn't been a part of it, and for that post Christie didn't choose a former prosecutor, instead tagging Rich Bagger, who was elected five times to the state Assembly starting in 1991 and to one term in the state Senate in 2001. He started to work at Pfizer, the drug giant, in 1993 and resigned from the legislature in 2003, one year into a four-year term, to devote full time to the Pfizer job, where he had risen to vice president. Owing to his background, he was the most political of Christie's three top aides. He liked running the day-to-day operations and was a policy wonk. Bagger returned to the biopharmaceutical industry after two years of working in Trenton, to become a senior vice president for Celgene Corp. Christie, not wanting vacancies that would be difficult to fill in an election year, nor the appearance that people were fleeing, had asked his senior staff and cabinet at the end of 2011 to commit to remaining for another two years or to leave at that time.

Around the State House, the powerful threesome—Bagger, Chiesa, and O'Dowd—had been known as the "triumvirate."

"We are going to have a very strong chief of staff and a very strong chief counsel," Christie said in making the staff announcement. "I have delegated a great deal of authority as United States attorney to the people in my front office then, and it served me extraordinarily well. I will delegate a great deal of authority to these folks as well."[16]

Paul Fishman, who succeeded Christie as U.S. attorney in 2010, didn't like having his staff drained off by Christie so he took a page out of Christie's own playbook with a call to the governor's office. He got very different results. "Paul Fishman said to me, 'I understand you had a conversation with Jon Corzine about that, and I'd like you to stop.' And I said, 'Well, you're not me, and I'm not Jon Corzine.' And Paul understood exactly what I meant by both statements."

Christie's staff is 180 degrees from the dysfunctional operation under Corzine.

"Everybody pulls together to a degree that I haven't seen fairly often in my prior experiences. It's a group of people who enjoy each other's company. It's fairly helpful in a high-intensity job," Bagger said.[17]

Christie, fiercely loyal to friends and colleagues, demanded the same of the people around him. "I told them I always will have their back. I won't throw them under the bus unless they lie to me. Only one lied to me, and he is gone," Christie said. That was a reference to Christie's first education commissioner, Bret Schundler. Senate president Steve Sweeney admits he laughed when Christie rolled into Trenton with all those prosecutors in tow. It reminded him of Corzine's reliance on former Goldman Sachs colleagues. What, he asked, do they know about governing? After seeing them in action, Sweeney changed his mind.

"I said to people, 'He's making the same mistake Corzine did. He's bringing in all these deputy attorneys general. They don't understand government.' I said it to him, too, I said, 'I think you're making a major mistake.' But I was wrong. The people that Chris has brought in are task-oriented people. They put cases together. They try things. They're task-oriented. The people that Chris has, if you say, 'Get something done,' they're going to work day and night to try to accomplish the task. The people Jon brought in were loyal to Jon. The people that Chris brought in are obviously loyal to Chris, but different skill sets. I think that Chris brought in a lot of very solid people around him that are extremely loyal, and I think it's made a big difference, to be honest with you."

They worked like a well-oiled machine. An example is the precedent-setting attempt to reform state employee health benefits and pensions. While Christie conducted town hall meetings, did interviews, and held news conferences to criticize the leadership of the state's employee unions, Bagger crafted the reform policy, Chiesa drafted the legislation, and O'Dowd, who was the governor's liaison to the legislature, worked the back rooms to win support. Democrats such as Speaker Sheila Oliver rave about their relationships with O'Dowd.

"It is an extremely tight ship. The tightest ship I can remember. No question about that," said state Senator Dick Codey, whose ship sailed after Jim McGreevey's sank.[18]

Insiders said Christie takes input from his trusted aides, encourages open debate, but in the end makes decisions himself. What he won't allow is for that debate to take place in public or the press, just as Christie's parents wouldn't permit Chris and Todd to fight in front of neighbors.

"I am not a micromanager. I have no interest in being one. I'm not a hand-wringer, and I don't have a difficult time making decisions. So I don't think I'm going to select people who suffer from any of those maladies, either," Christie said.[19]

"He encourages the whole team where we can have the open discussion and debate to bring out all the different aspects of an issue leading up to making a decision. He expects people to say what they feel, to disagree with each other. It's not uncommon for him to go around the table and ask everyone's view," Bagger said. [20]

That can be intimidating, joked Lieutenant Governor Kim Guadagno, herself a former prosecutor and sheriff. "You can image how fun that seat is with all those federal prosecutors sitting at [the table]."[21]

Before he took office, Christie said his choices for top leadership positions wouldn't be wallflowers. He said they would be encouraged to tell him—in private—when they think he is wrong and try to convince him why.

"I've said—and I don't remember who said it years ago, but I absolutely subscribe to this—that a small band of people who are intent upon leading can really change the course of history. And the reason why I'm convinced of that is we know it's the only thing that ever has."[22]

Sandy and Bill Christie
at their wedding. *(Family
photographs courtesy of Joe
Grasso and Chris Christie)*

(Left to right): Sandy
Christie, Nani (Anne)
Grasso, Joe Grasso,
Grandma Minnie
(Domenica) Scavone,
and Bill Christie.

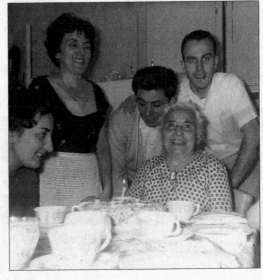

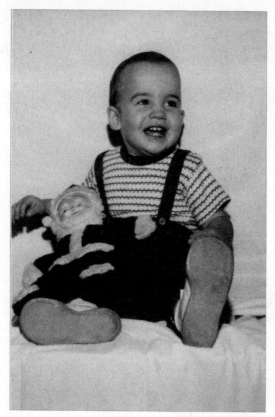

Young Chris Christie.

(Back Row, left to right): Sandy, Bill; *(front row, left to right):* Dawn, Todd, and Chris at the Jersey Shore.

(Left to right): Chris Christie, U.S. Senator Bill Bradley, and Bob Guarasci at the William Randolph Hearst Foundation's United States Senate Youth Program. *(Hearst Institute)*

Chris Christie in high school baseball uniform.

As I look back on our three years together, I see how we've grown together as a class. We have faced many obstacles on the road to success in our high school years, but none have been large enough, if we pulled together, to stop us from being successful. Obviously, our class as a whole has achieved many things academically, athletically and socially. We've run successful class functions, we've been one of the top classes academically, and our sports teams have played everywhere from our own gym to the Meadowlands.

More importantly though, is a spirit that prevails through each member of the Class of 1980. We have faced many challenges- save Open Lunch, save Graduation, adjust to a new principal, and rebound after the setbacks that any class experiences. I hope that this spirit will always live on within each of you and that you may call on all the great memories whenever you wish. As a group of nearly 600, we will never be all together in the same room again; but as long as this spirit lives within us, we shall never really part.

Good luck and God bless,

Chris Christie

Chris Christie
President, Class of 1980

Chris Christie's message to his 1980 senior class of which he was president.

Joe Grasso, Sandy Christie, and Nani (Anne) at Nani's ninetieth birthday party.

Todd Christie, Dawn Clarke, and Chris Christie at Dawn's wedding.

(Left to right): Jon Corzine, Chris Daggett, and Chris Christie at governor's race debate. *(Bob Ingle)*

Christie and his wife, Mary Pat, at the September 11 ten-year anniversary, September 11, 2011. *(Corbis Images)*

Chris and Mary Pat Christie, Hurricane Irene aftermath, August 29, 2011. *(Corbis Images)*

(Left to right): Chris Christie with John Sununu, former New Hampshire governor and former chief of state to President George H. W. Bush, in New Hampshire for Gov. Mitt Romney's presidential primary campaign. *(Bob Ingle)*

At a Mitt Romney rally in Iowa, December 30, 2011. *(Corbis Images)*

New Jersey Governor Chris Christie announces he will not run for president, October 4, 2011. *(Corbis Images)*

CHAPTER NINE

Putting the Bully in the Bully Pulpit

Some politicians love running for office but don't find the day-to-day running of government exciting enough. New Jersey's Jim McGreevey and Alabama's George Wallace are examples. Chris Christie relishes governing more than being on the campaign trail. In his administration even the dull and frustrating things that bore the rest of us held his attention.

Take, for instance, the state's bountiful supply of independent authorities—each with a well-intended purpose, but also serving as a mostly unchecked pit for patronage and government largesse. Governors have long had a team in their chief counsel's office keeping tabs on the shadow government. Christie's squad shone a light on their spending—with torches, not flashlights, to help the new governor send a message to the bureaucracy that the party was over.

In his first month in office, Christie vetoed the minutes of four authorities, thus rendering moot whatever they were trying to do. He also forced the head of the Passaic Valley Sewerage Commission to resign over his $313,000 annual salary. The governor is paid $175,000. Later, almost a hundred people were fired, stepped down, or arrested from the commission. Minutes for authorities, boards, and commissions had rarely been vetoed by governors, but he did so more than two dozen times in his first two years—including a $420,000 tax credit to the producers of MTV's

Jersey Shore, a show he often mocked in interviews for using a bunch of New Yorkers to perpetuate stereotypes about the Shore.

The Delaware River Port Authority is another patronage dump, a bi-state operation of Pennsylvania and New Jersey that has four toll bridges across the Delaware River and a commuter rail line. Passaic Valley is in the north, the DRPA operates in the south, land of Democratic Party boss George Norcross. Christie went to Camden to talk about things with the DRPA board, and longtime patronage protesters thought change finally is coming. Running the DRPA was a former Republican senator, John Matheussen. How he got the post is a story right out of the Soprano State.

State senators are important to party bosses in New Jersey because they can block any nominees they want to from their district because of "senatorial courtesy," an unwritten political tool so old nobody knows where it came from. Norcross worked with Governor McGreevey to get Matheussen a job as state transportation commissioner. Matheussen rejected it. Then his name was briefly floated for the state Supreme Court. He finally landed the DRPA post where he started at $195,000 a year, way more than his $49,000 salary as a state senator. Here's where it gets interesting. Matheussen became the first DRPA employee to be allowed to remain in the New Jersey pension system, which is more lucrative than Pennsylvania's, where DRPA employees had been placed since the 1930s. The difference? As a part-time state senator, he would have qualified for a $12,000 annual pension. With the DRPA salary after three years his pension would be $60,000 and increasing as his salary rose. Matheussen was replaced in the state Senate by Republican assemblyman George Geist and a move to then get Geist appointed to the Superior Court bench that fell apart. Then, Norcross and his minions raised $4.4 million to win the $49,000 a year seat for Democrat Fred Madden by sixty-three votes.

So Christie showed up at the DRPA and everyone expected fireworks. They were disappointed. He came out and said Matheussen would be his man in charge of reform. That led some to believe Christie had struck a deal with political boss Norcross and, at least in the eyes of Norcross foes, the governor's armor wasn't so shiny anymore.

Christie's relationship with the legislature was equally combative. It had started nicely enough at his inaugural address, which included a memorable and unscripted moment when he called the Democratic leaders of the legislature, Steve Sweeney in the Senate and Sheila Oliver in the Assembly, to join hands with him in a sign of friendship. The lawmakers, like Christie that day, had been—at least publicly—expressing an interest in cooperating with the governor, even though they were from different parties. "The Senate is not going at this to embarrass or to try to wedge-issue this governor-elect," Sweeney said.[1] "I do not believe in the stark, combative, adversarial partisanship that has gripped so much of our public debate in recent years, especially in our State House. I don't believe that attitude solves problems," Oliver said.[2]

That cooperation began fraying quickly, then was shredded when Christie called a special session three weeks into his term to lay out to lawmakers his plan for the state's budget deficit—not the annual structural one that gets solved each year, but an actual $2.2 billion midyear shortfall that Christie says jeopardized the state's ability to make payroll in March. Corzine had taken some steps to gird for the shortfall, some of them at Christie's behest. But Christie that day froze spending, cut the subsidy to New Jersey Transit, erased the pension contribution, and withheld $475 million in state aid to schools—all, he said, without the input or need for approval by the legislature. It turned out some legislative assistance was needed, but the well was poisoned. "So much for a handshake," Sweeney said.[3] "This is not a monarchy. That's not how you govern, with edicts. This was martial law. He's made things much more adversarial now," said Senator Barbara Buono, the majority leader.[4] Christie said sleight of hand is for magic acts; he planned to govern like a one-termer—unafraid to flex the muscles of his office, use the line-item veto to revise budgets downward, or issue conditional vetoes to rewrite bills and send them back to the legislature. Other governors threatened it, Christie actually did it.

His first budget faced a structural deficit of $11 billion, and its cuts included rolling back the earned income tax credit from 25 percent of the federal benefit to 20 percent for its 485,000 recipients. That saved the state $45 million but scaled back tax credits that benefit low-wage workers, even providing refunds to some who don't owe taxes. The EITC was created by

President Ronald Reagan. In 2012 Christie proposed reversing that cut as part of a plan, which didn't pass, to cut income taxes by 10 percent for all. "I didn't claim to fix that problem in one year, and we're not going to fix it in one year. It is a structural problem that needs to be attacked over a number of years," Christie said. "What I've always said is that I want us to be in sustainable, good fiscal shape by the end of my first term. We're on a path to get there."[5]

When McGreevey was governor and desperate for money, he and the Democrats in the legislature increased taxes on the wealthy—a hike known by its shorthand name as a millionaire's tax. It applied to households (not necessarily individuals, but households) earning $500,000 or more, so really it was a half-millionaire's tax. Corzine, wanting to limit deep spending cuts in an election year despite the state's recession-battered budget, and the legislature passed their own millionaire's tax in 2009—three new temporary tax rates that began at $400,000 of household income. They engineered it to die on December 31, 2009. It did. Lawmakers had a few sessions left to send Corzine a renewal. They didn't.

It's not that they weren't busy. Between that date and the time Christie took office January 19, 2010, the legislature passed 165 bills. Some of the crucial issues occupying their attention were permitting real estate brokers to provide rebates to purchasers, revising the Landscape Irrigation Contractor Certification Act of 1991, and establishing an Apparel Procurement Board to set standards for state purchases of clothing. Six of the laws enacted on Corzine's way out the door weren't even introduced in the legislature until the first week of 2010, then got approved within days. The temporary millionaire's tax, important as Democrats and special interests would later claim it was, wasn't revived by any of the 165 bills.

This was a dirty trick, the kind of political land mine scheming politicians leave for their opponents. Christie ran on a no-tax-hike pledge and the idea was to introduce the new millionaire's tax after he took office and force him to sign it, breaking his word, which of course Democrats would use against him.

It didn't work, he didn't sign it. His critics, especially the New Jersey Education Association, the teachers union, literally spent millions on advertising to discredit him, claiming he'd cut taxes for his millionaire friends. It was a lie. The tax rate had not changed since Christie took office.

Spending cuts continued in Christie's second year, including cuts proposed for Medicaid through a restructuring designed to save the state $300 million a year, which in an early version of the plan would have restricted access to the program for people earning only 25 percent of the federal poverty line—a threshold that at the full 100 percent level is inadequate in high-cost New Jersey, as it doesn't account for state-to-state variances in the cost of living. At the same time, Christie and the legislature cut business taxes to the tune of $185 million the first year, growing to more than $600 million in cuts annually by the fifth year, to encourage expansion and job creation. Democratic efforts to raise taxes on millionaires— actual ones, not half-millionaires—also continued in Christie's second and third years, ending with the same veto. "It's a victory for the wealthy, the first two years for him, because he has protected that class at the expense of everyone else," Sweeney said.

A story by coauthor Michael Symons in the *Asbury Park Press* about the challenges that the state's budget policies were creating and conversations among antipoverty groups about how to change the discussion drew the interest of Christie's musical idol, Bruce Springsteen. The rocker, also known as America's blue-collar poet, wrote a letter to the editor of what he called his "hometown newspaper" in which he came the closest he'd ventured to date in criticizing Christie, about whom he generally declined to answer questions, outside of telling *Vanity Fair* "let's just say that he and I are coming from different places."

"The article," Springsteen said in his letter to the editor, "is one of the few that highlights the contradictions between a policy of large tax cuts, on the one hand, and cuts in services to those in the most dire conditions, on the other. . . . These are voices that in our current climate are having a hard time being heard, not just in New Jersey, but nationally. Finally, your article shows that the cuts are eating away at the lower edges of the middle class, not just those already classified as in poverty, and are likely to continue to get worse over the next few years."

Christie knows the words to Springsteen's music, but chose not to take the ones in the letter to heart, asking interviewers such as ABC News' Diane Sawyer to consider the source. "Are you surprised to hear that from Bruce? I mean, you know, Bruce is liberal. Doesn't mean I like him any less. But you know, Bruce believes that we should be raising taxes all the time on everyone to do all the things that he'd like to see government do. That's fine, it's his point of view and he's absolutely welcome to it, and I have great respect for it, because he speaks out. And unlike other people who don't, he speaks out. That's great for him."[6] Springsteen didn't actually say anything about raising taxes anytime for anyone, but the framing helped Christie by making the matter political, not personal.

Christie is known for his almost perfect attendance at Springsteen concerts, having once even flown to London to see a show. He ordered flags at state buildings to be lowered to half-staff when E Street Band saxophonist Clarence Clemons died in 2011, and he'll sometimes crank up a Bruce song between meetings at the governor's office. "I love Bruce Springsteen, and I really enjoy his music. I go to a concert from time to time," said longtime pal Bill Palatucci. "But I'm not a crazy fanatic like the governor where I've got to go to every single thing the guy does. But I've been to a Springsteen concert or two with the governor over the years, just a couple. It's not particularly enjoyable to go with the governor unless you know every single word of every single song. While I certainly love a Bruce Springsteen concert, I love to bring my wife. It's just a little easier. It's half-intimidating and half-annoying to be there with someone who knows every single word to every single song. You can't keep up."

The teachers union was a big backer of Corzine in the campaign and had spent millions since trying to discredit Christie with the phony millionaire's tax issue, so there was no love lost on either side. It worsened when Christie began promoting education reform that included a change in teacher tenure, a long-established job protection that supporters said protected teachers from political meddling. It also effectively guaranteed lifetime employment to educators after three years on the job. Many teachers leave the occupation in those three years, either feeling overwhelmed or underappreciated, or are let go by their districts. But it's expensive and difficult to fire a teacher after that fourth year begins, no matter how ineffective they are or outrageously they behave. Christie also pushed for merit pay based on performance, saying it was ridiculous to pay teachers based on their education level and time on the job alone.

In New Jersey, until a 2012 law changed things, most of the roughly six hundred school districts had elections in which voters can approve education budgets. They were held in April and largely went unnoticed by the majority of the electorate, thereby strengthening the voice of people who do vote because they're connected to the system or would otherwise benefit personally. In a series of town hall meetings, Christie pushed his reform agenda and began to encourage people to vote down school budgets in districts where teachers didn't agree to freeze their pay. In one a teacher rose to challenge him, resulting in one of those YouTube moments. The governor told her no one was forcing her to teach. Voters seemed to like it. They defeated school budgets in record numbers—more than 58 percent of tax levies defeated, the first time since 1976 that more than half the school budgets were defeated. Turnout was nearly 27 percent; it had never before reached 19 percent.

Did the governor cause that? It seems so. The following year, Christie didn't campaign against school budgets, and a larger-than-normal share of them passed—80 percent, the most in eight years. Turnout fell by one-third, though it still topped historical norms.

Between those two elections, Christie and the legislature agreed on a budget cap law that said municipalities and school districts—with certain exceptions, such as for increases in enrollment, health care costs, and deferred pension payments—could not raise property taxes by more than 2 percent without permission from voters. Voters seemed to be more generous when the final say was theirs. In 2011, just eleven districts put "second questions" before voters looking to exceed the cap. Even among the sixty-nine districts looking to raise taxes more than 2 percent for reasons permitted under the cap law, 70 percent got voters' approval.

As part of Christie's plan to build support for his cap proposal, his office would regularly announce lists of mayors who'd endorsed the plan—a few counties at a time, generally grouped geographically. By the time a version of the cap passed, Christie had announced support from 225 mayors. While each announcement ratcheted up the pressure, the process was a slow build because most of the endorsing mayors were Christie's fellow Republicans (around 85 percent of them) and most were from small towns with less political heft. The movement gained steam and big-city Democratic mayors started to come on board from places like Atlantic City and Trenton. (In another of those only in the Soprano State stories, one endorsement was quietly erased after having been announced and listed online. It was that of Carlstadt mayor William Roseman, accused of leaving his ex-wife on his town's health and prescription plans for seven years after they divorced. He agreed in July 2012 to perform community service as part of a pretrial intervention program that cleared him of criminal charges.

The tide turned when Newark mayor Cory Booker, a Democrat friendly enough with Christie to have exchanged text messages with him through the campaign, gave the governor's plan his backing. Booker, a rising political star who opted against running for governor in 2013 in favor of seeking the U.S. Senate in 2014, endorsed Christie's property tax agenda at a news conference on June 21, 2010. That was a Monday. Word had gotten around as the weekend approached that Booker and Christie would do an event together as the new week began. Not coincidentally, Senate president Steve Sweeney made a rare and seemingly sudden Saturday announcement that he'd be countering Christie's plan—at this point, more than a month old—with a proposal of his own that included a 2.9 percent cap on property tax hikes.

Still, nothing had passed by the time the legislature approved the state budget in late June—typically, the time when its summer recess begins. Christie instead ordered the legislature into a special session to address property tax reform. Lawmakers convened July 1 to hear Christie give a speech on the topic. Then the Democrats, except for Sweeney, didn't even come to Trenton for Day 2 on July 2. A day after that, Christie and Sweeney—dragging Assembly speaker Sheila Oliver along—announced they'd reached a deal on a new cap law—setting the cap at 2 percent, rather than the 2.5 percent Christie wanted, allowing a few exceptions and doing it through a law, rather than through the state constitution.

The first municipal spending cap votes were held in April 2011, though few municipalities—only fourteen of the state's 566 cities and towns— sought voters' permission to exceed the 2 percent cap. Most towns, said Bill Dressel, the State League of Municipalities' chief lobbyist in Trenton, "realized it would be almost political suicide to talk about tax levy in-creases."[7] Christie's plan had worked.

Interestingly, six of the towns seeking to exceed the cap had mayors who endorsed Christie's cap in 2010. Eleven of the fourteen mayors who asked to exceed the cap were Republicans.

After getting the 2 percent cap, Christie wasn't done with school spend-ing. He put in place a salary cap on school superintendents' contracts—through a rule, without the legislature's input. It would mean $9.8 million in savings statewide for school districts, around 10 percent of the com-bined $100 million they were paid in 2010. That was followed by warnings it would lead to massive turnover and discourage candidates from seeking the jobs. The public responded it would drive them to the state line to make their exit easier. Caps vary by a district's enrollment and roughly range from $125,000 to $175,000, with an extra $2,500 available in dis-tricts that include a high school. The top-end $175,000 figure was chosen because that is what the governor made for running the whole state. Some school superintendents, who told the school boards what to do instead of the other way around, had much higher salaries and got perks like cars and clothing allowances. Several years back, the State Commission of Investi-gation did a study of seventy-one of the six hundred school districts and found that while the reported salary was $181,000 the actual compensa-tion neared $252,000.

Christie's move angered not only the superintendent-types who reveled in the status quo but also well-to-do suburbs for which overpaying a school super was a status symbol of sorts. A few fought back against Christie's restraints, such as Parsippany–Troy Hills, a township in Christie's Morris County backyard. The district renewed the contract for its superintendent, LeRoy Seitz, months before it expired in an effort to lock him in just be-fore the new rules took effect, at a salary of more than $216,000, with 2 percent increases through 2015. Christie took to publicly, and repeatedly, calling out Seitz as "the poster boy for greed and arrogance." The Parsippany school board sued but lost.

He wasn't the only Morris County figure who'd fought back after being zapped by Christie with that same salary cap. James O'Neill, superintendent in the Chathams' district, who had once been considered a finalist to become Christie's first education commissioner, said the caps were about Christie's political agenda, not finances or education. "He's doing this to the very communities that elected him," O'Neill said in an interview with Bloomberg, noting that 126 of the 205 school chiefs whose salaries were sliced work in communities that Christie won in 2009. "What he's telling us is that those people were all smart enough to elect him, but they're not smart enough to choose who will be superintendent."[8]

Lynne Strickland, executive director of the Garden State Coalition of Schools, which lobbies for suburban districts, said towns used to managing their own affairs feel threatened. "There's an intense roar that's sort of rising here," Strickland said.[9]

Governing wasn't all about cuts. Atlantic City casino jobs fell from 50,000 to 33,000 in five years due to competition from Indian-owned casinos and Pennsylvania's legalizing gaming. Casinos handled $5.2 billion in wagers in 2006, down to $3.6 billion in 2010. Under Christie, casino rules were reduced. Millions of dollars saved by deregulating casinos was put into cleaning up a new tourism district and marketing the resort city that had come to be called Camden By The Sea after the poverty-stricken, crime-plagued town across the Delaware River from Philadelphia. State inspectors no longer were required to patrol the gaming floors, and 115 of 144 inspectors were laid off. To get Revel casino's $2.5 billion construction project restarted—after the economy tanked it just stood there, shiny, all-glass and half-finished—the state agreed to reimburse more than $260 million in business, sales, and hotel taxes to Revel over the next twenty years. Despite this gift to building trade unions, Revel sought bankruptcy protection in February 2013, just ten months after opening.

Christie shrugged off the expected criticism about the state spending money to rescue a casino project when money was scarce, saying Atlantic City needs a rescue. "If you're satisfied with what's going on in Atlantic City now, you won't like this. But if you're satisfied with what's going on in Atlantic City now, you need your head examined," he said.[10]

For all the talk about the faltering economy, it took a backseat. Two months after including the economy in his fall 2010 "reform agenda," the

Web page for it was still blank and "under construction" until the pesky news media pointed it out. When Democrats passed a package of bills to aid the economy, Republican lawmakers objected to a $2 million proposal letting jobless people collect transportation and child care stipends as well as unemployment checks while getting on-the-job training with potential employers, based on a Georgia program. Christie vetoed that and others in the package. (He vetoed the Georgia-imitation plan a second time in early 2012.) Christie felt lowering tax rates, targeting tax credits to businesses, and reducing regulation would turn the state's economy around—and the state's economy added more private sector jobs in 2011 than it had since 2000. But Christie's first year had been sluggish, and the state's private sector job growth rate over his first thirty-five months in office ranked thirty-fourth nationally. Factoring in government job cuts in the state, primarily in local school districts, New Jersey's overall job growth ranked thirty-ninth.

In January 2011, Christie—who'd been pro-choice until 1996, but he says changed his mind after hearing his daughter's heartbeat during a prenatal visit when Mary Pat was thirteen weeks pregnant with their second child, Sarah—became the first New Jersey governor to address abortion rights opponents at their annual protest at the State House to mark the anniversary of the *Roe v. Wade* decision. "What we need to do each and every day is to live our lives in a way that encourages everyone to understand why this cause is so important," Christie said. "To show that we respect the life of every human being, and that every human being is one of God's creatures and deserves the love and respect that God gives to all us."[11]

His critics said Christie was pandering to the right wing of his party with an eye toward garnering their support in a future campaign for national office. Some thought the same when he tossed up a series of roadblocks in the implementation of a medical marijuana law that had been signed into law by Corzine the last day before Christie took office. Christie said he worried the law could lead to problems like those experienced in California and Colorado. His administration advanced rules that limited the strength of the marijuana that can be grown and sold, and eighteen months after the bill's enactment most of the six medical marijuana centers that are planned haven't found homes, as local residents fend off the new businesses.

Critics' objections only heightened when he expressed skepticism at a Toms River town hall meeting about global warming. He later said he believed climate change is real and that humans are contributing to it in some degree—at the same news conference where he angered environmentalists by pulling New Jersey out of a cap-and-trade cooperative of Northeastern states called the Regional Greenhouse Gas Initiative. Christie had earlier removed New Jersey from a lawsuit filed by multiple states seeking to force power companies to cut greenhouse gas emissions. Once again, he seemed to be ahead of the curve when the Supreme Court ruled against the states in June 2011.

Environmental groups had grown exasperated with Christie by his second year, sooner for some of them. The Red Tape Review Commission, among his first initiatives upon taking office, recommended rolling back environmental regulations. A clean energy fund saw its funding cut, transferred instead to balance the state budget. Funding for state parks was slashed. His Department of Environmental Protection adopted a rule allowing its commissioner to waive virtually any rule. There was a bear hunt, with funding for nonlethal strategies for managing the state's bear population clawed out of the budget. He stacked the panel that enforced the Highlands Act, which put large portions of rural northwestern New Jersey off-limits to development to protect drinking water, with opponents of the law—one of whom was quickly installed as chairman.

Storm water rules were weakened. Protections for threatened and endangered species were proposed to be removed from more than fifty square miles of habitat. He signed a law that froze zoning rules in place once a developer applies to a planning board, and signed a law allowing ten years to pass (rather than six) between master plan updates, meaning protections likelier to grow out-of-date can be locked in by developers. He signed some bills designed to protect the ecologically fragile Barnegat Bay but vetoed the one some felt most important. He slashed transit funding but refused to allow gas taxes to rise. His administration revised the state's energy plan, scaling back its goals for renewable energy.

Many state politicians complain about New Jersey's Supreme Court, especially due to a series of rulings starting in the 1970s that resulted in about 60 percent of the state's education budget going to just thirty-one of its six hundred school districts. Christie said he would do more than complain about it—that he'd change the makeup of the court.

Under New Jersey's constitution, a justice gets appointed for seven years, then is renominated, and if confirmed has tenure until he or she turns seventy years old and must retire. Since the arrangement was established in 1947, nominated justices were always confirmed and always granted tenure (although one justice, Peter Verniero, sidestepped being denied tenure by leaving the court early).

The first to come up for renomination under Christie was John Wallace, whose credentials were better than most on the court. In addition, he was the court's sole black member, and his seventieth birthday was only about two years off, meaning Christie would get the chance to replace him in 2012. But Christie did not renominate him because he had been a part of the liberal-leaning court that Christie had pledged to change—even though on issues such as gay marriage he hadn't voted with the court's liberal wing.

The state constitution says Supreme Court justices and Superior Court judges "shall hold their offices for initial terms of seven years and upon reappointment shall hold their offices during good behavior." Democrats interpret that as meaning Wallace should have been renominated unless he had misbehaved in office. Christie said it's a governor's decision whether to renominate a judge. Wallace was a personal friend of Senate president Sweeney and had administered the oath of office when he became Senate president. Sweeney, irked by Christie's action, refused to let the Judiciary Committee hold hearings on Christie's nominee, Anne Patterson, a friend who lives around four miles from the governor.

"That was the first run-in. And [people thought] because the guy's from Gloucester County, I cared," said Sweeney. "That wasn't the case, I told Chris, I said, 'Look, don't do something stupid here. The guy's a quality justice. You're going to get to pick four in your first term. The guy's going to retire in two years. You get that seat. It's not like you're reappointing somebody that's going to be there for fifteen years or ten years or even seven years. You're going to get that seat in two years. There's no reason not to reappoint him. He's a moderate. He went to your alma mater.' I was joking with him. And when he did it, he had no real reason to do it except that now I figured he's going to become Mr. Conservative. If you'll remember, he got real conservative in the primary against [Steve] Lonegan, but that wasn't really him. He wasn't that."

Sweeney was in his car when Christie called to tell him he wasn't going to renominate Wallace—and that he'd be announcing that publicly to reporters in an hour. That annoyed Sweeney because it gave him no chance to discuss it further.

"And you're having a press conference?" Sweeney asked.

"I'm doing my constitutional responsibility, and you need to do yours," said Christie, referring to the Senate's power to advise and consent on nominations.

"Okay," Sweeney said. "I'm advising you right now that I don't consent to what you're doing and you're not going to get a hearing on your nominee."

"You have a constitutional obligation," Christie said.

"I do, to advise and consent. And I don't consent," Sweeney said. "I'm not going to consent to this."

Sweeney said, "He took a well-respected, probably a little-bit-to-the-right-leaning justice—he was not a liberal by any means. He ruled in favor of the death penalty. Not by any means was he a liberal justice. And I said I'm not going to go along with it. And I think he expected me to go, 'Oh, okay.' We took away the only African American judge on the court. New Jersey's the most diversified state in the nation, and we're going to have an all-white court?"

Another justice, Roberto Rivera-Soto, who was not going to be renominated due to a series of embarrassments he caused the court—such as getting involved in a dispute between his son and the son's high school football captain—agreed to step down when his term ended. Sweeney suggested that Anne Patterson would get a hearing for Rivera-Soto's seat. Christie said no way. "I won't nominate anybody for that position until Anne Patterson gets a hearing for John Wallace's spot. I'm not going to give up the governor's prerogative to name a Supreme Court justice. If I were to do that, we should just allow the Senate to nominate who they want," Christie said.

There was more stalemate with temporary justices coming in from the appeals division and sitting justices having to recuse themselves for conflicts. The court was becoming more of a joke than usual. Months later, Christie went along with the switcheroo that was first suggested by Wallace's friend Sweeney.

Christie angered many of the Democratic women in the legislature, but thrilled social conservatives, by eliminating so-called family planning funding from the state budget. The name's a bit of a misnomer; the program provides health care services such as pap smears and mammograms to women and doesn't fund abortions. But because some of the funds went to Planned Parenthood centers, conservatives say the funding essentially enables such centers to be able to use other revenues to provide a service they find morally reprehensible. Christie argued that low-income women can access the health services they need at other clinics, primarily Federally Qualified Health Centers, in repeatedly vetoing Democrats' efforts to provide $7.5 million in family planning funds.

Democrats framed the family planning cuts as part of a bigger picture in which Christie has some sort of problem with women. He'd bluntly, inaccurately, told reporters that Assembly speaker Sheila Oliver had told them "a lie" by claiming her efforts to meet with him to discuss a policy proposal had been rebuffed. Her aides quickly produced emails showing her asking for a meeting and getting ignored. "That has irreparably affected my ability to work with this governor," Oliver said. "For him to cast aspersions on my integrity and say I would lie? That showed me I really cannot have a trusting relationship with this governor. Because he will distort the truth. He will stand up and lie. It was a game-changer for me, a total game-changer."[12]

Christie blamed Assemblywoman Bonnie Watson Coleman for a murder allegedly committed by a parolee released from prison early under legislation she sponsored. In asking reporters to call out Senator Loretta Weinberg for hypocrisy, he said, "Can you guys please take the bat out on her for once?"—not literally encouraging violence against women, of course, though that's what critics claimed. Then again, an NJEA staffer wasn't really praying for his death in an ill-conceived email joke in 2010, but Christie harped on that for months.

Here's where the vendetta-against-women angle falls down: Christie skewered men just as easily. He'd set the tone before taking office by accusing Assemblyman John McKeon of "political lying."[13] He called a nominee for the New Jersey Sports and Exposition Authority "probably the singular most unqualified candidate you could find."[14] (The nominee, Middlesex County sheriff Joseph Spicuzzo, wound up being indicted by state prosecutors in an unrelated bribery scheme, which hadn't yet gone to trial as of March 2013.) He called Assemblyman Joseph Cryan "disgusting."[15] He suggested that Senator Raymond Lesniak give back his legislative salary for spending too much time in France.[16] He called Assemblyman Reed Gusciora "numbnuts."[17] And he escalated a war of words with Senator Dick Codey over blocked nominees by stripping him of the security detail he had as a former governor and removing a Codey relative and a longtime friend of Codey's from government jobs.

The fireworks in the budget Christie proposed in 2011 exploded at the end of the process, rather than the beginning. They actually came on the heels of his crowning legislative achievement, an overhaul of public worker pension and health care benefits passed despite opposition from most majority Democrats. The bill was signed June 28, at a ceremony where Christie said the change wouldn't have happened without Senate president Steve Sweeney's five years of work on the issue. "I'm really, really honored to be his partner and be his friend," he said.

But there was trouble brewing. The deadline for adopting a new state budget was near, and Democrats had decided to radically rewrite Christie's proposal and pass it without negotiating with him. A year before, they'd left it to Republicans to sponsor Christie's budget and supplied the few votes needed to get it passed. This time Democrats, led by the progressive wing of their party, put together their own budget, approved it in committees June 27 and passed it June 29.

That seemed way too easy and unconfrontational. And it was.

On Thursday, June 30, a few hours short of the midnight deadline, Christie stunned Democrats, and probably a few Republicans, when he used his line-item veto to cut out $913 million of it. He even cut money from the budget he himself had put into it in February, four months prior. Among the things he did was slash funding from salary accounts for legislative staffers, while leaving his own office's salaries untouched. Months later, he basically acknowledged he did so out of spite—he was angry that Democrats removed funding for oversight from the Department of Environmental Protection. He also quietly transferred the money back in, when Democrats planned to inflict all the cuts on Republican staffers. A Senate employee said the Republicans asked Sweeney if he would intervene with Christie on behalf of GOP staff.

With political mouths still agape, Christie was off for two weeks, which included private vacation time with the family and an annual conference in Sun Valley, Idaho, hosted by Allen & Company, a private investment firm founded in 1922. It is a gathering of leaders from business, politics, and other spheres of influence. An invitation tells the world you have arrived, as attendees for the twenty-ninth conference included the likes of billionaire investor Warren Buffett, Microsoft founder Bill Gates, Facebook founder Mark Zuckerberg, and Oprah Winfrey. Fox Media mogul Rupert Murdoch attended, too, although he probably wished he hadn't, since as the conference began one of his papers in England, *News of the World*, was in the midst of a scandal regarding hacked telephone calls of private citizens and public figures. Reporters, kept at a distance for most events, were all over him at every opportunity. He left for England in an unsuccessful attempt to douse the flames.

The New York Times reported that the most popular scheduled conference events were a chat with Gates and Zuckerberg, a Charlie Rose interview with Winfrey, a panel on doing business with China, and a general session with Christie in which he was interviewed by former NBC anchor Tom Brokaw.[18]

Newark mayor Cory Booker was there. A year before, a chance meeting in a conference buffet line led to Zuckerberg's offering a $100 million matching grant for Newark schools. It was announced on Winfrey's show amid much hoopla, which some said was to drown out the opening of a movie, *The Social Network*, that showed Zuckerberg in a bad light. Booker and Christie had lunch with Zuckerberg at the Allen & Company conference.

"We sat down, had lunch and just gave him a quick update on the progress," Booker said. He also said Zuckerberg was pleased with progress being made in Newark schools. Christie probably mentioned now that the budget was signed and health care benefits and pension reforms were law, he would tackle education reform.[19]

Unfortunately for Christie, back home storm clouds were gathering and set to dump rain on his much anticipated education agenda. Sweeney was fuming. Reporters and State House regulars saw it as political theater. The script would go something like this: Democrats took the budget Christie sent forward in February and added to it. Christie used his line-item veto to cut it. Democrats would shout and scream and vow an override, knowing that wasn't likely to work because it needed three Republicans in the Senate and seven in the Assembly. Republicans were so afraid of Christie they wouldn't override any veto, even if a vote had been set to rescue their own staff.

Theater it may have been, but Sweeney said the governor veered way off the script and made deeper cuts than anyone expected. "We had conversations about the budget and the governor was very clear that he was going to take his pen to do some things. And the only commitment we asked of him was 'Let's talk about it. We know you have to do some things. But you don't have to do all these things.'"[20]

Where Democrats tried to restore money for some of their favorite projects, like legal aid for the needy, the governor rejected the additions and cut more on top of what he already had cut. Sweeney saw that as vindictive: "Listen, you can punch me in the face and knock me down, do what you want. But don't be vindictive and punish innocent people. These people didn't do anything to him. It's like a bank robber taking hostages. And now he's starting to shoot people. I liken it to being spoiled. He was angry because he wanted a mutual budget. But do you hurt people because of that? Do you take $8 million in AIDS funding away? Legal services is drowning as it is, and you take away another $5 million? I'm just so angry that he hurt people like this to prove a point. He is a cruel man."[21]

It went beyond political differences, it became personal. One of the programs cut was the Early Childhood Intervention Program, a service providing therapy for the developmentally disabled and others. Sweeney's daughter, Lauren, was born with Down syndrome. "When my daughter left a neo-natal unit after 75 days, the first person she saw was someone from the early intervention program," he told reporters. "And it's critically important for disabled children to have that program."[22] Sweeney, who stood proudly by the governor when the historic benefits reforms were signed into law, now called Christie a "rotten bastard," a "punk," a "prick," and the Mr. Potter character from the movie *It's a Wonderful Life*. A closer look at what Christie did shows the verbal attack was overkill and Sweeney later admitted it was over the top, although he wouldn't apologize for saying it. The childhood intervention program was scheduled to be financed at just under $100.5 million. Instead, it was trimmed to $92.6 million for the year that started July 1, 2011. In the budget year that had just ended, the adjusted appropriation for it was $86.6 million. So, the new appropriation was $6 million more than the prior year's, although $8 million less than Christie had asked for in February. While Christie cut the appropriation that he himself originally proposed, the program wasn't in any danger.

Sharp exchanges between Christie and Sweeney weren't uncommon, but underneath it they remained friends. In an earlier spat, at a time they had stopped communicating during a feud, Sweeney's daughter, Lauren, had remained more humane and apolitical. She had met Christie a few times—at the State House, at the governor's mansion—and when she heard the governor wasn't feeling well asked her father to dial the governor's number. Sweeney told her daughter they weren't getting along at that particular time, but she didn't want to hear it. Her call went to voice mail and she told the governor she loved him and that she wished he was better. A short time later, Sweeney's home phone rang. It was Christie.

"Chris?" Sweeney said.

"Yeah," Christie said. "Steve, I don't want to talk to you. We've said enough to each other to last. I want to talk to Lauren. Put her on the phone."

"But . . ."

"'I want to talk to Lauren. Put her on the phone," Christie said.

So Sweeney did. "And Lauren and he had a wonderful conversation for about ten minutes. You could hear him talking to her, and she's talking," he said. "And afterwards, he hung up."

No one doubted Sweeney's sincerity, especially when it comes to his daughter, but this battle was much deeper than that. Sweeney stuck his neck way out to help Christie get the reforms and budget through the legislature. This caused Sweeney to come under fire from his own party and the unions that help keep Democrats in office. Unions started an advertising campaign aimed at Sweeney, who felt betrayed by Christie. "I sat in my office all day like a nitwit, figuring we were going to talk," he said.

They didn't talk for nearly a month, when Sweeney called Christie to extend well wishes when an asthma attack—his worst since law school, brought on by a wave of hot, humid days and his weight—briefly hospitalized Christie in late July. It would be another ten days before they cleared the air. "He had his office call me to sit down, and I went and sat down with him. My conversation—I'm just going to leave it as we had a very clear conversation between the two of us, and we said we're going to move on. I said things that, I really wish I thought more before I said the things that I said, but I will not apologize. I felt that way. I was upset. He hurt people, I felt. I just thought he hurt defenseless people, and that's me. That's how I am. But he and I had a good conversation. And we didn't hit each other. There was no blows landed, and we moved on." And today? "I'm sure he looks at me a little bit differently, and I look at him a little bit differently. But we've still got a job to do, and we're going to do it."

The line-item veto skirmish marked a new direction in discourse. His enemies had tried to paint Christie as a bully and it didn't cost him much support. In fact, it gained him popularity across the country and reinforced his tough "Jersey Guy" image at home. After the vetoes, the term "bully" was dropped, replaced by "mean-spirited." "Being mean-spirited . . . means you can make decisions based on personal political calculations in spite of what may be good for the state. Whether or not you agree with Christie's cuts, this line of attack can have some traction among female independent voters who have been wavering in their support for the governor," noted political scientist Patrick Murray.[23]

The override votes were scheduled to take place over two days. The first was Monday, July 11, 2011. We have a proud tradition of open government in this country in which anyone can sit in the balcony above a legislative chamber and watch laws being made. But what we're seeing from up there is just the final act. The details and strategy have been worked out ahead of time when the party caucuses met behind closed doors. That's where the fighting takes place and the deals are made. Sometimes reporters know ahead of time the result, they just can't predict what will be said before voting buttons are pressed. Such was the case for the veto overrides. It had become clear that the Republicans would not offer Democrats the three votes needed for the two-thirds override. That was the case for fourteen of the fifteen attempts. The exception was a vote to provide funding for family planning clinics. Her caucus allowed Senator Jennifer Beck, whose district was changed in the once-a-decade redistricting effort, to vote with the Democrats on that one, which failed by two votes instead of three.

The next day was same song, second verse, except no Republicans crossed over. Democrats said they would return in August and try again on the rest of their list but they had accomplished their goal—enough campaign slogans, sound bites, and issues to unite Democrats against Republicans in the fall elections.

The Democrats knew going in they would fail in their override attempt; their hope was they would succeed in another area—branding Christie and his Republican colleagues in the legislature as heartless and uncaring about people less fortunate than they. If successful, that's election campaign gold in a competitive race, which New Jersey has very few of, Beck's district being a potential exception. It also gave cover to a Democratic senator, Brian Stack, who had been a dependable ally of Christie's, much to the dismay of fellow party members. He was allowed to sponsor four of the override resolutions, which he was glad to do because he knew they were going nowhere.

In two years, Sweeney had gone from promising not to try to "wedge-issue this governor" to collecting enough wedges to fill a Trivial Pursuit playing piece. Millionaire's tax, family planning funds, another millionaire's tax, the line-item vetoes, and, finally, at the start of 2012, gay marriage.

On the eve of the new legislative session, the one that would take state government up to the 2013 elections, Democrats announced at a State House news conference they would introduce in both houses a marriage equality bill, which would be given top priority. The last time a gay marriage bill came up was in January 2010, when a Democratic Senate failed to pass it, getting just fourteen of the twenty-one votes needed, and the Democratic Assembly wouldn't even post it for a vote. Governor Corzine said if the legislature sent it to him, he would sign. New Jersey's civil union law was being challenged in court and the feeling was if it made it to the state Supreme Court the civil union law would be tossed, replaced with same-sex marriage.

Sweeney, who was majority leader in 2010 when the bill failed, didn't cast a vote then. He called it a "terrible mistake" and said he has changed his mind. "This is about doing what's right and ensuring full equal and civil rights for New Jerseyans. Two years ago I made a mistake in abstaining on marriage equality—a mistake that means same-sex couples continue to be denied the very basic civil right to live their lives as they wish. But today isn't about me correcting my mistake, it's about correcting a mistake for thousands of loving couples across the state who want nothing more than to be treated equally as their neighbors."

Christie was on record as favoring civil unions but opposing same-sex marriage, and the unexpected turnaround was seen by some as an attempt to embarrass Christie in the national press, maybe make him a little less attractive among all-important swing voters when a presidential candidate came looking for a running mate. It was noted in the news conference that four out of the six states Christie had visited recently, including Iowa and New Hampshire where he campaigned for Mitt Romney, had same-sex marriage laws. Sweeney said a bill becomes law in forty-five days even if a governor doesn't sign it. "If the governor cannot raise himself by signing a law to ensure a basic civil right for all residents, we would hope that he would not lower himself by vetoing it."

Christie seemed unlikely to let a bill pass without acting on it. Asked at one point if he would take that approach with a difficult bill allowing adult adoptees access to their original birth certificates, he said that wasn't his style. (He wound up vetoing the bill.) And Christie had told CNN's Piers Morgan he can't envision a situation where he would change his mind about same-sex marriage. "I don't think so. I believe marriage is an institution between one man and one woman. I think it's special and unique in society. And I think we can have civil unions that can help to give the same type of legal rights to same sex couples that marriage gives them. But I just think marriage is a special connotation. And I couldn't see myself changing my mind on that. But I am in favor of making sure that homosexual couples have the same type of legal rights that same—that heterosexual couples have."[24]

Asked by Morgan whether homosexuality is a sin, Christie said he doesn't think so.

"My religion says it's a sin. I mean, I think—but for me I don't—I've always believed that people are born with the predisposition to be homosexual. And so, I think if someone is born that way, it's very difficult to say then that that's a sin," Christie said. "But I understand that my church says that. But for me personally, I don't look upon someone who is homosexual as a sinner."

In January 2012, Christie preempted the state Senate's consideration of the marriage bill one day later by nominating Bruce Harris as New Jersey's first openly gay associate justice on the state supreme court. Harris, the mayor of Chatham Borough, had a stellar academic record and solid career in public-finance law but no judicial experience. The other high-court choice Christie nominated the same day, Phillip Kwon, a former federal prosecutor under Christie who followed his administration to Trenton, also had never been a judge.

Each, however, met the diversity standard Democrats said they wanted after the court's two minority members had departed in 2010 and 2011. Kwon, who was born in South Korea, was poised to become the modern state supreme court's first immigrant and first Asian-American. Harris was believed to be the only gay, black Republican mayor in the United States at the time of his nomination. The Senate ultimately voted both down.

Asked the day the nominations were made if he would sign or veto the same-sex marriage bill, Christie threw cold water on speculation his opposition might be softening and quipped, "I'm not somebody who changes position with the grace of a ballerina, so I wouldn't be all atwitter with expectation." But he also used the phrase "marriage equality" to describe the same-sex marriage bill, the terminology preferred by advocates for such a change.

A day later, Christie made his intentions clear, with language that was anything but. He told reporters he would veto the bill—and did a few weeks later—and urged lawmakers to put the issue before state voters in a November ballot referendum. Democrats refused, reiterating that the issue is a civil-rights matter not appropriately decided at a ballot box. Christie said, "The fact of the matter is, I think people would have been happy to have a referendum on civil rights rather than fighting and dying in the streets in the South." After a backlash that even drew civil-rights legend U.S. Representative John Lewis to New Jersey, Christie said he understood that such a referendum would have failed and that he was saying that 1960s activists would have liked to have a hospitable enough environment for a referendum to be an option. He said he offered the idea to Democrats as a path around his opposition. "If they really cared about the issue, and they know the way this is going to end, then why don't they give same-sex couples in New Jersey the opportunity to make their case to the public?"

There was opportunity for Sweeney, too, who is eyeing a run for the U.S. Senate, in both the line-item veto overrides and the gay marriage bill. He saw a chance to put his name-calling tirade behind him, come off as reasonable and levelheaded while standing up to the governor in a move that would please some of his labor union critics. While Christie was hobnobbing with the rich and famous out west, Sweeney announced he would not move forward on two education reform bills important to the governor.

Christie wanted to pay teachers based on performance, merit pay, and do away with the last-in, first-out rule that protected the more senior teachers during layoffs. Sweeney said those bills would not come up for a vote.[17] Both were opposed by the New Jersey Education Association. At the same time, he left the door open to bringing up two of Christie's biggest issues—tenure reform and school vouchers.

The NJEA didn't want to see Christie's reform of the tenure system. The union also hates school vouchers, but Sweeney said both would be on the table.

In addition, he said he won't call up a bill Christie opposed, which would require local voters to approve charter schools, because in Christie's view such a requirement would end them. The guy who received national news coverage for calling Christie a punk and a bully a few days earlier now sounded diplomatic: "I don't have much of a choice but to deal with him because I have to. I can't shut the government down or shut down discussions on policy or programs that are important because my feelings got hurt or I hurt his feelings."

CHAPTER TEN

You'll Thank Me Later

Ask anyone what he knows about Chris Christie and the answer will likely contain words like bold, abrasive, pugnacious, strong-willed, determined, or aggressive. Standing up to his critics is what made Christie a national figure.

No battles have endeared Christie more to conservatives around the country than his tangles with the state's public employee unions. Christie got started quickly: In his first public appearance as governor-elect, in a visit to the Robert Treat Academy charter school in Newark, he singled out for criticism the New Jersey Education Association, which had spent about $3 million supporting Jon Corzine for reelection in ads he says lied about his positions. He was specifically talking about its opposition to charter schools, a skirmish he first fought with them as a lobbyist a dozen years earlier. "The forces that are arrayed against us on this are significant and powerful—although I think they just learned in this last election, not as powerful as they think," he said.[1]

Some of Christie's most cutting remarks came at the expense of the teachers union. He said upon arriving in the State House that he recognized the NJEA as the neighborhood bully no one—until he arrived—would stand up to. He said a teacher was using children like "drug mules" by having them ask their parents whether they intended to vote on the local education budget. He also took those critiques beyond the state's borders. In a speech to the Brookings Institution in New York in April 2011, he called the New Jersey Education Association "bullies and thugs"[2] that cow the legislature into following its demands. He made similar remarks at Harvard's Graduate School of Education, calling the union a "political thuggery operation" that is "fat, rich, and entitled."[3]

On his first full day in office, he issued an executive order trying to include unions under the state's pay-to-play rules, the series of laws first put in place in 2004 intending to limit campaign contributions from state contractors—a contracting reform as much as a campaign finance move. Christie felt it was unfair that the rules limited to $300 donations from businesses with more than $17,500 in public contracts while leaving unaffected the pipeline of union cash that benefited mostly various Democratic campaign committees. So he changed the rules to say any union that negotiates a contract for its members is considered a state contractor and therefore covered by the rules. (He also included legislative leadership committees under the pay-to-play restrictions; the legislature had conveniently left out the powerful PACs run by its own leadership in adopting the reforms.)

Executive orders aren't as permanent as laws, since they can be changed by a follow-up order from the same or a future governor, and they're only supposed to govern how the executive branch of state government operates. Four labor unions responded to the order by filing suit, saying Christie overreached by changing pay-to-play rules without the legislative branch. On May 7, 2010, an appeals court agreed, saying that while the idea might be wise, such public policy changes can't be dictated unilaterally. "The desired changes in the law would, in essence, require not only a pen, but also an eraser," the opinion states.[4]

Christie's battles with the unions continued beyond that court fight—into his crusade to get voters to reject budgets if teachers didn't consent to pay cuts, and into his lengthy effort to get lawmakers to pass what he called his property tax "tool kit." Christie had said as a candidate—often, since reporters pressed him frequently for a property tax plan—that there is no single, magic-bullet solution to the state's property tax bills. Attacking the issue would require multiple efforts to chip away at the cost drivers, he said. Those plans became evident in May 2010 in his tool kit—which public employee unions saw as a hammer aimed directly at them, since it included things such as capping at 2 percent the size of the raises that an arbitrator can award when contract talks break down, as well as changing civil service rules to allow cities and towns to drop out of the system while guaranteeing certain protections. The arbitration changes were enacted, though Democrats made sure they expired after four years, meaning they'll be in effect for one round of the town-by-town union contracts. Civil service changes weren't taken up by the legislature, which said there weren't cost savings in it; Christie and allies said neighboring municipalities can run into roadblocks in trying to share or merge services if one town is covered by civil service and the other isn't.

Christie's attempts to change the way state worker unions operate pleased conservatives across the country, who probably didn't realize he had an unlikely ally on the other end of the political spectrum. President Franklin Roosevelt, wealthy champion of the working man, nevertheless was critical of private union tactics being adopted by government employee unions. In a 1937 letter to Luther C. Steward, president of the National Federation of Federal Employees, FDR said, "All government employees should realize that the process of collective bargaining, as usually understood, cannot be transplanted into the public service."

Militancy in particular, he saw as a problem: "I want to emphasize my conviction that militant tactics have no place in the functions of any organization of government employees. Upon employees in the Federal service rests the obligation to serve the whole people, whose interests and welfare require orderliness and continuity in the conduct of government activities. This obligation is paramount. Since their own services have to do with the functioning of the government, a strike of public employees manifests nothing less than an intent on their part to prevent or obstruct the operations of government until their demands are satisfied. Such action, looking toward the paralysis of government by those who have sworn to support it, is unthinkable and intolerable."[5]

George Meany, legendary president of the AFL-CIO, agreed. In 1955 he said, "It is impossible to bargain collectively with the government." The labor movement was about getting workers a larger share of profits they helped produce, but government workers don't produce more profit, they only ask for more money.[6]

The idea that collective bargaining didn't fit in with public service held until 1959 when Wisconsin opened the door to it. It spread and public employee unions grew strong at every election. The dues collected that could be used to buy advertising to support or oppose candidates and the large number of workers who could attend rallies and take part in get-out-the vote activities changed the landscape in Wisconsin and other states, including New Jersey, where Election Day is a holiday for state employees.

The Communications Workers of America and the New Jersey Education Association had become accustomed to getting their way by the time Christie arrived on the scene. They called it negotiations, but it really wasn't. Politicians, eager for the cash and manpower contributions, rolled over and played dead. Taxpayers got the funeral bill.

Politicians were at fault in other ways, too. Starting with Governor Christie Whitman, the state's contribution to employee pension plans was not in cash but an IOU. In the mid-1990s pension funds were in great shape and borrowing from them offered a way to live higher off the hog without paying for the pork. By the time Christie became governor in 2010, the pension and health care funds were more than $100 billion short of what they needed. Employees got lawmakers to boost their pensions by 9 percent and trim their contributions; local governments were deferring their payments, the state regularly skipping its contributions. No money was ever put aside to pay future health care costs for retirees; those were just absorbed on a yearly basis and growing rapidly. The gloomiest prediction, by Northwestern University professor Josh Rauh, was that the pension funds could go insolvent by 2018.[7]

In 2005, Senator Steve Sweeney, himself an ironworkers labor leader, warned something had to be done. Instead of being treated like Paul Revere for his call to save the pensions, state employee unions saw him more as Benedict Arnold, the infamous traitor, and condemned him, even putting up an inflatable rat used on job sites where nonunion labor worked.

As a candidate, Christie told firefighters and teachers that pensions for current employees wouldn't be altered. As governor, he said he didn't realize the depth of the problem when he had said that. Christie said change had to come for the benefit of the taxpayers and the unionized state workers as well, who he said would thank him in fifteen years when they realized he saved their retirement income. But in the present, the battle lines were drawn.

Before it hit the fan in New Jersey, however, the public worker union reform fight hit the headlines from Wisconsin, the state where collective bargaining for public employees began. Newly elected Republican governor Scott Walker tried to end collective bargaining for state employees. That resulted in protests resembling the antiwar crusades during the Vietnam years.

Wisconsin and New Jersey are alike in some ways and very much different in others. Wisconsin is huge, mostly rural, leans to the left but is predominantly moderate politically and its people are friendly with a Midwestern politeness. New Jersey is small, densely packed, leans to the Democratic, although also predominantly moderate, and is accustomed to in-your-face discussions whether the subject is politics or pizza.

One of the key differences between Walker and Christie was that Walker had a legislature of his own party. Christie faced an Assembly and Senate dominated by Democrats. That meant he had to compromise and seek help from Senate President Sweeney and Assembly speaker Sheila Oliver. On NBC's *Meet the Press* Christie told host David Gregory that the three of them were able to make compromises "that didn't violate our principles and that's the key. You can't ask people to violate their principles." He said the plan was developed nine months before it was passed, which gave him time to have thirty town hall meetings to sell the plan and promote public pressure on the legislature to move on it. He called it a national model for reform.[8]

"I think it's a lot different than what happened with Scott [Walker] because he came in, he had a legislature of his own party and he did it right away," Christie told *Politico*. "My approach had to be different, by the nature of the state I live in. It's a more Democratic state than Wisconsin. I have a Democratic legislature."[9]

Larry Sabato, renowned University of Virginia political scientist, said Christie surprised people who thought they had him pegged. "It's stunning mainly because it is a bipartisan deal, and that's not Christie's national image. He's seen as confrontational and partisan. The deal belies that and people are taking notice in light of what's going on in other states."[10]

The town hall meetings were key to keeping up the pressure on the legislature, Christie said. In them, a crowd of mostly supportive citizens listens to a lengthy Christie lecture, delivered without notes, as the governor strolls around a cordoned-off square surrounded by constituents. That's followed by a Q&A session, which invariably produces an exchange—often fiery, sometimes just a good yarn—that his staff deems worthy of putting on YouTube.

Montclair State University political scientist Brigid Harrison said the format plays to Christie's strengths as a trial lawyer and former prosecutor. "That is why he is so darn good at it. It is kind of a Perry Mason personality. It's almost like a scripted jury trial, and it's one of the reasons these town halls prove so effective—a nice, concise, cohesive story that people are familiar with and tend to like. That's why we have courtroom shows on TV."[11]

The reform, which is predicted to save the taxpayers $120 billion over thirty years, was signed into law on June 28, 2011. It made several major changes—significant, to be sure, though not ones that would be considered radical by private sector unions like Sweeney's ironworkers, who were hit hard by the economic downturn. State workers had golden benefits. For instance, until 2007 when Governor Corzine required state workers to pay 1.5 percent of their salary toward their health care premiums, most state workers paid nothing during their working years and after they retired, when the health care continued for them and their families. Even after the 2007 reform, 96 percent of workers chose the most expensive plan, as their cost was the same no matter what. Christie joked that layoffs should start with the 4 percent who chose a worse plan.

The changes froze cost-of-living increases for pensions, until the funds got back to having 80 cents on hand for every $1 in projected obligations. Public workers have to put more of their salaries toward the pension—eventually reaching 7.5 percent of pay for teachers, 9 percent for state troopers, and 10 percent for local firefighters and police officers. All employees will have to pay more toward their health benefits, on a sliding scale that varies from 3 percent of a health plan's cost for workers making less than $25,000 to 35 percent for people paid over $110,000. The retirement age was raised to sixty-five for new workers. Employee unions gained seats on labor-management boards that oversee the pension and health benefits plans, and they gained the right to sue the state if it fails to pay into the pension fund.

You would have thought Christie, Sweeney, and Oliver were forcing each state worker to hand over their firstborn. There were noisy rallies around the State House with speeches by Democratic politicians wanting to make points with an eye toward the election in five months in which every member of the Senate and Assembly faced the voters. They called it the Second Battle of Trenton, though there had already been two of those in the Revolutionary War. (Why didn't some history teacher in the NJEA point that out?) A small band also crossed the Delaware, à la George Washington, but unlike him they came across a bridge. Then there was Camp Collective Bargaining, about one hundred brand-new pup tents on a lawn at the rear of the State House. There was no one in any of them, but it looked impressive from news helicopters. The tents came down hours after they were pitched; Christie's attorney general, Paula Dow, wouldn't allow the NJEA to keep the tents up after dark, saying she couldn't guarantee campers' safety in the Trenton night.

Chants of "We will remember in November" filled the hot, humid Trenton air. Which raised the question, what exactly did the unions think they could do about it? Vote in more Republicans who wouldn't be sympathetic to their cause? Union leaders saw the folly in that so they took on George Norcross, the South Jersey Democratic boss, and Joseph DiVincenzo Jr., a power broker in North Jersey, who was the real boss of Speaker Oliver when she was in her county job in Newark.

"You can't look at those Democrats who voted in favor of his bill as individuals; you have to see them as controlled," said Communications Workers of America state director Hetty Rosenstein. "We think that kind of boss politics is failing New Jersey. That's part of what we're assessing here as we go forward."[12]

Of course, the boss system in politics has been in place for decades in New Jersey, but the public employee unions didn't recognize it when they were getting their way.

A Senate committee passed out the reform bill on a Monday, and the Assembly had its hearing the following Thursday. The night before the Assembly's hearing, union leaders were offered a better deal than they ultimately got, but they rejected it. They could have had a 3 percent of salary cost for health care that would never increase, more health plans to choose from, which would have lowered costs to employees, and a nonimposition clause, meaning the governor could not impose a contract on workers, a right New Jersey governors have had since 1968. Public employees don't have the right to strike. Union leaders walked away from it. Why?

Some think it had to do with plans in place for the Assembly hearing the next day. After a union leader spoke, union members in the room started chanting to disrupt the proceedings and were escorted out of the room and given citations by state troopers. It was well photographed because the union had leaked its plans earlier so that newspeople could be in the right place to capture it all. It was a photo op that would not have come off if the compromise plan had been accepted the night before.

John Donahue of Harvard University predicted more skirmishes. "We are going to see more battles like this. The big picture history is going to record of this period is that we lost the middle class in the private sector in the 1980s and 1990s, and it is politically unsustainable to have a middle class public sector and not a middle class private sector." Donahue, who served in President Bill Clinton's Labor Department, added, "Government can't be a middle class island in a divided world."[13]

The CWA's Rosenstein said the loss of the middle class in the private sector is because of the destruction of organized labor in the private sector.

Crisis Management

New Jersey experienced a dizzying accumulation of peculiar events in Christie's first few years in office—multiple floods, a crippling blizzard, a summer-long heat wave, a rare direct hit from a tropical storm just barely below hurricane force when it came ashore, even the swaying and rumbling from an earthquake that struck in Virginia.

It was while Hurricane Irene was approaching and Christie was relaying emergency instructions at a news conference that the governor veered off script into one of his more famous rants, when he told sunbathers who were ignoring his evacuation request to "get the hell off the beach in Asbury Park."

"I was just pissed, you know?" Christie said.[14] "I was upstairs for those 14-hour days at the Regional Operations Intelligence Center, and I'm watching TV and there's a guy from CNN standing on the Boardwalk in Asbury Park, and 10 hours earlier I told everybody to get off the islands, get back to safer ground. I said it really nicely: 'It is in your best interest to move to a safer place during this very dangerous time.' And then I watched this guy from CNN standing on the Boardwalk in Asbury Park. He didn't bother me too much, but behind him there were people building sand castles. There was a guy putting sunscreen on his wife or girlfriend, and there was another guy that grabbed his surfboard and running out to the water. I said, 'Who are these idiots?' And I said 'OK, time for a press conference,' and I went down there and I just figured I had to take a much more Jersey approach to the problem.

"When we were going through this it was an interesting experience for my family because we actually happened to be on vacation that week at the Jersey Shore," Christie said. "And after I delivered my line I then went back to Island Beach State Park to see my family, and I saw my 11-year-old son, Patrick, first when I pulled in the driveway of the house. I got out of the car and he said: 'Dad, I can't say the word you said, but we're off the beach.'"

Christie's seizing the moment in August 2011 as Hurricane Irene bore down on the Garden State reminded some of the moment eight months earlier when he did the opposite during a blizzard.

Christie, often absent at home while governing the state, had promised his children a trip to Walt Disney World during Christmas week in his first year in office. Problem was, Lieutenant Governor Kim Guadagno was scheduled to go on a family vacation at the same time, a cruise to Mexico with her ill father. Rather than force her to miss the trip, and unwilling to cancel his, both left the state.

And New Jersey got socked by a major blizzard.

That left Senate president Steve Sweeney in charge for four days as the state dug out from more than two feet of snow that started falling December 26. Sweeney didn't even find out until December 22 he was on call; although Christie knew about the scheduling conflict for months, he didn't let the senator know. As forecasts worsened and other states declared states of emergency, New Jersey lagged—until after Christie's flight took off from Newark. Cars got stranded and abandoned in snowbanks on state highways and exit ramps, making clearing the snow virtually impossible. Christie's transportation commissioner later compared conditions on Route 280 to the Donner Pass—the Sierra Nevada mountain route where in 1846 California-bound emigrants got their wagons stuck in the snow and forty-five of eighty-one pioneers died, some alleged to have resorted to cannibalism. An executive order lifting the emergency was issued by Sweeney—even though roads at the Shore remained impassable. Similar nothing-to-see-here, please-disperse orders lifting emergencies hadn't been signed by Christie after floods earlier in his term.

Christie tossed kerosene on the controversy by saying he'd talked with Sweeney on the phone from Florida, when he hadn't, and blaming mayors for snowbound citizens. He said he had no regrets about keeping his promise—though months later did finally express some. "It created a perception among people that maybe I didn't care, which was a mistake to allow that perception to be created. I think the things we've done this year have shown people that I really do care and was trying to be a good father and a good husband."[15]

Christie got tripped up a second time in the travel area, as well.

In the spring of 2011, when his oldest son's high school baseball team was advancing through the playoffs, Christie used a state police helicopter to travel to two games. The trips weren't on his official schedule but burst into the news when photographers shot pictures of Christie's arrival near the field at the second game—followed by his hundred-yard car ride to the bleachers.

That wasn't the worst of it: Christie then left the game early, with his wife, to fly back to the governor's mansion in Princeton to meet with some political donors from Iowa who flew east to implore him to run for president. The governor and his staff did a brilliant public relations job of framing the matter as one about a father wanting to see his son—ignoring, with great success, the part about bigwigs begging him to seek a job he'd repeatedly disavowed wanting.

Family obligations are difficult for any parent to meet, let alone one responsible for a state of nearly nine million residents. Just a few weeks earlier, Christie had skipped the annual Legislative Correspondents' Club Show because he needed to attend his daughter's recital—believed to be the first time in the 120-plus-year history of the club that a governor who was in the state at the time didn't attend. (If he'd flown the helicopter back to central Jersey for the show, would the press have jumped on the baseball/Iowa story as much? Could it, without looking hypocritical?)

New Jersey governors have frequently been criticized for their use of the state helicopter. Ironically, a panel that reviewed gubernatorial travel protocols after Governor Corzine's near-death experience suggested helicopters be used more. Nevertheless, Christie's opponents had a field day, with the Assembly even holding a committee hearing on the topic. Assemblyman John Wisniewski, the Democratic state chairman, dubbed the chopper Hypocrisy One: "This is a governor who as U.S. attorney railed against elected officials blurring the line, but he continues to have selective memory and outrage when it comes to his own activities."[16] The superintendent of the state police, Colonel Joseph Fuentes, defended the trip, saying the pilots would have been in the air for training, regardless of the destination. "There is no additional cost to taxpayers or the state police budget, nor is there any interference with our daily mission, by adding the state's chief executive to any of these trips," he said in a statement.[17]

Records showed Christie had flown in the helicopters around thirty-five times. With the controversy raging, Christie sought to end it by reimbursing the state $2,151.50—plus a bit over $1,200 more from the Republican State Committee—for the chopper use. Christie said his son expressed thanks to him for coming to the game and that he wasn't out joyriding around the state. "It's not like I'm using it as a perk of office. I use it only when my schedule demands really that I use it," he said.[18] Assemblywoman Valerie Vainieri Huttle, a Democrat, seemed to question his paternal bonafides: "Leaving in the fifth inning to meet with wealthy Iowa political donors says something about the governor's priorities."[19] Christie sought to end the story, but he did so unrepentantly: "She should really be embarrassed at what a jerk she is to say something like that."[20]

Judge Thyself Superior

Under Christie's reforms, judges were required to contribute 12 percent of their salaries toward their pensions, up from 3 percent. Other state employees contributed between 6.5 percent and 10 percent. The state had around 430 judges. They don't get regularly scheduled pay hikes, but from 2007 to 2009, Superior Court judges received three annual $8,000 raises, for a total of $24,000 in two years.

A month after the reforms were passed, Superior Court Judge Paul DePascale of Hudson County filed a lawsuit claiming that forcing judges to pay more for their benefits was a violation of the state constitution. The article he cited states a judge's salary can't be reduced during his term. It was designed to prevent the legislature and governor from retaliating against an unpopular ruling by cutting a judge's salary, which must have been a reality sometime in the state's distant past.

Other state employees tried to join in, but since-retired Superior Court Judge Linda Feinberg, the Mercer County assignment judge hearing the case, wouldn't allow it. Most people, even those without law degrees, know salary means salary—the gross pay, not take-home or net. Moreover, there was nothing forcing a judge to accept the benefits package and accompanying deductions. And besides, couldn't judges use the same argument to say paying income taxes reduced their salary? In October, Feinberg issued a fifty-nine-page ruling that found having to pay deductions for health care and retirement did affect salary. She ordered the money that had been deducted be returned to judges. In that respect she made money off her ruling.

Christie reacted swiftly. "This outrageous self-serving decision where a judge is protecting her own pocketbook and those of her colleagues, is why the public has grown to have such little faith in the objectively of the judiciary. This is a blatant attempt to exact for themselves special treatment because they have the power to do so." He said the decision would be appealed—to other judges with built-in conflicts, of course—and if that didn't produce a better decision he wanted the legislature to allow a public vote in a November referendum to make it clear that judges should be affected by the law just like other public workers. "We are not going to leave this in the hands of a self-interested judiciary. We'll put this in the hands of the people who pay these bills."[21]

County-level Superior Court judges were paid $165,000 a year. Chief Justice Stuart Rabner was paid $192,795 and associate justices were paid $185,482. To drive the point home, Christie said a judge contributes less than 10 percent of the actual cost of his or her pension; other state employees provide around half. Retiring judges have an average pension benefit of $107,540 a year (average over a lifetime, $2.3 million) off an average lifetime contribution of $59,300. A retiree would recover his contribution in less than seven months.

This was far from the first time the New Jersey judiciary had conveniently twisted the state's basic governing document to serve its own policy goals. Chief Justice Deborah Poritz, a Christie Whitman appointee, frequently tried to support what she wanted by referring to a constitutional phrase that said the state had to provide a "thorough and efficient education."[22] It actually says thorough and efficient "system" of education. The system is in place, that's schools, teachers, and so forth. No state can guarantee education because that involves too many variables. On another occasion she glossed over that the constitution required the school system was for children "between the ages of five and 18 years."[23] Why would she do that? Because she was in the process of ordering New Jersey to provide preschool for three and four year-olds.

After Christie proposed the constitutional amendment to define salary, Senate president Sweeney said he would wait to see what happened in the courts before considering it. Assembly speaker Oliver was reluctant: "It sets a very unhealthy precedent."[24] After the Supreme Court also ruled the law can't apply to judges, lawmakers quickly agreed to the referendum. An overwhelming 83 percent of voters saw things Christie's way.

The Rise and Fall of Schundler

Bret Schundler joined the Christie cabinet as education commissioner. He was no stranger to Jersey politics, having been the first Republican mayor elected in Jersey City since 1917. He held the office from 1992 to 2001. He's actually a converted Democrat who had run Gary Hart's New Jersey campaign for president in 1984. After Hart lost the primary, Schundler got a job in the sales department at Salomon Brothers, although he had no experience in the financial field. He moved to another firm and was successful enough to retire at thirty-one. He ran unsuccessfully for the state Senate in 1991. The next year Gerald McCann had to quit as Jersey City mayor because of a criminal conviction unrelated to his office and Schundler won a special election to finish the remaining eight months of McCann's term. He won a full term with 60 percent of the vote and a second in 1997 although the city remained solidly Democratic. He had the reputation of someone who could not be bought in a place where corruption was a way of life for most of the twentieth century.

Frank Hague, Jersey City mayor from 1917 to 1947, was known as the granddaddy of Jersey political bosses. When he died his wealth was estimated at $10 million although the mayor's salary was never more than $8,500 a year. His desk had a special drawer, which could be pushed toward the person sitting in front of him so that bribes could be easily deposited.

Schundler ran against Jim McGreevey for governor in 2001 and lost. In 2005 he lost the Republican gubernatorial primary to businessman Doug Forrester, who was beaten by Jon Corzine in the general election.

When Christie nominated Schundler for education commissioner, there were smiles throughout the GOP, but some privately asked each other if the two strong-willed self-made men could get along.

From January to August things went well—but then came the Race to the Top, a federal grant program that could have garnered as much as

$400 million for cash-strapped New Jersey schools. The state narrowly missed out on the money because the application asked for a comparison of education spending for 2008 and 2009 but the state submitted figures for 2010 and 2011. The error cost the state 4.8 points on a 500-point scale. That was more than the difference between New Jersey and Ohio, which was the lowest-scoring state to be awarded a grant. In a State House news conference, Christie said Schundler did provide the right numbers and criticized the Obama administration, which Christie said was too bureaucratic in its response to the error. The Obama Education Department responded with a video of the New Jersey team's interview with the program's judges, which showed otherwise.[25] That wasn't the only problem.

Federal education secretary Arne Duncan had said states had to have a bold plan or buy-in from the education community, which included the New Jersey Education Association, which was no friend of Christie's. Hedging his bets, Schundler worked out a compromise with the NJEA to makes changes to the proposal—"merit pay" was dropped in favor of "bonuses" and the initiative was described as a pilot program in which up to 50 percent of those bonuses could be spent on schools, not individual teachers. Schundler also dropped language that would have based layoffs on teacher effectiveness rather than seniority. Layoffs would be last in, first out. Schundler said he briefed Rich Bagger, then the chief of staff, and messaged the governor about the agreement.

The next morning Schundler said he got an angry call from Christie telling him radio talk show host Jim Gearhart was saying the governor caved in to get union support for the application. "He said the leaders of the NJEA had demeaned him and that it was utterly intolerable for him to be viewed as having given in to them. The money was not worth it," Schundler recalled.[26]

The application was redone to stick with Christie's initial proposals, which cost the administration the teachers union support and probably the $400 million. The error of including the wrong budget years seemed to have grown from confusion in redoing the application so many times under deadline pressure. Schundler himself replaced the correct information with the wrong data.

Saying Schundler lied, Christie fired him. The Democrats sprang into action and called for hearings and subpoenas. Until now, it was starting to look like the governor didn't make mistakes, so this gave them hope in a weird kind of political way. Schundler testified when the Senate subpoenaed him and said Christie—who said "he believed it is always better to be on offense than defense," according to Schundler—told the public the exact inaccurate information he'd warned him not to.

"So if the Governor had given us time to discover how the error occurred, and then fired me for it, I would still feel devastated, losing a job I loved, but I would not feel I had been defamed," Schundler told lawmakers. "Telling the truth is important to me. And the accusation that I misled the governor to hide a poor interview performance is utter nonsense.

"I mentioned that the governor told me he likes being on offense, not defense. As a former prosecutor, that it is not surprising to me. Prosecutors construct their argument and press it," Schundler said. ". . . The governor ignored my correction of his mental script. Whether accidentally or on purpose, he went ahead and said what he had wanted to say from the beginning. He shouldn't have. Good prosecutors don't support their argument with claims they know are false. And they don't make charges against people they know are innocent."

Christie said Schundler's version of events is "absolutely incorrect," though Schundler was under oath. "Bret Schundler and his antics are in my rearview mirror," he said.[27]

"All along, Schundler had always been the one wild-card in the appointments that Christie made," said Joseph Marbach, former Seton Hall University political scientist, now provost at La Salle University. "There was a lot of concern: Would he be able to control Schundler? And I guess the answer is no."[28]

Tunnel to Macy's Basement

As big a deal as that was, the $400 million was small potatoes compared to Christie's run-in with Washington over what was called the nation's largest mass transportation project by supporters and "the tunnel to Macy's basement" by critics. For years there had been plans to build a new rail tunnel from Jersey to Manhattan. It and an accompanying rail line from somewhere in the vicinity of the stalled Meadowlands mega-mall, Xanadu, were speeded up during the final year of the Corzine administration so that Corzine and others could pose with shovels for reelection material. It was pitched as a monumental public works project and a boon to rail traffic, although the latter claim was dubious given the relatively few who would use it.

It was a dumb idea. The New York end of the $9 billion tunnel did not terminate at Moynihan Station, slated to replace Penn Station under Madison Square Garden, but about 180 feet under Macy's department store. Riders would take a steep escalator ride to the surface and walk two blocks if they changed trains. It wouldn't connect to Grand Central Station or any of the rail lines on Manhattan's east side. To add to the unattractive nature of the plan New York refused to pay its share. It would have been paid for by New Jersey, Washington, and the Port Authority of New York and New Jersey, so in effect, Jersey paid twice. But there was more: Under the agreement with the federal government, New Jersey alone was responsible for any cost overruns, which were estimated to be $2 billion to $5 billion, but given the history of such projects, that was a very conservative guess.

The pay-to-play crowd had all but spent the money it planned to rake in and the Democrats saw a chance to make Christie look bad. "If this project gets stalled, it would be an unmitigated disaster for the people of New Jersey,"[29] said state assemblyman and Democratic Party chairman John Wisniewski, as if the state's taxpayers getting stuck with billions of dollars in cost overruns would be a walk in the park. Wisniewski called hearings before his transportation committee.

Phillip Craig, testifying on behalf of the New Jersey Association of Railroad Passengers, called the tunnel "a compromised, mediocre project that will not meet" the region's train needs and will not yield maximum benefit for the money spent. "Most importantly [it] is not affordable given the State of New Jersey's financial condition."[30]

Likewise, Jeff Tittel of the Sierra Club, who supported the train-tunnel concept but not the version that was proposed, said, "Currently, the different groups in charge of mass transit are acting like spoiled children with their own set of choo-choos." Other environmental groups, and groups claiming to be, took part in disseminating false information.[31]

Democratic senator Frank Lautenberg, rarely seen in New Jersey, showed up for a press conference to defend Corzine's Big Dig. He spread false information as well, telling one constituent in a letter the rail line went to the new Moynihan Station.

First Lady Mary Pat Christie got involved in lobbying against this one; she came at it from personal experience: "I just thought whoever came up with that plan didn't commute for 25 years"[32] as she did.

Christie canceled the project, then was asked by Washington to reconsider after alternative financing plans were considered. He did, but killed the largest mass transportation project again after saying New Jersey taxpayers would still be on the hook for the overruns.

"In the end my decision has not changed," Christie said. "I cannot place upon the citizens of New Jersey an open letter of credit. What proponents are asking me to do is hand over a blank check. I simply will not do that."[33]

CHAPTER ELEVEN

The White House Can Wait

From the beginning of his political career it was clear Chris Christie was ambitious and ever aiming for something higher. He took on a veteran state senator in a race than ended before it began. He lowered his sights to a county office and won, then announced less than four weeks after taking office he was thinking about running for the state Assembly.

He knew how to milk the U.S. attorney's office for every ounce of publicity and while he said he didn't have other ambitions, nobody in the New Jersey news media or in politics bought it. When he decided Jon Corzine was beatable, he got into a crowded Republican primary and won, then took on Corzine and won again.

It wasn't long after he became governor that the buzz around the State House was he would seek higher office yet again. Even as he denied interest, he laid the framework for the rest of the country to discover Chris Christie.

Almost every memorable utterance made it to YouTube thanks to his communications staff. It was good stuff, too—the governor calling out a columnist and editorial page editor for being thin-skinned, or telling a complaining teacher she didn't have to do that job if she were so unhappy. He repeated the stories about growing up and the advice from his parents, mostly his mother. And while New Jersey reporters waited patiently to pose questions at press availabilities after news conferences, he was all over the broadcast and cable networks. Press Row in Trenton watched as he did appearance after appearance elsewhere and concluded if he really weren't getting ready to run for national office he would have declined invitations to do those shows.

And there was Christie's staff and style that brought on, as beloved legendary catcher and New Jersey resident Yogi Berra would say, a feeling of déjà vu all over again for folks familiar with his days as a prosecutor.

As outstanding as his U.S. attorney stint had been, there was another career that was remarkably similar, and some think could have been a model for Christie. In 1983, Rudolph Giuliani was named U.S. attorney for the Southern District of New York. The son of working-class parents, Giuliani got a law degree in 1968 and voted Democratic, but he wound up in Washington working in the Ford administration's Justice Department where he was associate deputy attorney general and chief of staff to deputy attorney general Harold "Ace" Tyler. During the Carter administration, he joined a law firm where he was chief of staff to his former Justice Department boss, Tyler, who later was critical of Giuliani, calling his tactics "overkill."[1]

After Reagan took the White House for Republicans, Giuliani, who had changed his voter registration to Independent, then to Republican, was named U.S. attorney. He gained a national reputation by prosecuting Ivan Boesky and Michael Milken of Wall Street and went after organized crime and government corruption. He was credited with 4,152 convictions and fine-tuning the aforementioned perp walk that Christie later would use so well to his advantage.[2] When Christie's office indicted Republican Jim Treffinger, the Essex County executive, officials arrested and hand-cuffed him outside his home at 8:30 a.m., with tipped-off news media staking out the property. He then had to wear leg irons and handcuffs. Treffinger suggested the practice, which hadn't been used in past arrests of public officials, "might have been specifically invented" by Christie for his case and called it "harassment and intimidation." Treffinger knew he was being investigated and had asked prosecutors five times to let him voluntarily surrender, if charges were to be filed. Christie responded: "I am not going to take advice from Jim Treffinger on how to be United States attorney, given his conduct as reflected in the indictment."[3]

Treffinger wasn't the only one to question the perp walks and Christie's overall courtship of media attention and positive press. Robert Del Tufo, a former U.S. attorney and New Jersey attorney general, was a Christie supporter left uneasy by the perp walks. "He is doing an extraordinary job. He's made prosecuting corruption a priority and has energized the staff by proving he is committed to these cases. But I can't condone the show business, that's not something that should be done." Christie shrugged it off. "No one complains when an unarmed drug dealer has the cuffs slapped on him or is shackled in court," said Christie. "Who is doing the most damage to society? Politicians who break the law and the public trust aren't entitled to special treatment."[4]

Giuliani left the federal government as the Reagan era ended amid criticism that he prosecuted cases for political gain, and went into private practice. In 1989 he ran for New York mayor, calling himself a reformer in televised debates.[5] Giuliani got the endorsement of the *New York Post*, but the other three daily papers backed David Dinkins, who won by 47,000 votes out of 1.9 million cast.

Four years later, Giuliani ran for mayor again. Unemployment had spiked due to a national recession and frustrated New Yorkers were growing tired of mostly petty nuisances that eroded the quality of life—peddlers, panhandlers, prostitutes, and the squeegee guys who tried to shake down motorists waiting at stoplights. The former prosecutor promised to use the police department to clean it up. This time Giuliani beat Dinkins by more than 53,000 votes and became the first Republican mayor in New York since John Lindsay in 1965.

In 1997, Manhattan borough president Ruth Messinger, a Democrat, challenged Giuliani, who ran a campaign based on his image as the guy who cleaned up the city. It worked; a Quinnipiac University poll showed him with a 68 percent approval rating. Seventy percent of New Yorkers were satisfied with their life and 64 percent said things were better than four years prior, according to the poll.[6] Giuliani romped, capturing 59 percent of the vote.

As mayor, Giuliani grappled with a budget deficit but lowered taxes. He favored the privatization of failing public schools and a voucher system to give parents more choice in where to send their children. Sound familiar?

The downside was he had a tendency to pick fights—also familiar—that sometimes put him in a bad light. He tore into the reputation of an unarmed black man killed by an undercover police officer. He had an affair and announced at a press conference he was separating from his wife—without first informing her.[7]

The public had tired of Giuliani's fighting jaywalkers, street vendors, and seemingly anyone who looked at him funny. He didn't seek reelection and looked like he was finished politically when on September 11, 2001, terrorists attacked the United States, using four commercial jetliners as weapons, two of them flown into Manhattan's World Trade Center Twin Towers. With President Bush first looking paralyzed before school kids, then taking the long way back to Washington from Florida, and Vice President Dick Cheney hidden away in a bunker, Giuliani stepped up to the plate with eloquence and authority, becoming the face and voice of government in New York and everywhere else. When no one could be sure what came next, he took to the airwaves for reassurance: "Tomorrow New York is going to be here. And we're going to rebuild, and we're going to be stronger than we were before. . . . I want the people of New York to be an example to the rest of the country, and the rest of the world, that terrorism can't stop us."[8] On that day, people around the world were all New Yorkers. Later, Oprah Winfrey would dub him "America's Mayor."

He became an instantly recognizable hero over the globe, although back home there were questions about his administration's decisions, such as locating the Office of Emergency Management on the twenty-third floor of one of the buildings destroyed, despite pleas to put it in Brooklyn, which was considered less of a target.

In 2008, he entered the race for the GOP nomination for the White House but finished fourth in the New Hampshire primary and didn't do much better in later contests. His staff focused on the Florida primary in late January, where he finished a distant third, trailing John McCain and Mitt Romney. Giuliani withdrew from the race and endorsed McCain.

Consider the similarities:

Giuliani and Christie both built their reputations as tough-talking reformers. They both made ample use of the perp walk in front of the media and both were accused of using prosecution as a political weapon. They both supported privatizing failing schools, private school vouchers so parents can send their children where they want to, and charter schools as ways creating competition in education. Christie, like Giuliani, didn't walk away from a confrontation, seeming to enjoy the experience. They both gained national reputations as leaders. The 9/11 attacks that restored Giuliani's political viability had a similar effect for Christie, whose nomination for U.S. attorney was not blocked despite limited qualifications, in part to defer to President George W. Bush's choice for the crucial post.

Kathleen R. Madaras, who was an aide to Giuliani, said she noticed the similarities long before Christie was governor. "It's like he took the first ten chapters of the Giuliani songbook."

Maybe it's more than coincidence that Christie's political team features three high-profile workers from the Giuliani presidential campaign.

Giuliani campaign manager Mike DuHaime, a New Jerseyan, is political adviser to Christie. Maria Comella, Giuliani's deputy communications director for the presidential campaign, is Christie's deputy chief of staff for communications. Bill Stepien was Giuliani's national field director; he managed Christie's campaign and is now his deputy chief of staff for legislative and intergovernmental affairs.

One person who doesn't think Giuliani influenced Christie is Christie.

"I followed Rudy like everyone else did when he was U.S. attorney, especially as a lawyer, and I had a lot of respect for the stuff that he accomplished over there. But it wasn't like I sat down and said, 'Gee, I want to be like Rudy Giuliani.' That wasn't it at all. In fact, I didn't have a role model for how I wanted to conduct myself in the job," Christie said. "What happened and what evolved over time once I got in there was I spent a lot of time with my predecessors. I took them out to lunch, I took them out to dinner. I picked their brains about what they thought they'd done well, what they thought they'd done poorly, where they thought the office was at this point in its history, what they thought needed. I spent a lot of time with a few—Fred Lacey, Herb Stern, and Sam Alito. And then [Michael] Chertoff was my nominal boss, because he was the head of the criminal division at the time, so he and I had a number of conversations about ongoing business matters that would often stray into talking about the office and the history of the office. But I spent a lot of time, probably the most time, with Lacey and Stern, and then a decent amount of time with Sam Alito to get his advice on things. Sam was much more reserved about it, as you might imagine, than Fred and Herb were.

"So Giuliani was not really a role model or an influence. It was more those guys became influences to me, once I got into the job," he said. "Remember, in the beginning, none of them were all that excited about me getting the job. The only one who reached out to me during that interim period, of my predecessors, to try to be helpful, was Herb Stern. All the rest of them, they kind of waited until I actually got in, and then when I reached out to them they were willing to be receptive to talking to me."

Role model or not, Christie wasn't about to make the mistakes Guiliani made in his White House run. If he were going to get into the race he had to be sure he could go all the way. As 2011 approached, questions about his plans increased. He said if he got into the race he could win, but he didn't plan to get in because his kids were still in school and he liked being governor of New Jersey; he had promises to keep. The more he resisted the more Republicans wanted him.

As he publicly rejected the idea, his activities told a different story. He continued to conduct cable and network interviews although it was not clear what that had to do with keeping campaign promises in New Jersey. He traveled to Iowa for an education speech and to Colorado to deliver the keynote to an audience of wealthy conservative donors brought in by David and Charles Koch, owners of Koch Industries and founders of Americans for Prosperity, a national conservative group whose New Jersey leader is, ironically, Steve Lonegan, the rival Christie beat in the GOP primary for governor. Lonegan regularly runs ads critical of the state's Supreme Court or of Democrats, but not of Christie.

The Koch brothers inherited a business from their father and grew it into a conglomerate to where it is the second largest privately owned company in the country with annual revenues approaching $100 billion. The holdings include forest products giant Georgia-Pacific, Stainmaster Carpet, oil refineries, ethanol, and pipeline building. Americans for Prosperity in 2010 circulated a document to politicians asking them not to support climate change legislation. Christie did not sign it. He did, however, pull out of the ten-state Regional Greenhouse Gas Initiative program (RGGI) several months after meeting with David Koch. Christie called RGGI a failure that would result in higher energy taxes and render the state uncompetitive with neighbors not in the program such as Pennsylvania. RGGI was an effort by the supporting states to tackle climate change issues by charging companies for polluting emissions but allowing them to buy credits from firms that don't pollute, which would theoretically offer economic incentive to reduce reliance on fossil fuels.

Christie's action prompted criticism from his mentor, former governor Tom Kean, who speaking at a Rutgers University conference termed what Christie did with RGGI a "shame" and called on informed citizens to "confront those who don't believe in the science of it for the ignorant people they are."[9]

Critics saw a pattern developing. Christie's scaled back renewable energy goals, scaled back rebates for solar panels at residences, vetoed a bill that would have banned fracking, a process of using pressurized fluid to release gas and petroleum for extraction. "All these policies come directly from the Koch brothers agenda," said the Sierra Club's Jeff Tittel, a constant Christie critic.

The Colorado speech, which cost the New Jersey Republican State Committee $63,000 in expenses[10], was not disclosed on Christie's public schedule. It was closed to the media, and tight security was in place to keep what was said there among the people in attendance, but *Mother Jones* magazine obtained an audio recording of Christie's remarks. He said the Democrats were stupid to push a "millionaire's tax" two straight years when they knew he would wipe it out with a veto. That wasn't new; at home he had said the same, adding that if Democrats got by with a millionaire's tax they would try raising the gas tax next.

What he said next in Colorado was new—and incendiary back home, where furious Democrats were already questioning the loyalties and priorities of their party's legislative leaders. He said Democratic Assembly speaker Sheila Oliver had stuck her neck out to get controversial state employee pension and benefit reforms through, on the condition that he line up Republican votes to keep her in power if her caucus tried to oust her from her leadership post. In Jersey, denial was swift and strong. An angry Oliver said it wasn't true: "Governor Christie is making an assertion that I called him for his help in retaining my speakership? Governor Christie is more mentally deranged than some of us thought. Never happened."[11]

Mentally deranged? Well, that's New Jersey politics. Oliver had a legitimate concern about distancing herself from the governor. Hetty Rosenstein, state director of the Communications Workers of America, a state employee union, summed it up thusly: "If you're going to go and get the support of the Republican Party to remain speaker . . . then you shouldn't be in the leadership of the Democratic caucus. It would be an incredible betrayal."[12]

After a year of chewing up and spitting out Democrats with regularity, Christie flipped the script. He started talking about bipartisan accomplishment in his 2011 State of the State and hit the theme often, comparing progress in Trenton with dysfunction in Washington. In a speech about leadership at the Mecca of Republican politics—the Ronald Reagan Library in California—he said, as Reagan had, there is a need to compromise to get things done. You don't compromise your principles, but it means not getting everything you want. That seemed partially aimed at radio talker Rush Limbaugh, who said Christie's reputation as a compromiser gave him pause about Christie's qualifications.

Everyone has a favorite Reagan story, Christie told the library audience, which included Nancy Reagan. His, perhaps not surprisingly, was one with organized labor in the crosshairs. "For me, that story happened 30 years ago, in August 1981. The air traffic controllers, in violation of their contracts, went on strike. President Reagan ordered them back to work, making clear that those who refused would be fired. In the end, thousands refused, and thousands were fired.

"I cite this incident not as a parable of labor relations but as a parable of principle. Ronald Reagan was a man who said what he meant and meant what he said. Those who thought he was bluffing were sadly mistaken. Reagan's demand was not an empty political play; it was leadership, pure and simple."

The speech caught Christie watchers, accustomed to hearing him talk about things Jersey, by surprise when he took the conversation offshore. "The image of the United States around the world is not what it was, it is not what it can be and it is not what it needs to be. This country pays a price whenever our economy fails to deliver rising living standards to our citizens—which is exactly what has been the case for years now."

One of the criticisms of Christie's political background during the White House speculation was that he has no foreign experience. In October 2011 at a news conference with Israel's ambassador to the United States, who grew up in the same town as Christie, the governor announced that he and his wife, Mary Pat, would travel to Israel on a trade mission. He would be the seventh recent New Jersey governor to do so, most of them thinking they had a chance at higher office. One of those was Jim McGreevey, who said in 2000 on a trade mission he met Golan Cipel, a former Israeli sailor working in public relations for the city of Rishon Le Zion, and brought him six thousand miles to work on his gubernatorial campaign. After the election he named Cipel his security adviser despite the fact that as a non-American he couldn't get a security clearance. Cipel was also the love interest alluded to when McGreevey resigned in 2004.

As for Washington, Christie said, "President Obama prepares to divide our nation to achieve re-election. This is not a leadership style, this is a re-election strategy. Telling those who are scared and struggling that the only way their lives can get better is to diminish the success of others. Trying to cynically convince those who are suffering that the American economic pie is no longer a growing one that can provide more prosperity for all who work hard. Insisting that we must tax and take and demonize those who have already achieved the American Dream. That may turn out to be a good re-election strategy for President Obama, but is a demoralizing message for America. What happened to state Senator Obama? When did he decide to become one of the 'dividers' he spoke of so eloquently in 2004?"

Christie had ramped up the criticism of Obama throughout 2011. In November, after Congress's supercommittee failed to come up with a deal on how to reduce the deficit, he went after Obama for not trying to forge a compromise, calling him a bystander and asking him "What the hell are we paying you for?"[13] In December, in an interview on MSNBC's *Morning Joe*, he called the president "someone who still is searching around in a dark room trying to find the light switch of leadership"[14] and blasted Obama for having compared himself with President Theodore Roosevelt.

"That was such ridiculous, pabulum-filled pander. For Barack Obama, who is probably the weakest president I've seen in my lifetime, to stand up and utter his name in the same breath as Teddy Roosevelt? Are you kidding me?" said Christie. "For him to sit there and say, 'it's time for us to step up our game,' 'it's time to meet the moment'? Well, you know, Mr. President we've been waiting for you to meet the moment for three years."

He made a more effective, forceful case against the president than any of the announced GOP 2012 presidential contenders.

"I believe that the Occupy movement and the Tea Party movement come—their genesis—is from the same feeling, which is an anger that government can't get things done," Christie said. "And so, now, that is the last similarity between the Tea Party movement and the Occupy movement. But I believe that the cause for their anger comes from the same place. They look at Washington, D.C., and they look at a president who is a bystander in the Oval Office. You know, I was angry this weekend, listening to the spin coming out of the administration about the failure of the supercommittee. And that the president knew that it was doomed for failure so he didn't get involved. Well then what the hell are we paying you for?

"It's doomed for failure so I'm not getting involved? Well, what have you been doing exactly?" he said. "I mean, I will tell you that I think both parties deserve blame for what's going on in Washington, D.C., both parties do. They're spending more time talking at each other than talking with each other. We all know what the solutions to these problems are, we've done them in New Jersey in many areas, but we don't have the political will to get them done. And in New Jersey, the reason why they got things done is because I called people into a room and said we're going to solve this problem and I had people of good will on the other side who said they believed it was their obligation, regardless of party, to get done things like pension and benefit reform."[15]

That wasn't always his message regarding how to deal with lawmakers.

Among the ways that Christie has whacked at Obama for a perceived lack of leadership is for his refusal to lock congressional leaders in a room to avert a federal government shutdown. "He should get in and lead and bring them together," he told ABC's Diane Sawyer in 2011. "It certainly had a powerful effect when I did it in New Jersey. I think it would be powerful if the president did that. It's time to lead." But as a candidate and as governor, Christie has mocked his predecessor, Jon Corzine, for bringing a cot to the State House and refusing to leave until a budget agreement was reached. He said he would go to the governor's mansion, open a beer, order pizza, watch the Mets, and return when lawmakers reopened the government.

While Christie has worked bipartisan miracles on things like pension reform, his work has not been as much of a compromise as it may appear to those outside New Jersey. In Senate president Sweeney and Assembly speaker Oliver, Christie has Democrats who largely share his views or at least are closely allied with party bosses who do. That wasn't the case with the 2012 fiscal budget, from which Christie cut about $1 billion. The Democrats tried an override and failed. Sweeney then had heated words for the governor, as did Oliver. He called the governor a prick, she said he was deranged. Christie has compromised around the edges but not on his core beliefs—and only on issues he puts on the agenda. He's exhibited little compromise in areas Democrats have sought to advance. He signed fewer laws in his first three years in office than any New Jersey governor in 164 years. He vetoed roughly 180 bills in three years. More than a quarter of his nominees stalled in the state Senate.

A *New York Times Magazine* article called him "The Disrupter."[16] In days past he might have been seen as pretty down-to-earth normal but in this political age, especially next to the assortment of GOP candidates in the spotlight for the 2012 presidential sweepstakes, just talking sense makes him seem a maverick. To his supporters, his normalcy, that Everyman guy-next-door persona, is part of the Christie charm. He's doing what the rest of the country likes to think it would do in his shoes. He calls reporters out for inaccurate articles, he tells radio phone-in questioners it is "none of your business" where his kids go to school, and when faced with rushing back to Jersey or allowing the Senate president to run the state in the middle of a blizzard, he chooses to stay at Disney World with the kids because he promised them the trip. He says things are in bad shape, that we're going to have to sacrifice but down the roads things will be better. He admits he has had a weight problem most of his life and he is working on it—how many millions can relate to that? He forsakes the too serious, politically correct, and phony niceness politicians exude in public for the persona of a regular Jersey guy. What you see is what you get.

It's that fascination that has catapulted him to the front of the line of Republican fund-raisers. In his first twenty months in office, he made more than thirty political appearances outside New Jersey and in one trip in late September 2011 raised over $620,000 from non-Jersey sources, according to state Election Law Enforcement Commission records. His former boss and former U.S. senator from Missouri, John Ashcroft, who was a part of the controversial artificial limbs monitoring program investigated by Congress, donated $2,500, as did the CEO of Ashcroft's law firm, David Ayres. Also from his Missouri trip came $25,000 from August Busch III, former head of the Anheuser-Busch brewery.[17]

Even though he kept saying he wasn't running for president, there was plenty of tease in the other direction. A *Wall Street Journal* column said Christie had been having dinner with foreign policy experts.[18] In the fall of 2011 he scheduled a speaking engagement with another Republican not running, Governor Mitch Daniels of Indiana, and they offered criticism of the GOP announced candidates. A $1.5 million ad campaign sponsored at least in part by two fellow University of Delaware classmates seemed like a campaign ad; it opened with a shot of the Capitol in Washington. The committee sponsoring it was organized under IRS rules as a federal nonprofit 501(c)(4) issues advocacy group, meaning it is not subject to disclosure of donors to the IRS and the donors aren't subject to state pay-to-play laws that restrict contributions made by companies that do business with New Jersey. Although in his gubernatorial campaign Christie pushed for transparency and tighter financial disclosure laws, he would not criticize the committee paying for the ad promoting him when reporters asked about it.[19] He earlier had benefited from a similar group calling itself Reform Jersey Now, whose board consisted of Christie backers and other Republican Party regulars. The group disbanded the day it finally revealed its donor list—which included contributors who couldn't have otherwise given to the party or Christie, given New Jersey's campaign finance restrictions on donations from government contractors.

Christie's Reagan Library speech came at the height of speculation that he might reverse earlier denials and enter the presidential primary. After the warm reception for the speech, the rumors got even hotter. Polls showed he would do well and with the donors he had been courting there was no doubt he could bring in the cash. He said that the kids and Mary Pat were behind whatever decision he made—and acknowledged that he had begun reconsidering a White House run a few weeks earlier, when Mary Pat woke him up at six one morning and said, "If you want to run, go for it. Go for it, and don't worry about me and the kids. We'll be fine."

"We had made this decision, but I felt like the decision had to be made again," Mary Pat said. "I don't think that Chris ever felt that way—he felt that his decision was made. But it's hard to explain when you're in a meeting and you're getting letters from all over the country. It just was really stressful. I felt like, 'Oh my gosh, are we really reopening this again? Do we really have to think about this again?' And so, I wanted to stop thinking about it. So it's true. I turned to him, and I was ready to make the decision. So I was like, 'Okay! Do it. Do it. I can't take this anymore, just do it.'"

"I think she really at that point," the governor said, "rather than there being any sense of indecision about it, she would just rather have me go. And I think she thought the only reason I wasn't going was because I thought that she was against it."

Mary Pat had been a part of conversations with the high-profile people encouraging her husband to run. He said that if she were totally opposed to the idea she would have signaled that by not going and listening.

"I always kind of figured that if I really did want to do it, that if she were opposed, that I could kind of talk her into it and say, 'Look, come on, this is really important to me. I really want to do it. Be with me.' And that she would be. I never doubted it," Christie said. "When people were writing all this stuff out there about it's really Mary Pat, his wife doesn't want him to do it and therefore it won't happen, we would kind of laugh about that. It was true that she really didn't want me to do it, but there's a big difference between what she really would want me to do and what she was willing to participate in.

"That morning freaked me out actually," he said. "She's right. I really felt like I'm listening to people, I'm listening to staff, I'm listening to donors, I'm listening to other political operatives around the country, but in my own mind I had never really felt like the answer ever really turned from no to yes. Or even no to maybe. It was just kind of like, 'Okay, I need to re-evaluate my no and just make sure that I am really comfortable with it.' So when she turned to me, about three weeks before I made the October 4 announcement, and said, 'You should do it. If you want to do it, you should do it. Just do it. Don't worry about me and the kids. We'll be fine.' I mean—I'll remember this for the rest of my life. She was getting out of bed, and she turned over her shoulder and said, 'Don't worry about me and the kids. We'll be fine.' And she walked off to go to the shower. I was like, 'You've got to come back here!'"

They often talk at that early hour because Mary Pat is up and off to work in Manhattan some days and the governor is reenergized after a full night's sleep.

"It is my favorite time to talk. And she's actually pretty indulgent, given that she really has to get to work," he said. "But she came back after she showered. I said to her, 'Are you telling me you think I should run? Or are you giving me permission to run?' She kind of like said, 'Well. I mean, you definitely have permission to run. And, ah, maybe you should run.' I'm like, 'Holy crap!' Now I'm really in trouble if she's telling me she thinks I should run. Now she think I should run? My fear was that maybe I really am missing something here."

Christie had said over the course of the previous year in many colorful ways that he wasn't running. Sometimes he joked, such as when he asked reporters if there was a way short of suicide for him to make clear he wasn't running. Other times he was serious about it, particularly in a May 2011 speech at Princeton University, where he said he wasn't ready and would be filled with self-doubt if he won.

"Just because there's a bit of a siren song being sung from the Potomac—I know who I am. I made a commitment here, I'm going to keep my commitment here. And I also know something else: I'm not ready to be president. And I have people make all kinds of arguments to me about, well, President Obama's experience or President Bush's experience or President Clinton's experience. You see, you miss the point. All those men decided that they looked in the mirror, and in their heart they felt they were ready. Unless and until you can do that, you have no business, in my opinion, in asking for anybody's vote. And I know I'm not ready. And the worst thing in the world—people say to me, 'You could win.' And I say, 'Well yeah, I know I *could* win.' But that's like the dog catching the garbage truck, right? What happens if I actually catch it? (Laughter.) And I win. You know, that's when things really start to get nerve-wracking. . . .

"I think that I've been able to govern the way I've governed, aggressively, because I'm not filled with self-doubt. I will tell you that if I were ever at this moment just elevated to the presidency, I would be filled with self-doubt. And you can't lead if you have self-doubt. It's different than introspection. We all should have introspection. It's different. . . . I can't allow flattery to get in the way of common sense, and I can't allow opportunity to trump my own good judgment. And so that's why I say no. I say no because in my heart, as much as my ego might want to say yes, my heart tells me no."

Still, Christie says he wasn't concerned during the reconsideration about how such statements surely would be used against him if he'd jumped into the campaign.

"I never worried about that because what I've learned in this job is that if it's not that, it's something else. So if it isn't that that I'm going to get picked on for, I'll get picked on for something else. I could deal with that, so, no, that didn't bother me all that much," Christie said. "And in fact, in our internal conversations about it, nobody spoke to me about being bothered all that much by that. I had raised it. I've given like thirty different answers saying I'm not going to run, including I'm not ready. How do I get by that? And everybody I talked to, just everybody I talked to, kept telling me, 'Don't worry about that. That will be the story for the first week that they'll talk about, and they'll play that over and over again. But the reality's going to be you're running, so, okay. Now they're going to have to delve into are you ready.' I remember Maria [Comella] saying to me, 'Just have an answer ready about why you think you're ready.' And I said, 'If you're running, you do think you're ready.'"

The list of people wanting Christie to go for the White House was long and impressive, including people promising to help raise tens of millions of dollars for a campaign and some who had been at the highest level of government and were known internationally.

"Henry Kissinger was incredibly—what would the right word be?— encouraging. Very bold about it and really assertive and had obviously taken the time to think it through. He's incredibly smart. I posed what I thought were challenges or issues. You know, he's good. You can see why he's Henry Kissinger," Christie said. "Everyone from Henry Kissinger to Ken Langone [Home Depot] to Stan Druckenmiller [hedge fund operator] to Dick Grasso [former New York Stock Exchange chairman] to Rudy Giuliani to—I can't even begin to come up with all of them. People were calling— Steve Wynn from Las Vegas. You know, I was getting phone calls in here. Rosemary would come in, 'Steve Wynn's on the phone.' Steve Wynn? I get on the phone, and he's like, 'You have to run.' I'm like, 'Oh, my God. Really?' I had a lot of conversations with political folks—other governors, who really felt it was important for me to do it.

"It was overwhelming. It was completely overwhelming," Christie said. "A meeting we had with Ken Langone and the group he put together in New York was completely overwhelming. And I don't overwhelm easy. But I was sitting there thinking to myself, how the hell did I get into this chair, at this moment, with Henry Kissinger, Stan Druckenmiller, Langone, John Mack from Morgan Stanley?"

Charles "Chuck" Schwab flew from California for the New York meeting. When Christie went to Iowa for a fund-raiser for U.S. Representative Steve King, the coach of the University of Iowa's football team, Kirk Ferentz, told the governor, "You know, you have to do this."

There were regular people, too, who offered their encouragement.

"We went out to Notre Dame. Andrew [his oldest son] was looking at the school, so we went out to visit for the weekend. We're at the basketball game on Friday night, and this guy taps me on the shoulder and says, 'Governor, God, you know, I love you. We love what you're doing. You're a great leader for America.' 'Well, thank you.' 'Can I take a picture?' Sure, we take a picture. I said, 'So where are you from?' And he said, 'Montana.' And I said, 'Where in Montana?' And he goes, 'Oh, a little town called Hysham. You probably wouldn't know it,'" Christie said.

"And he said, 'My daughter's over there.' And he's got his family over there, and they're all waving to me. 'Hysham, Montana?' I said. And he's telling me his daughter's high school graduating class—she was the same year as Andrew, so she's there looking at Notre Dame also—is thirty-two people. So how big can Hysham, Montana, be? Isn't gonna be that big," Christie said. (According to the 2010 census, it has 312 residents.) "The guy was inviting me to come and hunt and fish on his ranch—'if you want to go someplace where nobody knows you.' And I'm like, 'Well that ship has sailed, because obviously you do. It's not like nobody will know me. You know me.' So, it was all those folks. When that stuff's happening, it's really overwhelming."

After the Christies returned from the Reagan Library the governor knew he needed to make a decision soon. That need was reinforced by a FedEx package addressed to the Christie kids sent to their house by a Nebraska farmer, who told the children they needed to convince their father to run for president and that they would be remembered in history for it. The Christies found the letter both cool and creepy.

"I already kind of made up my own mind that I had to decide that weekend. Logistically and every other way, I had to put this to rest, one way or the other," said Christie. "And then that letter came Saturday morning, and the troopers walk in with the FedEx delivery. And I opened this up, and I said, 'You are not going to believe this.' I handed her the letter. And it's telling the kids, 'When the history of this time in our country is written, they're going to write about the fact that the Christie children approached their father on an October weekend . . .' Mary Pat looked at me and said, "Chris, we've got to put this to an end one way or the other.'"

While the nation was speculating about the governor's future, his father, Bill, was going back and forth as well. One day he was sure his son would be in the race, the next day it looked like he wouldn't. He was ready to do his part: "I'll make 8,000 calls a month." And he would have some help. Bill's second wife, Fran, and he have eight kids and thirty grandchildren between them.

Christie knew he had a prime opportunity to win the White House, one that might never come up again. Obama was in a shaky position, the Republican field had not excited voters, he had a good chance to compete in typically Democratic states in the Electoral College. But he didn't think that was reason enough to run. He'd once run for offices nobody in Morris County wanted him to seek, and Republicans thought they'd ended his political career by gleefully booting him after one term in county office. That experience back in the mid-1990s had influenced him when he was being encouraged to run for governor after Governor Jim McGreevey's resignation. Now some in his party thought he ought to be leader of the free world.

"When I walked out of the freeholders' offices in '97, I really never thought I would run for public office again. I just felt like my skills probably weren't best utilized in running for elective office and that if I was going to be involved in public life again, it would probably be in some type of appointed position," Christie said. "After the Morris County experience, I just felt like I must not be cut out for this. I thought I was cut out for it, but I guess I'm not. Mary Pat and I talked about that. I wasn't happy about it, but I really had kind of concluded it wasn't going to happen. And I think that made me very reluctant about '04–'05. I think Mary Pat was reluctant about '04–'05, too, as I remember."

Christie, however, says those who try to draw an exact parallel between what happened to him in his early years and his decision about running for governor in 2005 and the White House in 2012 are wrong.

"It isn't, 'Oh, I ran for the Assembly in '95 and I was called a young man in a hurry and I lost, therefore I'm not going to run in '05 and risk that and I'm not going to run in '12 and risk that,'" Christie said. "Because I know I'm different now. My résumé is different. How people view me is different than they did back then. What's right about it is that that '95 experience, '95–'97 experience, informed the judgments I made about it, but it wasn't like an 'if this, then that' routine. It was more, okay, what did you learn from that about you?"

Christie reached a decision and felt an obligation to tell the people first who worked so hard encouraging him. He made about twenty calls.

"My first call was Ken Langone, who had kind of been the leader of the band. He got on the phone and he said, 'Yeah? What? You got something to tell me?'" said Christie. "And I said, 'I'm not doing it, Kenny.' 'Oh, Governor. Don't tell me that, Governor. Don't tell me that!' And he's like yelling at me on the phone. And I'm like, 'Kenny, it doesn't feel right. I don't feel right to leave here. I'm not doing it. I'm announcing it this afternoon.' And I said, 'I wanted you to know before anyone else knew. You're my first phone call.' And he said, 'Oh, I'm crushed. I'm crushed.'"

On October 4 the governor ended the guessing at a packed press conference in his outer office in Trenton. In a speech that was pure Christie— funny, self-deprecating, lengthy, at times eloquent—he said 2012 was not his time. As is his usual style, he did it without notes or a TelePrompTer. He spoke from the heart and kidded with friends and foes in New Jersey: "You're stuck with me."

The reality is Christie appealed to more elements of his party than the other candidates. Some in the Tea Party movement liked his cut-the-government stance and his direct, tough at times straight talk, though others were wary about his conservative bonafides. Christie is mindful, however, that the Tea Party folks can be radioactive. U.S. Representative Joe Wilson of South Carolina, who famously yelled "You lie!" at President Obama during a joint address to Congress, traveled to Christie's home county to support him when he was running for governor. The event was organized by NJTeaParty; Wilson wouldn't accept a fee, saying he came for Christie "because he is a patriot and a hell of a decent guy." The candidate himself wasn't there; Christie was holding a separate event two miles away. He joked he didn't want to give Democrats a photo op. He later told Fox News, "No, there was no campaigning with Joe Wilson."[20]

Coauthor Michael Symons, writing in *USA Today*, summed it up like this: "Republicans nationally remain enthralled by Gov. Chris Christie, the gregarious, pugnacious, budget-balancing, union-fighting fiscal conservative. Whether they're ready for the Christie who opposes rolling back gun-control laws, believes it's wrong to demagogue about immigration or Muslims, and endorses President Barack Obama's education plans might prove another matter."[21]

The governor opposed a move in Congress that would effectively override New Jersey's strict laws against concealed weapons although New Jersey's entire Republican House delegation voted for it. The "right-to-carry reciprocity" bill would allow anyone with a valid permit to carry in their home state the same right in any other state. In New Jersey holders of carry permits from other states must lock their guns up when entering the Garden State.

"I believe that each state should have the right to make firearms laws as they see fit. I don't believe it's right for the federal government to get into the middle of this and decide firearms laws for the people of the state of New Jersey," Christie told *The Record* in July 2009.[22]

A week before the 2009 election, Christie said in an interview—on Fox News with Sean Hannity, of all places—that he supported some gun control measures. He was asked by Hannity if there are any issues where he is "moderate to left as a Republican."

Christie: "Listen, I favor some of the gun-control measures we have in New Jersey."

Hannity, shaking his head: "Bad idea."

Christie: "Listen, we have a densely populated state, and there's a big handgun problem in New Jersey. Now, I don't support all the things that the governor supports, by a long stretch. But on certain gun control issues, looking at it from a law-enforcement perspective, seeing how many police officers were killed, we have an illegal gun problem in New Jersey."

Hannity: "Should every citizen in your state be allowed to get a licensed weapon if they want one?"

Christie: "In New Jersey, that's not going to happen, Sean."

Hannity: "Why?"

Christie: "Listen, the Democratic legislature we have, there's no way those type of things—"

Hannity: "Would you support it?"

Christie: "Listen, at the end of the day, what I support are common-sense laws that will allow people to protect themselves, but I also am very concerned about the safety of our police officers on the streets, very concerned. And I want to make sure that we don't have an abundance of guns out there. But listen, the issues in this race are taxes and jobs and spending."

Hannity: ". . . Stupid."[23]

In a move just before Christmas in 2010 that looked like a nod to gun rights supporters, Christie commuted the seven-year prison sentence of Brian Aitken, who had been convicted for possessing guns—locked, unloaded but in his car trunk, as well as thirty-nine hollow-point bullets, which are illegal in New Jersey—he had bought legally in Colorado. He didn't have a required carry permit but says he was in the process of changing residences, which exempted him from that requirement. Evan Nappen, Aitken's attorney, called Christie "a hero to gun owners across the nation."[24]

Christie is conservative by New Jersey standards, perhaps the most conservative the state has had in the governor's office. "But even in moments where he's flexed conservative muscles, such as withdrawing New Jersey from a multistate cap-and-trade program aimed at curbing global warming emissions, he raised eyebrows on the right because it was paired with his assertion that climate change is real and influenced by human activity," Symons wrote.[25]

Rutgers University political scientist Ross Baker notes by national standards, Christie is middle-of-the-road. "A great deal of the enthusiasm for him among conservatives has more to do with his confrontation style with unions than with anything else," Baker said. "It's consistent with the belief that you need a fighter, somebody that is aggressive. And that is all true of the governor. But I think he would run into problems with social conservatives."[26]

Mainline Republicans liked that he is intelligent, articulate, and easily wins over listeners. He can bring voters and donors to the GOP tent. He attracted a few dozen high-rollers to a fund-raiser at the California home of Meg Whitman, CEO of Hewlett-Packard—which provided Christie's uncle, Joe Grasso, a few laughs, even though he was far away at the time on a humanitarian mission.

"Thom Weisel, my partner, was at the meeting at Whitman's house. I was in Cumana, Venezuela, and when I came back Weisel, who was a founder at Montgomery [Securities], called me: 'Joey! Why didn't you ever tell me Chris was your nephew?'" Grasso said. "Chris told me what happened. There were thirty-nine people at Meg Whitman's house, and she was raising money, and each of the participants, they were all venture capital guys, and Thom got to speak to him. And Chris said to him, 'I know who you are.' He said, 'What?' Chris said, 'My uncle is your partner.' And Thom said, 'Who's your uncle?' And Chris told him. And he said, 'Joey's your uncle!'

"Thom Weisel is probably the best salesman in the world," Grasso said. "So he calls up and says, 'Joey, you've got to get him to run.' He gives me this whole spiel. I said, 'Thom, if you as the best salesman I know couldn't talk him into it. . . . But I'll do this for you: Give me your cell number, I'll give it to Chris and have him call.' 'You know I could raise him $150 million.' I said, 'Thom, he's not running.' 'The country needs him.' He went on and on. [My wife] Victoria asked, 'What the hell were you doing on with him for so long?' He wouldn't stop about what a real person Chris was and that the country needed him."

On October 11, one week after he took himself out of the race, Christie held a news conference with Mitt Romney and endorsed him. With nothing on his public schedule to give a hint of what was coming, Christie and Mary Pat flew to New Hampshire where Christie said, "I'm here in New Hampshire today for one simple reason: America cannot survive another four years of Barack Obama, and Mitt Romney is the man we need to lead America and we need him now."[27]

While Christie spoke Romney stood slightly behind him and to the right as viewed on TV with a bemused look. Three days prior, the opening skit on NBC's *Saturday Night Live* was built around a Romney speech to Republican donors who kept asking in various ways if there were any chance to get Christie into the race. Jason Sudekis, the actor playing Romney, stood in the same place with the same look as the actor playing Christie, Bobby Moynihan, praised Romney and told the questioning audience to apologize for hurting Romney's feelings. He then asked the Romney character to cover his ears and when he did told the audience he would be on the ticket in 2016. He playfully called the Republican donors in the skit "meatballs." The audience loved it.

What few knew was the same day the *SNL* skit was broadcast, Romney paid a quickly arranged visit to Christie and Mary Pat at their Mendham home. It started with a call from Russ Schriefer, Romney's media consultant, who played the same role for Christie in his gubernatorial campaign, on the day Christie declined to run.

Christie recalled the phone conversation: "Schriefer reached out that day, on that Tuesday, to Bill Palatucci and said, 'Do you think the governor would be willing to take a meeting with Governor Romney sooner rather than later?' And Bill said, 'I'll check with the governor and I'll let you know.' So I told Bill, basically, 'Tell them that Romney can give me a call, and we can talk.' So he called me on that Thursday and said, 'Thanks for not running. I think it was the right decision,'" Christie said with a laugh. "And, as he had many times over the last year, said to me, 'I really would like to have you on the team. It would be important to me. And on Saturday, I'm going to be in Washington giving a speech, and then I'm going to Boston for the weekend to go home. Ann and I would love to stop by, after my speech in Washington to see you and Mary Pat.' So I said, 'Well, let me talk to Mary Pat,' because Saturdays are usually pretty crazy, with kids' sports and other stuff. So I called Mary Pat and said, like, 'Mitt and Ann want to come over for lunch. What do you think?' And she's like, 'Yeah, we can work it out.'"

The governor's public Saturday schedule released Friday night had him speaking to a Hispanic group on one of his favorite topics, education. When he didn't show, a state senator was told one of the Christie kids was ill and the senator was asked not to repeat it. Later, a Christie spokeswoman said "something personal" had come up.[28]

"Originally I was supposed to be able to do both," Christie said. "I was going to do the Latino Leadership Alliance speech, and then Romney wasn't supposed to get to our house until like two o'clock. But for whatever reason, he was an hour and a half ahead of schedule. So I'm literally getting ready to leave for the Leadership Alliance and I get a call from Bill Palatucci saying, 'I know you're not going to want to hear this, but Romney's an hour and a half ahead of schedule, and he'll be at your house by 12:30, quarter to one.' And I say, 'Well, I'm supposed to be at this Latino Leadership Alliance thing, what am I supposed to do?' I got on the phone with [Bill] Stepien, and I said I can't really leave Mitt Romney hanging at the house. So Step called down to our people that we had advancing the thing and said, 'Just let them know that the governor had an issue, and he can't make it.' My Hispanic outreach guy spoke for me that day, Abe Lopez. So Abe gave them the talk, broad outlines about education and stuff. And then Mitt and Ann came a little bit before one o'clock."

Mary Pat recalled, "They landed, and somebody said, 'Well, they'll go get lunch first. We'll stall, we'll go get lunch.' We're like, yeah, Mitt and Ann Romney are going to go and have lunch in Morristown."

The governor didn't like the idea, either. "'Stall them? I just canceled this speech. No, don't stall them, get them here now!' And so then he had a body guy who didn't have a GPS. And they got lost. They're calling me from the road, where are you?"

The Romneys eventually found the Christies and the meeting turned into a picnic on the patio—a stack of sandwiches and a bowl of chips in the kitchen, the two couples sitting outside, the Christies' children taking part for a while.

"Andrew and Sarah sat there for a while and listened. Patrick kind of Rollerbladed over at one point and wanted to say hello to Mitt Romney. 'Can I say hello to Mitt Romney?' 'Yeah, Patrick, you can say hello to Mitt Romney. Call him Governor Romney, okay?' So they came kind of in and out of the conversation," Christie said.

"It was not a policy-heavy conversation. It was basically just us getting to know each other and about how we met, how they met—kind of like the normal kind of conversation you would have with another couple who you're going out to dinner with or something for the first time, you're being brought together for some reason and you're trying to orient each other with each other," he said. "And that's the kind of conversation up until about the last half an hour of it when he finally got down to business. It was the last half-hour of the conversation, not even a half-hour, probably the last fifteen minutes of the conversation, because I made it pretty short."

Mary Pat found Romney formal. "But he was lovely. He was asking the kids stuff, he was asking me about the pictures. But he seemed genuine. I've got to tell you, I really think that he is, and his wife's great. But definitely, he is stiff and formal."

Christie felt Romney filters what he says—"He's formal but not un-friendly," said Christie, who says he has advised the candidate to be "edgier and bolder"—while his wife, Ann, says what she feels. "What struck me was this is obviously a guy who has a number of children of his own and a number of grandchildren of his own, and so he knows how to deal with kids. That came very naturally to him, dealing with children. Probably more naturally than it was dealing with us in the beginning. He was really—not that he was unnatural with us, but he was really easy with the kids. He went back and forth with them pretty nicely."

Bill Palatucci said after being around Romney and Christie several times in private situations he noticed, "They like each other's company. They are two very different guys, but they really get along. And you get no sense that Romney at all feels upstaged or threatened. He's thrilled to have this guy at his side. So whether that turns into this may be an invitation to join the ticket, we'll have to see. But the starting point is just one real friendship."

The lunch meeting at Christie's house seemed like a VP vetting, which made sense to political veteran Palatucci. "If I were Romney I would be testing that relationship in a number of different settings."

The Christie-for-VP speculation wasn't limited to New Jersey political reporters looking to spice up their 2012. On the afternoon of the New Hampshire primary, the *National Journal*'s Josh Kraushaar wrote a column about the particular importance for Romney, if he were to win the nomination, of picking a running mate who excites the base, effectively attacks Obama, and doesn't alienate independents. Kraushaar devoted 161 words combined to six prospective candidates—Senator Marco Rubio of Florida, Governor Susana Martinez of New Mexico, Governor Brian Sandoval of Nevada, Governor Nikki Haley of South Carolina, Governor Bob Mc-Donnell of Virginia, and Senator Rob Portman of Ohio. He then spent the next 250 words on Christie alone, saying he "occupies a category all to himself."

"He's a conservative rock star, whose acid attack lines against Obama cast aspersions on his performance in office, not his pedigree to hold it. He's built up his own impressive résumé, cutting entitlements and taking on unions, all while holding a strong approval rating in a solidly blue state. He's got both suburban and working-class appeal. There's no coincidence that the one Romney event in New Hampshire that generated a 2008-like atmosphere was last Sunday night's rally Romney held with Christie. The big risk with Christie is whether Team Romney would want to have a running mate that would overshadow the nominee and risk being occasionally off-message," wrote Kraushaar.[29]

"A Romney-Christie ticket would also put two Northeasterners on a ticket for a party that's concentrated in the South and Mountain West. Picking Christie would be akin to Bill Clinton shedding his party's liberal image by picking another Southern Democrat, Al Gore, to run with him in 1992. Tapping Christie would allow Romney to brand the Republican ticket as a pair of can-do executives with a record of getting things done— much like the Clinton-Gore ticket's youth emphasized the generational gap between the two tickets."

Romney and Christie have had a working relationship for some time. They have common experiences, both became Republican governors in Democrat-leaning states. Romney endorsed Christie for governor and gave $25,000 to New Jersey Republicans. In December 2011, Christie, his brother, Todd, and Palatucci returned the favor and then some, raising $1.1 million for Romney at a dinner event in Morris County. Christie praised Romney as mature, intelligent, thoughtful, honest, and for having "the integrity of his principles." Romney told the gathering: "I've watched Chris Christie from afar just in awe of his accomplishments. This guy's just amazing. The whole nation's watching this guy."

Romney was the first GOP contender to visit Christie.

While in New Hampshire to endorse Romney, on the afternoon before the Bloomberg News–sponsored GOP debate, Christie and Romney sat with NBC News' Jamie Gangel for a joint interview in which the subject of the vice presidency for Christie came up. Romney gave Christie an opening through which he could have emphatically ended such speculation.

Romney: "Well, of course, he'd be on anyone's short list. He may take himself off the list and say: 'No way,' he'd have no interest."[30]

Christie could have. But he didn't. Asked if they'd be a good match, Christie left the ball in Romney's court:

"Honestly, like I said before, I don't know that I'd be anybody's good match in that regard," Christie said, laughing. "But ultimately, that kind of thing is up to the person who's the presidential nominee to decide who they think is the best person for them and most importantly the best person for the country."

America noticed. The Project for Excellence in Journalism, which studies media trends, said presidential politics—driven by Christie's announcement not to run, and to a lesser extent Rick Perry's hunting camp with the N-word rock, and Sarah Palin's decision not to seek the White House—was the second most covered story of the week. The economy was first. In third place was the death of computer legend Steve Jobs. While Christie's announcement had aired live on national cable television, one place it didn't appear was on NJTV, the TV operation that took over after the governor forced the state-run New Jersey Network off the air. NJTV was showing *Angelina Ballerina*, a cartoon show, to its Jersey audience.

The next month, Christie was back in New Hampshire to thank Romney's Manchester volunteers for their efforts. Romney himself was in Michigan preparing for the latest in what seemed to be an endless series of GOP debates. Then Christie went to Nashua, where he was introduced by former New Hampshire governor John Sununu, who was chief of staff to President George H. W. Bush. Sununu called Christie one of the great practitioners of "the Sununu theory of governance called warmth and charm." Christie spoke without notes and, picking up on Sununu's line, said those who weren't committed to Romney had better be the next time he comes to New Hampshire: "I was real nice to you tonight, I won't be next time." He could have just as well have called them "meatballs," like in the *Saturday Night Live* skit; the crowd roared its approval.

During a radio interview on that trip, he sidestepped questions about being on the Romney ticket as vice president.

He elaborated for the Manchester *Union Leader* newspaper, saying he can't imagine Romney or any presidential nominee asking him to be his or her running mate. "I just don't think it's my personality to be a number two to anybody and be standing behind them nodding my head. I don't think that's me. I can't imagine any presidential candidate looking at me and saying, 'He'd be perfect for this.'"

But that door remained ajar.

"I won't say 'absolutely not' because I think it's rude and presumptuous to say for something that I haven't been offered if offered I wouldn't take it. But I just can't imagine it's going to happen."[31]

Christie had the makings of a productive vice president. On the campaign trail he is tenacious, going after political enemies with gusto. They could have sold tickets to a Christie–Joe Biden debate. He could do an administration's in-your-face, tell-it-like-it-is work while the president remained in the Oval Office being presidential. He wouldn't be happy going to state funerals and cutting ribbons at new federal buildings; Christie would want to play an active role, probably getting foreign relations experience, something missing from his résumé, although, as the Reagan Library speech showed, he can speak eloquently of our place in the world. And he would, as he always did before, have his eye on the next rung on the ladder.

University of Virginia political scientist Larry Sabato said a Romney-Christie ticket could have done well in the Electoral College. "If they were on a ticket together, then the Republicans could compete in Pennsylvania, Michigan, Wisconsin, and New Hampshire. Suddenly, Obama's got a big problem. He has to worry about some of what he thought was his base." Then there is New Jersey, "dependably blue" since 1992—but that wasn't true for the most part of the second half of the twentieth century. New Jersey went for the GOP in every presidential race from 1968 through 1988.

Christie said he knows his reputation is tied to what he accomplishes in New Jersey, meaning it is dependent on a legislature controlled by Democrats who might decide to start denying him victories in advance of his 2013 reelection or potential run for national office.

"Let me just say this. If, in fact, they're worried about their political future or mine, the best way to do it is for us to do our jobs," Christie said. "Because I'll tell you, I will call them out on this. If they want to become like the Republicans and Democrats in Washington, D.C., who sit around and just yell and scream at each other, posture and get nothing done, I will call them out for that.

"The reason why people, I believe, are happy with the job that I'm doing is because I brought people together, because we forged bipartisan compromise, because we've gotten things done," Christie said. "They have to also look at the results. Over two years, I've produced results. I've produced budgets that have passed the Democratic legislature. I've produced a cap on property taxes, cap on interest arbitration, pension and benefits reform that nobody thought was going to get done.

"But also, I think we should have political fights in public. We should let people know where we stand, and then if we can find a boulevard we can travel on to compromise," Christie said. "There's always a boulevard between violating your principles and getting everything you want. I don't expect to win everything I want. I will not violate my principles. Sometimes that boulevard's wider. Sometimes it's narrower. My job is to navigate the car on that boulevard. I've done it for two years, and unless they want to become like the Republicans and Democrats in Washington, D.C., where all they care about is posing and preening for the camera and not getting things done, then they're going to continue to work with me. If they don't want to continue to work with me, I'll bring my cause to the voters and we'll see how we do."[32]

Many conservatives said they wouldn't vote for Romney, and those same folks might not see Christie as their cup of tea, either. Even Rush Limbaugh—who early in the governor's term quipped, "Is it wrong to love another man? Because I love Chris Christie."—was throwing up red flags after Christie's Reagan Library speech, saying he sounded too much like Senator John McCain. Though Obama entered 2012 in a shaky position, he wound up winning reelection by nearly five million votes. Republicans stung by the loss searched for a new direction, and while some conservatives don't think Christie can provide it, enough people like him to make clear he's positioned, at a minimum, to influence the party for years to come.

After a speech at the University of Delaware, when asked about running for president in 2016, he said, "That's five years from now. Five years ago nobody was clamoring for me to run for president of the United States. A lot can happen in five years in American politics and so I have no way of knowing.

"But my reason for not running this time was not because I was saying I never want to be president. It was because I didn't feel like now was my time. Because I hadn't finished the job in New Jersey. And I didn't feel comfortable leaving after twenty months as governor," he said. "That's kind of like going with one woman to the dance and then you see a better-looking woman come in the room and she comes up 'Hey you want to you dance,' and you go, 'Yeah sure, okay, you're better-looking, let me go with you.' You would have a name for a guy like that, right? So whether it's dealing with women or dealing with politics, I don't think there's a whole lot of difference."[33]

When asked why the media were so fascinated with him running for president, he relied on humor:

"I'm not so sure but I think they would find me fairly entertaining. From a media perspective, they thought, 'Look at this, like a big fat guy for president. Wouldn't that be unusual?'" he said. "And I would like to think that some of it also was that I've had a pretty good record as governor and they thought, 'Well maybe this guy looks like he could get something done, let's give him a chance.' But in the end none of those were good enough reasons for me."

In politics moods and opinions change quickly, a month can be an eternity. One day you're on top of the polls, the next you're a cellar-dweller. What if 2012 was the only chance Christie would get at the biggest of all brass rings?

"I'm comfortable, and I think Mary Pat's comfortable, with the idea that if it turns out that 2012 was our only real opportunity to run for president, that we're okay with having passed it by. And if it never happens, it never happens. It's not like I'm sitting here saying to myself, 'I must do this. I must do it. I just have to figure out when.' That's not it. It's if that opportunity comes again, we see where we are in our lives, what we feel, what the politics of the situation are, all things you would normally consider in a presidential race, and then make your decision."

A part of his consideration is that after Jim McGreevey was forced to resign in 2004, there were scores of people considered smart and informed telling Christie it was his time and his only time to run for governor. He ignored them, watched Jon Corzine win in 2005, then roared back in 2009 to defeat the well-heeled incumbent.

"There were lots of smart people saying to me, 'It's your only chance. McGreevey got run out of the office. The corruption, this, that. Perfect moment for you. This moment will never repeat itself again. Then you're going to have to run against an incumbent Jon Corzine. He'll be impossible to beat," Christie said. "You hear all that stuff, all of it. What you realize is, everybody's got an opinion. That's what cracks me up about politics. I say this to Mary Pat all the time. I feel like I've reached a pretty decent level in my life in understanding this business, and I've reached a good level. It's like—to me it's like baseball. Everybody who ever played Little League thinks they know how to tell Joe Torre how to manage the Yankees in Game 6 of the World Series. 'How could he do that? Why didn't he bunt the guy? When I was in Little League, I would have.'

"And I think the same thing about politics. I can't tell you the smart people who will come to me for advice and then do the exact opposite of what I advise them to do because they think, well, they understand, this isn't that hard. They know how to do this. I remember saying to one guy who's an investor, I said to him, 'You know, this would be like me coming into your office because we own stocks and bonds and looking over your shoulder and saying, 'No, no, no, no, no. Don't buy that. Buy this.' You'd look at me and kick my ass out of the office. But yet you feel free to come into my office and tell me that I should do this or that because you read the newspaper every day. You know, I do know a little more about this than you do,'" Christie said. "When I listen to all those people who say things like, 'This is your only chance,' all the rest of it, in that context—they could be right, but it won't be because they knew what they were talking about. It will be for a whole other set of reasons. And if that's the case, that's the case. I can live with it."

Christie said his governing style fits his personality—that it wouldn't work for everybody, because for some it would be forced.

"What you see is what you get," he said in an interview in his office. "Staff will tell you that what you see behind the podium when I'm giving press conferences is what they get in this room. If they ask me something that I think is stupid, I go, like, 'Are you kidding me?' And I just take it to them. If, on the other hand, they do something that I think is really great, they also get that kind of feedback from me in what I think is a really genuine and emotional way, that I really value the people around me. And I think that comes across to the folks. And I think that to the extent that I've gotten this popularity around the country, I think it's for that reason, in addition to the fact that we've shown we can accomplish things. I think people look at me and say, 'Man, you know, he's just saying it.' And I feel somewhat liberated to be able to do that because I'm a Republican in New Jersey, right?

"So, you know, I can't sit here and calculate because even if I did everything perfectly politically, I could wind up not being reelected if that's what I chose to do, if I chose to run, I could wind up not winning anyway, just given the demographics of the state and the way things work. So I think what you see is what you get. I think that's the thing that I'd like them to know about me the most.

"And I think that the biggest misconception that gets coupled with that, which bothers me substantively, not stylistically, all the discussion of my weight," Christie said. "Like I said one day out there, I'm not in denial about it. I have a mirror. I get it. I know. But that people draw a line between that and being undisciplined is just one of the most ignorant things that I can imagine, and it's so completely untrue. I don't think anybody would call me undisciplined. I work incredibly hard. I work smart. I know where I want to go. I keep things in the lane I want to keep them in, when I want to, and I move out of that lane when I want to.

"I think it was the central miscalculation of the Corzine campaign," he said. "In the end, I think if you go back and you analyze that campaign, the central miscalculation was, 'This fat guy is undisciplined. We're going to have a camera following him twenty-four hours a day,' which they did, 'and he is going to blow up. We're going to keep picking at him, picking at him, picking at him, and he's so undisciplined that he's going to make a huge mistake, and we're going to win.'

"And they're still waiting. It's now a year of campaigning and two years of governing, and they're still waiting for that moment to happen, for that defining, ugly moment that they think is going to happen because they drew a direct line between somebody's who overweight and somebody who's undisciplined," said Christie. "And it's just not true. It could be true, but it's not like night follows day. And so, I think for people in the country, I think most people in the country already understand that, because people who struggle with their weight around the country know that about themselves."

As for his reputation as an abrasive, blowhard egomaniac and whether that would play outside New Jersey, brother Todd knows him better than anyone other than Mary Pat and says that's not the real Chris Christie.

"He's got to be the way he is now. He's gotta be tough because historically if you look back at the politics of New Jersey, if you show weakness they're gonna eat you up alive," Todd said. "The downside of that is that people think you're a nasty bully. He's not like that at all."

At home, said Mary Pat, the governor is not the combative person in the YouTube videos. They don't disagree on much—except baseball, because she is a Phillies fan. "He's very assertive. He's an amazing father. He's a great partner." Her brother Brian calls Christie "a very loving man. He kisses me when we see each other, gives me a big Italian kiss on the cheek."[34]

His father, Bill, said he thinks the governor often responds in the manner things are presented to him. "He's always been the way he is now, you never heard anything other than a straightforwardness. I don't think that people are used to straightforward answers. I know it's genuine. It's not made up. That's the kid I know."

Others who have known Christie all his life agree on his basic personality traits, intelligence, and driving ambition to get to the top, all the way back to his days at Squiretown Elementary, a small school next to a working farm complete with a horse the children fed. The school's former principal Ralph Celebre said the Christie he remembers was beloved by everyone, even the school custodians, and was a smart, cheerful kid.

Joyce Cushman is a family friend and former school district employee. She remembers a day on the Squiretown playground when Christie was in the second grade.

"There was this little, tiny, dark-haired kid, standing in front of a flag-pole, and so earnest. He looked up and said, 'Mrs. Cushman, I'm going to be president someday.' I've never forgotten it because he was so serious. And I thought at the time, 'You know? This kid may do it.'"[35]

CHAPTER TWELVE

◆

A Rising Star in the Republican Galaxy

Since crossing paths in the 2009 election, the lives of New Jersey's two most recent governors could hardly have been more different.

Jon Corzine returned to Wall Street as chief executive officer of MF Global Holdings Ltd., a Manhattan-based commodities brokerage. He didn't make a clean break from politics, though, because his company issued a prospectus to sell five-year notes that contained a "key man event" clause, which stipulated that if Corzine left due to an appointment by the president of the United States prior to July 1, 2013, the notes would pay an extra 1 percent. Some wags said that promise was like a leggy blonde on the side of the road hiking her skirt to attract drivers.

Corzine got Washington's attention—but not the kind he wanted. On Halloween 2011, his company filed for bankruptcy protection and was suspended from doing business with the New York Federal Reserve. MF Global admitted using clients' money as its trouble mounted. Federal rules require client money and company money to be kept in separate accounts. Corzine was summoned before congressional committees to explain what happened. He has not been charged criminally but potentially faces civil actions. In February 2013, regulators from the National Futures Association opted against banning him from the industry for life, as some of its members had urged.

His reputation among journalists, politicians, and Wall Street colleagues headed south. He was further humiliated when President Obama's campaign and the Democratic National Committee returned more than $70,000 in contributions from him. The guy who had bought his way into the Senate and governor's office and Democratic Party inner circles was told his money was political poison.

Chris Christie didn't gloat; in fact, for a man whose family and friends had been dragged through the mud by Corzine's campaign, he was downright reserved.

"I don't think anyone could have predicted this," he said. "Plus, I've done enough of these white-collar cases to know they're a lot more complicated than they look from the outside, and I think it will be years before we really know what happened at MF Global, whether he knew or didn't know, what he knew, when he knew it. Sometimes the obvious things you leap to as a member of the public when you're a prosecutor turns out not to be the case, or sometimes it could turn out to be much worse. So I guess that seven years has led me to a disposition of not jumping to conclusions. Yeah, sure, I'm surprised. I didn't think there's anything in his background that I saw that would lead me to conclude that he would drive the firm into bankruptcy."

As Corzine's star diminished, Christie's grew to become one of the brightest in the Republican galaxy. After saying he would not seek his party's nomination for the White House, Christie hit the trail for the man who would eventually get the nod, Mitt Romney, and other Republican candidates for national and state offices. He raised money and charmed crowds across the nation. There were awkward moments, when audience members asked why he was supporting Romney instead of running himself.

While Christie insisted publicly that he wanted to remain governor, his schedule stirred speculation he could become Romney's vice-presidential running mate. A trip to Israel during 2012's Holy Week, which included meetings with Prime Minister Benjamin Netanyahu and President Shimon Peres, concluding with a short vacation in Jordan, added to the impression he was trying to develop his foreign-policy knowledge. At his first public appearance after returning home, Christie traveled into New York City to address the George W. Bush Institute Conference on Taxes and Economic Growth, where he voiced sentiments that, had they been uttered a few months later, would have reminded some of Romney's ill-fated, in-private "47 percent" remarks that went public and helped doom his campaign.

"I've never seen a less optimistic time in my lifetime in this country," Christie said. "And people wonder why. I think it's really simple. It's because government's now telling them, stop dreaming, stop striving, we'll take care of you. We're turning into a paternalistic entitlement society. That will not just bankrupt us financially. It will bankrupt us morally. Because when the American people no longer believe that this is a place where only their willingness to work hard and to act with honor and integrity and ingenuity determines their success in life, then we'll have a bunch of people sitting on a couch waiting for their next government check."

Christie had become enough of a political celebrity for comedian Jimmy Kimmel to crack jokes about him—about his weight, naturally—at the White House Correspondents' Dinner in April 2012. Christie laughed it off and said it wasn't a bad thing to have actress Sofia Vergara consoling him from one seat over; Vergara later attended a California fund-raiser for Christie's reelection campaign. Even simple things in Christie's life and work were becoming major media stories. When he attended a Springsteen concert after the Middle East trip, the *New York Post* said Christie had fallen asleep at the show; he insisted—taking offense, only half-feigned—that he had not nodded off but closed his eyes to absorb Bruce's spiritual "Rocky Ground." After the death of singer and actress Whitney Houston, who was born, raised, and lived in New Jersey, Christie ordered state flags lowered on the day of her funeral—setting off a national conversation about whether he was honoring someone who derailed her own career and life by abusing drugs.

And there were more examples of Christie's famous bluntness, which drew attention as his national profile grew. During 2012, Christie called a former Navy SEAL, who had become involved in local politics, "an idiot" after a shouting match at a town hall meeting. He called a newspaper reporter from *The Record* the same thing for asking an off-topic question at a news conference. He stalked down a Seaside Heights boardwalk, ice-cream cone in hand, hollering back at a heckler on a bicycle in an incident someone recorded and posted online. He told billionaire investor Warren

Buffett to "just write a check and shut up" about advocating for higher income taxes for the rich.

Despite those incidents, or perhaps in part because of things like them, Christie was indeed being vetted by Romney's camp as a possible vice-presidential running mate. He'd gotten a call from Romney in April asking if he could be vetted, filled out a twenty-plus-page questionnaire, turned over ten to twelve years of tax returns, and designated longtime friend Bill Palatucci as a go-between, so Beth Myers and the search committee didn't have to directly barrage Christie with calls and requests for documentation.

Christie found out he wasn't the choice just a few hours before word that Paul Ryan would be the running mate began leaking out on Friday, August 10. Christie was with Palatucci, flying back on a Wi-Fi–enabled private plane to Morristown Municipal Airport from Montana, where he had wrapped up a three-day fund-raising trip through western states for Romney and a few gubernatorial candidates. Palatucci got an email from Russ Schriefer, a senior advisor to Romney, who had handled the ads for Christie's 2009 campaign: Christie needed to call Romney right away. That wasn't possible for about ninety minutes, but Christie called from the airport terminal around 9 p.m. Romney told him he was going elsewhere for a running mate but asked if Christie would be willing to do the keynote speech at the Republican convention. The lateness of the time Christie was informed, and the fact that the keynote speaker's slot hadn't been filled publicly, suggest he was among the finalists for the V.P. post.

"I'd always said that I really didn't want, and I told him that—that it was not something that I really wanted and that I thought there were other people that were better suited for the job," Christie said, in a February 2013 interview. "I told him that when we discussed it. I was very candid with him about it. But I'm also a very competitive guy, too, so you hope if you were asked that if you got to the point where you decided to say yes, then you could make some difference. So it's not like I look back on the campaign and say, 'Oh, that was a good miss.' No, I don't look at it that way. I think every campaign becomes different based on the individuals you put into it. So who knows, could it have been different? I don't know. I certainly don't regret being considered."

Christie says he never thought he'd be asked and never seriously thought about how he'd respond if Romney did choose him.

He told former Governor Thomas Kean, in a chat in his Statehouse office while the vetting was at its peak, that he would turn down the offer.

"You know," Kean said, "I'm hearing from some folks, some sources I have, that this is getting serious. What if he asks you?"

"I think I'd say no," Christie said.

Kean laughed. "I'd love to be in the room for that."

Christie acknowledges that turning down the nomination wouldn't have been easy.

"I think it would be very difficult to say no if asked," Christie said. "But I would have had a lot of questions about my role and how he envisioned my role, because I think I'm a relatively young guy and I've got a really good job that I enjoy. So I would have wanted to have a really in-depth conversation about how he envisioned the role, both in the campaign and then ultimately if we were to win. So you don't know if that would have all worked out to both of our satisfactions, if he were really interested. But we never had to get there."

Christie got to work on his keynote speech, which he wrote with communications director Maria Comella, economic adviser Bob Grady, and Palatucci. Christie's staff had provided him transcripts of every Democratic and Republican convention keynote speech since the 1960s. He watched speeches on YouTube, if they were available. In all, they went through fourteen drafts of the speech, whittling it down from around 4,500 words to around 2,600. And for all his jokes about how expectations for the speech were unrealistically high, he did little to dim the spotlight, engaging in a round of pre-speech interviews on the networks' morning shows and even launching a convention-week blog with insider looks at his week in Tampa.

In true Christie style, where flag-lowerings and Springsteen concerts somehow become tangled tales, even the introduction to his speech was tinged with drama. Convention organizers, worried that Christie's speech would extend past 11 o'clock, when network coverage was ending, wanted to skip the two-minute, forty-second biographical video Christie's team had produced to run before the speech. Christie insisted, and organizers reluctantly relented—and while Christie finished on time, there were points where he zipped through the speech to do so. Then the speech, while well received in the Tampa Bay Times Forum, was largely panned, largely because Christie was two-thirds of the way through—sixteen minutes and twenty-seven seconds, in a speech of just under twenty-four minutes—before he mentioned Mitt Romney for the first time. "This speech not only was a bad speech," MSNBC's Rachel Maddow said afterward. "I think this was one of the most remarkable acts of political selfishness I have ever seen."

Christie said people were looking for ways to be critical. "I think the people that mentioned that were just people that were caught in an old analysis, which is: Is this guy a rival of Romney's, or is this guy a partner? Clearly I was a partner, but they wanted to make the story, so they made the story," he said.

Christie said none of the speech's earlier drafts mentioned Romney any sooner than the version he delivered.

"I think what people confused was a nominating speech and a keynote speech," Christie said. "I went back and listened to other keynote speeches. I went back and listened to Mario Cuomo's keynote speech, where he never mentioned Walter Mondale, not once. I went back and listened to Barack Obama's keynote speech for John Kerry, where he was fifteen minutes into the speech before he mentioned John Kerry. I went back and listened to those things because I wanted to make sure I wasn't coloring too far outside the lines in what was traditional. So I think all of that had much more to do with all the speculation about me running or not, and so people never quite got over the idea that Romney and I might be rivals rather than partners. So they would read into something like that."

Christie's defense is a little fuzzy on the details. Obama's entire keynote lasted around fifteen and a half minutes; he mentioned Kerry for the first time around 45 percent of the way through, a little more than seven minutes into the speech. Cuomo's speech, indeed, didn't mention Mondale—though as Christie acknowledged in an interview, "talked about Reagan, significantly." It was an attack on Reagan's record, comparing Republican and Democratic priorities as a way to frame the choice between the two parties. "I don't think people have found anything wrong with the governor of New Jersey waiting before he used the candidate's name," Cuomo told Fox Business Network on August 31, 2012. "It was that he spent those sixteen minutes talking about himself. That's not a mistake I made all those years ago."

Another criticism aimed at Christie after the keynote was the apparent divergence between one of the lines in his speech—"Tonight, we choose respect over love"—and one spoken earlier in the hour by Ann Romney— "Tonight, I want to talk to you about love." The line in Christie's speech was a familiar one to audiences who had heard his town hall tales, as he relayed advice from his late mother about relationships with women: Choose respect over love, because that has a chance of lasting, but love without respect is fleeting. "It applies just as much to leadership," he told the convention crowd. "In fact, I think that advice applies to America today more than ever. I believe we have become paralyzed by our desire to be loved."

"Two totally different topics, and while the words are the same, the contexts are completely different," Christie said in an interview. "Ann Romney's talking about a long-term marriage where she talked about how he shows his love to her and to their children. I'm talking about pandering politicians who care more about having folks kiss their rear ends and tell them how great they are because they always say yes as opposed to being more about being respected by them by giving them the hard answers they need to hear. So I never saw the conflict between the two, and she [told me she] didn't see the conflict in it either."

Critics panned Christie for the line, saying it undercut Ann Romney's efforts to help Americans warm up to the Republicans' formal, stiff nominee. Christie had never heard Ann Romney's speech, though. Originally, she was supposed to speak on Monday night but got rescheduled because the broadcast networks opted not to carry any of that night's programming. Ultimately, the convention schedule was scrapped that day due to Hurricane Isaac. She was plugged into the same 10 p.m. hour as Christie because it was the only hour the broadcast networks carried live. Responsibility for correcting the perceived conflict between the speeches would seem to fall on the convention organizers, who'd read drafts of Christie's speech and watched him rehearse it twice in Tampa, but didn't raise concerns about it—not about the love line, not about how long the speech went before the Romney mention, not about anything at all.

In that regard, Christie's RNC experience was like that of South Carolina Governor Nikki Haley, who was two-thirds of the way through her convention speech before she mentioned Romney. In a visit to *USA Today*'s workspace at the convention, she said convention organizers had approved her speech without making changes.

"They were clearly looking at it and listening to it," Christie said. "Their instruction to me from the beginning was 'Be yourself, that's why we want you.' So I don't think they wanted to do a whole lot of manipulating in the speech that they thought would make it sound less like me. I think they wanted it to sound as I sound. I wouldn't call them hands-off, because they did review it with us. But no, they didn't change a word of the speech in the end."

Although Christie said the day before delivering the speech that he didn't make changes to the text to adjust for following Ann Romney and that he wrote it without knowing who'd be on before him, the morning after the keynote he told delegates from Pennsylvania and New Hampshire he didn't talk more about Romney because she had done so. "I really thought that my job last night was to lay out both the stakes in this election and the choice in this election. And as it turned out with Mrs. Romney going first . . . it actually freed me up to put the choice in even more general terms than I was originally gonna do. It allowed me to be able to let Ann Romney talk about Mitt Romney the person."

Christie remained active in Romney's campaign after the convention. In all, over the course of roughly a year, Christie did two dozen events outside of New Jersey for Romney, including rallies in Iowa, New Hampshire, Ohio, and Virginia, as well as fund-raisers in thirteen states and Washington, D.C., which he says raised around $20 million for the campaign. He also did more than thirty other fund-raisers outside New Jersey in 2012 for gubernatorial candidates, congressional candidates and other GOP committees, including a fund-raiser and rally with Wisconsin Governor Scott Walker during his recall election. National politics dominated his fall calendar: Of seventy items on Christie's public schedule between the end of the political conventions September 10 and October 26, fifty were campaign-related events outside of New Jersey.

Back in Trenton, Democrats sought to turn Christie's frequent trips out of state into a political liability for him—suggesting he was so focused on building up his chances to be Romney's running mate, and accumulate favors for a later White House run, that he was neglecting his day job. That criticism didn't seem to register with the public, which gave Christie increasingly positive, mid-50s ratings in voter polls.

But for every governing win Christie managed, he was also tagged with a loss or no-decision.

Christie and Newark Mayor Cory Booker drummed up laughs and some bipartisan glow with a spoof video filmed for the annual New Jersey Legislative Correspondents' Club Show that played off Seinfeld's famous, derisive "Newman!" line and Booker's penchant for acts of heroism. "I've got this," he told Christie as he helped the State Police, changed a flat tire, brought a replacement guitar to Bruce Springsteen, and caught a baby dropped from the Statehouse rotunda, only to have Christie step in when Romney called into New Jersey looking for a running mate. But his stalemate and standoff with the Democrat-controlled Legislature deepened in 2012, when Christie signed fewer laws than in any year since at least 1844 in New Jersey. He vetoed nearly one bill for every two he signed. One-third of his nominees couldn't get a hearing or got rejected by the Senate.

Christie's Supreme Court nominees, Bruce Harris and Phillip Kwon, were rejected by a Senate committee—the first time that had happened in state history. Kwon was rejected primarily because of financial problems his mother had experienced in running the family business, a wine and liquor store. She forfeited nearly $160,000 without admitting liability to settle civil charges about whether she had deposited funds in a way intended to evade taxes, but more than $140,000 that had been seized was returned and no criminal charges were filed. More than six months later, the governor finally nominated two new candidates, but Democrats quickly made clear they weren't going to move quickly to confirm David Bauman, already a state trial-court judge, or Robert Hanna, the Board of Public Utilities president. Christie—ever loyal and not unwilling to leverage some patronage—made sure the rejections ended with soft, well-paid landings for both Harris, who became the New Jersey Turnpike Authority general counsel, and Kwon, who became Port Authority of New York and New Jersey deputy general counsel.

The state reached a contract agreement with the union that represents teachers in the Newark schools—a system run by the state, as part of a "temporary" takeover now in its eighteenth year—that includes merit pay, a first in New Jersey. He also signed a law that significantly revamps the tenure system for public school teachers in the state, though the system keeps in place the "last in, first out" policy of conducting layoffs based on seniority, not ability. The law has quite a bit in common with a plan advanced by the New Jersey Education Association that Christie had once ridiculed.

State workers agreed to a four-year contract that froze pay for the first two years, then provided raises below the likely rate of inflation. But Christie's continuing effort to stop paying retiring public workers for their unused sick days sputtered. The courts upheld the freeze to public workers' pensions cost-of-living increases enacted through the 2011 reforms signed by Christie, but they also overturned the portion of the law Christie signed in 2011 that applied the increased contributions for pensions and health benefits to judges, ruling that the provision amounted to a pay cut prohibited by the state constitution. Voters quickly overturned the ruling five months later by amending the constitution.

Efforts to remake Atlantic City's tourism district continued—but revenues at the casinos plunged another 8 percent, extending their losing streak to six years. Revel, the city's latest casino, opened in the spring after its $260-million rescue from the Christie administration a year earlier. By year's end, it was taking on additional loans in an effort to stave off bankruptcy. Christie signed a law allowing sports betting in New Jersey, despite a federal law that seemed to ban such gaming. Nobody signed up for a license to accept such bets, and the law drew a legal challenge from sports leagues such as the NFL, NCAA, and Major League Baseball.

Two of Christie's bigger legislative accomplishments in 2012 were victories, of sorts, for George Norcross, the Democratic Party boss from South Jersey. Christie signed a law allowing private nonprofits to build and manage schools in three cities, including Camden. The first one approved—two months after it had initially, shockingly, been turned down by the Camden school board—was the KIPP Cooper Norcross Academy. Later in the year, he signed a law that broke up the University of Medicine and

Dentistry of New Jersey. In Central Jersey, that translated to giving Rutgers University a medical school. In South Jersey, that granted Rowan University research university status, giving it access to more federal research dollars, and nearly caused the shotgun wedding of Rutgers' Camden assets, including its law school, into Rowan.

Lawmakers approved Christie's proposal to expand a "drug court" diversionary program for nonviolent offenders, but balked at the last moment on his companion plan to give judges more discretion to revoke bail for defendants accused of violent crimes. Christie successfully cleared the Republican field for his friend, state Senator Joseph Kyrillos, to easily capture the U.S. Senate Republican nomination—only to see incumbent Senator Robert Menendez win in the state's biggest Senate rout since 1984. His clumsy effort to advocate for a referendum on whether to allow gay couples to marry in the state—"People would have been happy to have a referendum on civil rights rather than fighting and dying in the streets in the South"—drew civil-rights movement legend Representative John Lewis to Trenton to object. A state appeals court reinstated an affordable-housing agency Christie had abolished without legislative consent. After repeated delays, the state's first medical marijuana dispensary opened in Montclair, but the long wait annoyed many advocates, who were also disappointed when Christie refused to commute the sentence of a man with multiple sclerosis, John Ray Wilson, sent to prison for five years for growing marijuana in his backyard.

Potentially more troublesome than any of that was the elusive "Jersey Comeback."

Christie declared New Jersey's economic comeback underway in his State of the State in January, trumpeting a reversal of the job losses that had plagued Governor Jon Corzine's tenure and extended into the early months of his term. Though a federal Commerce Department report later said New Jersey was one of seven states where the economy shrank in 2011, the governor said the state's economy and budget were aimed in the right direction and called for an across-the-board income-tax cut of 10 percent—delayed until 2013 and then phased in, which would have the effect of delaying the bulk of the $1-billion hit to the treasury until after his reelection but allowing him to campaign on the accomplishment.

Democrats refused, as the proposal ignored the state's most crushing tax for the middle class, property taxes, in favor of cutting one that, with the state's progressive rate structure, is truly burdensome only for the wealthy. For middle-class taxpayers, New Jersey's income taxes are lowest in the region. Even for someone with an income of $1 million, the tab's not among the ten highest nationally, according to a study done for *Forbes* magazine.

Senate President Stephen Sweeney countered with a hybrid tax-cut plan that indirectly lowered property taxes by allowing most taxpayers, though not wealthy ones, to deduct 10 percent of their property taxes off their income tax bill. Christie traveled the state declaring victory, as Democrats were now talking tax cuts, and reached a deal that basically adopted Sweeney's plan, with slightly higher income thresholds to make more people eligible. Senate Democrats howled when Sweeney—who quickly begged off, citing the need to recover from a colonoscopy—and Christie planned to announce their agreement before the senator ran it past his Senate colleagues.

That delay proved crucial. Democrats developed concerns—prescient ones, it turned out—about whether New Jersey would see the more than 7 percent gain in tax revenues counted on by Christie's budget plan. They agreed to set aside the funds that would be needed for the first installment on the phased-in plan, which wouldn't have taken effect until 2013 anyway, and said they'd pass the plan if state revenues met forecasts. Christie called a special session of the Legislature, forcing lawmakers to meet in July, but they didn't act on his call for action. And then revenues began missing their marks, month after month. The economy did, as well. In truth, New Jersey's economic performance had never been leading the charge; even at its peak, it was middle-of-the-road nationally. After peaking in May, the state shed private-sector jobs in June, in July, in August, in September, and in October.

Chapter Thirteen

"I'm Gonna Die in This Fleece"

Oh, October.

The month began with nobody but Christie believing Romney would revive his flagging candidacy by shellacking Obama in the first debate—a prediction, incidentally, he says he ran by Romney's aides before revealing it on national TV in an effort to shake up the race and buck up Romney's downcast supporters. It ended with Christie walking through a South Jersey island with Obama after saluting the president's leadership when New Jersey was ravaged by Superstorm Sandy.

The National Weather Service's first advisory about Sandy—then Tropical Depression Eighteen—was issued Monday, October 22, warning about a tropical storm that would cross Jamaica, eastern Cuba, and the Bahamas as it moved northeast. By Tuesday it was apparent the storm would gain hurricane strength but forecasters believed the storm would take a hard right turn away from the United States. A day later, that hard right turn had become a soft right. And by late morning on Thursday, October 25, though Sandy hadn't yet raked across the Bahamas, the long-term forecast called for a strike on New Jersey's coast as a post-tropical storm with 70-mph winds five days later, on Tuesday morning. That forecast varied little over the next five days, with the storm's center aimed at South Jersey or Delaware, meaning the only question for New Jersey was whether the brunt would be borne by the Atlantic coast or the Delaware Bay shore.

New Jersey hadn't been directly hit by a hurricane in a century, though it had been battered by destructive nor'easters, most famously in 1962, and dealt blows by a handful of tropical storms in the previous dozen years—such as Floyd in 1999 and Irene in 2011, the latter of which was believed to be a hurricane when it arrived, only to be downgraded when more closely examined later. Technically, a hurricane still hasn't made landfall in New Jersey since 1903, since Sandy had merged with a winter weather system and lost tropical characteristics.

This distinction was good for homeowners, as insurers weren't able to force them to pay much higher insurance deductibles. But it wasn't helpful for warning people about the dangers. Hurricane warnings were never posted, for instance. And Sandy was generally described as a Category 1 storm for most of its trek northward, at one point even weakening to tropical-storm status. However, that scale solely takes into effect the cyclone's wind speeds, ignoring other factors, such as the storm surge—which is what ultimately ravaged Moonachie, Sayreville, and the Monmouth and Ocean county shorelines—and the fact that the storm was 1,000 miles wide.

The message about the storm's seriousness got through to many people. Shore towns began voluntary evacuations on Friday, October 26, which later became mandatory. Christie—who spent the day campaigning in North Carolina for Romney and gubernatorial candidate Pat McCrory—directed North Jersey reservoir systems to be drawn down to make room for the expected deluge.

"I knew it was going to be bad, but it's very hard to imagine it until you see it," Christie said, eleven days after the storm struck. "When I was hearing the reports about the storm on Friday and Saturday and Sunday, and the National Weather Service was telling us what was going to happen, it almost was so catastrophic that I couldn't imagine they were right."

On Saturday, two days before the storm hit, Christie put on his blue fleece—the one that says CHRIS CHRISTIE, GOVERNOR, in case anyone wasn't sure who that was on their TV—and convened the first of what would become nearly two weeks of daily Cabinet meetings. He declared a state of emergency and ordered the barrier islands of South Jersey to be evacuated, including the Atlantic City casinos. And he headed to Middletown in Monmouth County, then to North Wildwood in Cape May County, to implore people to prepare for the storm and take it seriously.

He tried seriousness: "We have to be prepared for the worst here. I can be as cynical as anyone, but when the storm comes, if it's as bad as they're predicting, you're going to wish you weren't as cynical as you otherwise might have been." He tried a bit of comedy in urging people to be careful about getting power to their homes if it went out: "Anything that looks stupid is stupid, let's go by that rule. I think we all know what we're talking about, right? If you think you're being overly clever but you know it looks stupid, don't do it. You're going to wind up getting somebody hurt. That's a good general New Jersey rule." He tried speaking directly to people reluctant to leave because they'd scrambled a year earlier for Irene, which wasn't too bad. "I don't think it's too big of an inconvenience to try and save your life."

Sunday morning came, and it was clear Sandy wasn't going to veer away. Christie requested an emergency declaration from President Barack Obama, who signed it late that night. The governor suspended tolls on the Garden State Parkway and Atlantic City Expressway and urged people to get to safer ground. "Don't be stupid. Get out," he said. The meteorologist in charge at the National Weather Service office in Mount Holly, New Jersey, issued an ominous update that pleaded with people to listen to evacuation orders. "Think about the rescue/recovery teams who will rescue you if you are injured or recover your remains if you do not survive," he wrote in a briefing. "Call me up on Friday . . . and yell at me all you want. . . . I will be very happy that you are alive and well, no matter how much you yell at me." He told reporters, "There's no one living who has seen a storm like this. . . . It's basically the worst-case scenario coming true. It will be beyond anything anyone has ever experienced," he said.[1]

Even before Sandy made landfall Monday around 8 p.m., near Atlantic City and Brigantine, its impressive reach had battered New Jersey. Parts of South Jersey got a foot of rain. Wind gusts were recorded at around 90 mph in places. The storm surges in places like lower Manhattan and Sandy Hook smashed all-time records. "This is not a time to be a show-off. This is not a time to be stupid. This is the time to save yourself and your family," Christie said in a televised news conference.

Monday evening, Christie opened his televised briefing by excoriating Atlantic City's mayor, Lorenzo Langford, with whom he's had a long-simmering battle. He said the city, which is on a barrier island, had put people in danger by establishing shelters in flood zones despite his mandate to evacuate. "For some reason, the mayor in Atlantic City advised people to stay put—some in a shelter feet from the bay that is now flooded. . . . He said he didn't want his people leaving Atlantic City. I hope and pray there will not be any loss of life because of it." Public schools in the city had, indeed, been designated as shelters—of last resort. People who arrived earlier were taken by bus to shelters on the mainland. "Get out of the city if you can," Langford had said Saturday. "We want our residents to take every precaution to get out of town and, if they can't or, for whatever reason, they won't, at least go to a shelter located in the city."[2] Christie said people in Atlantic City would be better off at home than at those shelters. On Tuesday morning, on NBC's *Today* show, Langford said he'd like to "confront the governor mano a mano." "The governor is either misinformed and ill-advised or simply just deciding to prevaricate," Langford said. "That's not what happened, and isn't it sad: Here we are in the throes of a major catastrophe, and the governor has chosen a time such as this to play politics. I think it's reprehensible that he would stoop to the level to try to make a political situation out of something that is so serious as this situation." Christie dialed back the rhetoric and said, at a minimum, Langford gave the public mixed messages about shelters. "I feel badly for the folks in Atlantic City who listened to him and sheltered in Atlantic City, and I guess my—my anger has turned to sympathy for those folks," he told *Today*.

Any attention that might have been paid to Christie's battle with Langford was quickly consumed by his far different reaction to the storm response from the White House.

For months, Christie had been an active surrogate for Romney, eagerly ripping Obama for a perceived lack of leadership. In a variation on remarks he'd delivered a couple of times, Christie told Romney supporters at an October 19 rally in Richmond, Virginia, that Obama was "blindly walking around the White House looking for a clue." Christie—like Rudy Giuliani before him, an expert and arbiter of all things "leadership"—said

Obama was like "a man wandering around a dark room, hands up against the wall, clutching for the light switch of leadership, and he just can't find it."

Apparently, as Sandy knocked out the lights in New Jersey, it turned them on at the White House.

In a series of TV interviews the morning after Sandy arrived, Christie—who would have been campaigning in Nevada on that day, if not for the hurricane—effusively praised Obama, using words such as "outstanding" and "excellent" to describe his response to the storm. "The president has been all over this and he deserves great credit," Christie told MSNBC's *Morning Joe.* "I've been on the phone with him, like I said, yesterday personally three times. He gave me his number at the White House, told me to call him if I need anything, and he absolutely means it. It's been very good working with the president."

The change of tone was striking—and noted far and wide by political journalists. Christie had been a serious contender as Romney's running mate, attended campaign rallies with Romney in Iowa, New Hampshire, Ohio, and Virginia, and headlined at least fourteen fund-raisers for the campaign. Not only was he now complimenting Obama, he was doing so in the midst of a hurricane that was commanding the nation's attention—undercutting the "lack of leadership" charge and enabling Obama to be bipartisan. Obama even seemed to have figured out how to fix FEMA, an agency still mending its reputation after Hurricane Katrina. Christie professed not to care about the presidential election at that moment—and bristled at suggestions from apoplectic Republicans that he ought to, such as by joining Romney to tour storm damage. "I have no idea, nor am I the least bit concerned or interested. I've got a job to do here in New Jersey that's much bigger than presidential politics, and I could care less about any of that stuff," he told Fox News. "If you think right now I give a damn about presidential politics, then you don't know me."

Christie—still nursing a bad cold he'd picked up nearly two weeks earlier in a campaign swing through Indiana for gubernatorial candidate Mike Pence and U.S. Senate candidate Richard Mourdock—had gotten about two hours of sleep the night before. "Every time I fell asleep, someone woke me up. The president woke me up one time—which is fine, he gets to." Obama called Christie fairly regularly for a number of days; the governor noted he'd been invited to call Obama directly if he ran into trouble getting needed help from the federal government, though the offer wasn't exclusive to Christie. "I told the mayors and governors if they're getting no for an answer somewhere in the federal government, they can call me personally at the White House," Obama said on October 30. "We are not going to tolerate red tape. We're not going to tolerate bureaucracy," he said a day later. "And I've instituted a fifteen-minute rule, essentially, on my team: You return everybody's phone calls in fifteen minutes, whether it's the mayors', the governors', county officials'. If they need something, we figure out a way to say yes."

Christie said he's never had any personal conflict with Obama, even as he sharply critiqued his leadership style. They'd met at National Governors Association dinners at the White House—at the February 2013 post-Sandy dinner, Christie was seated next to First Lady Michelle Obama—and in New Jersey a few times. One of those meetings was in July 2010, when Obama flew to Newark Liberty International Airport en route to Tastee Sub Shop in Edison to talk up a small-business proposal.

"It was the summer, and we had asked the staff if I could bring my kids, because my kids were off, so they could meet him. And they said no, just you and Mayor [Cory] Booker, that's it," Christie said. "So kind of ironically, when he came down the stairs, he said, 'It's the summer, where are the kids?' And I said, 'Well they're at home.' He said, 'Why didn't you bring them?" And I said, 'Because your staff wouldn't let me.' And he got visibly angry about that, and he said to me, 'The next time you're in D.C. for one of the Sunday morning shows, let me know, and if I'm around, I'd like to make it up to the kids.'"

Six months later, Christie and his family were in Washington for Christie's interview on *Fox News Sunday* in which—ironically, given later events—host Chris Wallace noted his praise for Obama's speech in Arizona after the shootings that wounded U.S. Representative Gabrielle Giffords. Christie talked about the value of unscripted moments for people wanting to get to know their presidential candidates, and Wallace said—not corrected by Christie—that the governor had advised House Republicans, in a September 2010 visit to their caucus meeting: "When governors like me come and ask for more aid, don't give it to us. That's the worst thing you can do."

After *Fox News Sunday,* Christie and his family headed over to visit Obama. "We walked over to the White House and the president was very gracious, apologized to the kids for his staff messing it up and not letting them meet him at the airport, and said, 'I'll give you a better tour.' He gave them a tour of the West Wing himself and ended it in the Oval Office, and it was very, very nice. Took some pictures, and he was very gracious," Christie said. "I wouldn't want to overplay our relationship. It's not like we're buddies. But clearly there's no personal animus between the two of us at all. We have significant policy and leadership approach differences, but like I said at the beginning, we're both professionals in this business, and I think you try to separate the two if you can."

The two looked like old friends on Halloween, when Obama flew up to New Jersey's Atlantic City International Airport to join Christie for a Marine One helicopter tour of the coast and a walking tour of Brigantine, an island next to Atlantic City. The governor met the president on the tarmac, and the two exchanged handshakes and pats on the back. In the car, Christie mentioned a few issues that needed attention; Obama got on the phone immediately to get those matters resolved, the governor said he was "pleased to report." In the air, they talked a bit about the swirling political circumstances—as did a jokester who wrote ROMNEY in capital letters in the sand to greet the visiting president.

"I want to just let you know that your governor is working overtime to make sure that as soon as possible everybody can get back to normal," Obama told residents. "The main message I just want to send is that the entire country has been watching what's been happening and everybody knows how hard Jersey's been hit."

"He has worked incredibly closely with me since before the storm hit. I think this is our sixth conversation since the weekend, and it's been a great working relationship to make sure that we're doing the jobs that people elected us to do," Christie said at a press briefing, the presidential seal on the podium. "And I cannot thank the president enough for his personal concern and compassion for our state and for the people of our state. And

I heard it on the phone conversations with him, and I was able to witness it today personally. . . . I want to thank him for being here today, for bringing his personal attention to it. And it's my honor to introduce to all of you the president of the United States."

Obama was equally generous returning the praise, telling residents in Brigantine that Christie had been "working overtime to make sure that as soon as possible everybody can get back to normal."

"I have to say that Governor Christie throughout this process has been responsive. He has been aggressive in making sure that the state got out in front of this incredible storm," Obama said. "And I think the people of New Jersey recognize that he has put his heart and soul into making sure that the people of New Jersey bounce back even stronger than before. So I just want to thank him for his extraordinary leadership and partnership."

The day after Obama's visit, the president participated in the daily conference call New Jersey was holding for mayors and other elected officials. The cooperation was so extensive that some Republicans felt it was over the top. Stephen Colbert joked that "Barack Obama stole Mitt Romney's date to Disaster Prom."[3] Christie shrugged.

"I'm aware of all the atmospherics. I'm not in a coma," Christie said on October 31. "But the fact is I don't care. There will be some folks who will criticize me for complimenting him. Well, you know I speak the truth. That's what I do. I say what I feel and what I believe. And I'm just doing the same thing with the president of the United States."

Christie got a number of phone calls—"Plenty of calls, more than you would imagine, in the middle of the storm," he said—from angry Republican donors around the county, demanding to know why he was betraying Romney just days before the election. Months later, tensions had started to ease, though not for everyone. After a February 2013 fund-raising trip to California to support his reelection bid, he said, "There are some people who weren't there who I think otherwise would have been.

"It was just kind of confusing to me, to tell you the truth, and still is somewhat baffling today on one level," Christie said of the reaction. "I completely understand how everybody, myself included, in the Romney campaign would have preferred the storm to never happen, because it just sucked the oxygen out, for three or four days, of any discussion of politics and the presidential campaign. The news was dominated, as it should have been, by the storm. And I also understand how the Romney campaign would feel uncomfortable about the president getting some significant face time with their number-one surrogate. But that stuff was all unavoidable.

"Once the storm happened, and it was as catastrophic as it was, and the president of the United States calls and says, 'I want to come and see your people and its damage,' what would they have had me do? Say, 'No, Mr. President, we're six days away from an election; I'd prefer you not to come because I support the other guy'? To me that was just an absolutely unacceptable alternative," Christie said. "So when he called, I understood the politics of it. But I also understood that I had no choice. My choice was to serve the people of the state. And having the president come undoubtedly was going to be good for the spirit of the people of the state and good for our recovery, if he paid the right attention to us. And he did. And when he did, I—appropriately, I believe—complimented him. Now, I understand that that made some people in my party feel uncomfortable, but the fact, is the truth is the truth. And they loved me telling the truth about Barack Obama when I was giving him hell, but when I threw him a compliment, all of a sudden that wasn't appropriate. And I'll never quite understand that."

Christie's reaction to Sandy was an emotional one, rather than a political one, because the Jersey Shore was a staple of his youth—just as it has been for millions of New Jerseyans, many of whom spent weeks each summer at rented houses or Wildwood motels. Even teens who don't live at the Shore are anchored there—from days as little kids riding the carnival attractions and playing Skee-Ball, to prom weekends in less-than-sanitary cramped quarters, to returning to familiar haunts with their own children years later. Many of those places were gone—much of the shore violently washed away, never to look the same even if it gets rebuilt.

Christie understood all that. He'd spent summers in and around Seaside, taking in long weekends at relatives' houses in now-ravaged places like Ortley Beach. Any governor would have expressed sympathy for the Shore, drawn attention to its recovery needs. But imagine if Christie's predecessor had won a second term in 2009: While Jon Corzine would have toured and prioritized the Shore, he was an Illinois kid whose shore of choice seemed to be in the Hamptons. He'd have been helpful and empathetic—but wouldn't have conveyed that nostalgic sense of loss, that dreadful horror that goes beyond the property losses and deaths, that acknowledgment that part of what makes New Jersey and connects it across generations would never return.

"It's just incredible," Christie said, huddled inside a New Jersey State Police boat five days after Sandy and riding across Barnegat Bay, into which a number of homes had been dropped by the storm surge. "I've spent a lot of time in these waters over the years. My brother having a house in Point Pleasant Beach, we've water-skid and Jet-Skid in this area, so it's really familiar to me. To see these houses destroyed where they are, just amazing. I saw a lot of it from the air, and got a good impression, but seeing it down on this level is incredible. Like I said before, this is going to change the face of this area for a long, long time."

One of Christie's Shore damage tours ended at 46 Franklin Avenue in Seaside Heights, where the small house Christie and eleven friends rented for two weeks thirty-two years earlier after his graduation from Livingston High School in 1980 still stands. His friends sent him to the Shore to rent the house; he recalled promising the owner they wouldn't have more than six people staying there. "Right here, twelve guys, right after we graduated from high school, two weeks. Not good," said Christie, sporting sunglasses as his senior staff listened to him reminisce. "But a perfect location, perfect location because right next to the parking lot, where people were coming and going to the boardwalk. Perfect location. Scouting opportunities were fabulous." The house had two beds and a few couches; the group took turns on an alphabetical-order rotation either sleeping in sleeping bags, on a couch, or on a bed. Christie said he slept on the couch one night, then opted to remain in the sleeping bag for the time he could have used a couch. "I don't know what had happened on those couches, but it just didn't feel right," he joked.

"The Jersey Shore of my youth is gone," Christie declared the day after Sandy's destruction. "There is no question in my mind that we'll rebuild it. But for those of us my age, it won't be the same because many of the iconic things that made it what it was are now gone and washed into the ocean." Roller coasters in the ocean, boardwalks—some of them just a year old, installed after Irene barreled through—smashed and scattered. "The level of devastation at the Jersey Shore is unthinkable," Christie said. "It is beyond anything I thought I'd ever see. Terrible." Christie took a helicopter tour of the coast for four and a half hours, stopping a couple of times to see the damage up close. "I was just here walking this place this summer, and the fact that most of it is gone is just incredible," Christie told Belmar Mayor Matt Doherty while surveying damage on Ocean Avenue. He said that it was appropriate for people to be sad and to mourn—but only for a day or so, when the recovery would have to begin. "This is the kind of thing New Jerseyans are built for—we're plenty tough and now we have a little more reason to be angry after this. Just what we need in New Jersey, a chance to be a little more angry," he joked in Belmar.

To be sure, Christie's handling of the storm wasn't perfect. His administration's New Jersey Transit team opted to keep their trains in a yard in the Meadowlands that flooded, causing tens of millions of dollars in damage. Executives there said the Kearny yard hadn't flooded before, so they presumed it wouldn't again—which might make sense if Christie hadn't been exhorting people to take Sandy seriously because they'd never seen anything like it. Christie reacted angrily when reporters asked about NJ Transit's decision. He minimized problems with looting, even after mayors were telling him it was happening and getting him to dispatch National Guard patrols. He insisted for days that holding the presidential election eight days after the storm wasn't on his priority list, and when rules were bent at the last minute to allow people to vote by email or fax, confusion reigned about the requirements, and requests for such ballots swamped county elections officials. And his administration had dealt with months of pointed questions about the financial and ethical wisdom of the first contract his administration awarded—to the debris-removal firm AshBritt Inc., a deal potentially worth $100 million that piggybacked off a contract the company had with Connecticut, rather than being independently bid in New Jersey. AshBritt came with the recommendation of former Mississippi Governor Haley Barbour, a friend of Christie's who steered $7.5 million of Republican Governors Association funds into the 2009 campaign and now lobbies for AshBritt.

By and large, though, Christie was in control and at his best. When hours-long lines were leading to altercations at gas stations, which were having a distribution problem because of the lack of power, Christie instituted a 1970s-style, odd-even gas-rationing system that seemed to ease the problems. New York residents, in a Quinnipiac University poll, gave Christie higher marks for handling the storm than they gave Mayor Michael Bloomberg or Governor Andrew Cuomo. Jon Stewart, on *The Daily Show*, said Christie "kicked crazy ass during the storm."[4] Jordan's king called. Britain's prime minister emailed. More than anything, though, he endeared himself to residents by consoling them, hugging them, joking with them, reassuring them that they weren't alone in their plight. "We're a tough state. Other states would be crying right now. Not us, we're too tough," he said. "We'll rebuild the rest of it, but we can't replace you," he told one woman. In Little Ferry, one lady told Christie after hugging him: "You got a bigger attitude than me. I didn't think that was possible." Even public workers thanked him. "Can I hug you, Mr. Christie?" Katie Reilly asked him. "I'm a teacher and I'm giving you a lot of credit." Don't feel shy about pushing for help, he said: "I'm as big of a pain in the ass as anybody." Democratic antagonists joined him at many stops. "You're doing a great job," said Senator Paul Sarlo, whose Shore house in Lavallette was destroyed. In Middletown, he met a nine-year-old girl, Ginjer Doherty, who was visibly upset because her home had been lost. Christie says that of everyone he met, Ginjer made the biggest impression—she's the same age, same height, and has the same speaking style as his daughter, Bridget, he said. The girls share more than a passing resemblance, too. He told her that what matters most is that her mom, dad, and dog were alive. "It's a sad thing," he told her. "I'm sad, too. But it's okay to be sad." Christie got Ginjer's cell phone number and called regularly—so often, he later joked, that she had to tell him she's fine and that he didn't need to check in.

Hours after meeting Ginjer, his daughter, Bridget—whom Christie hadn't seen much since Sandy hit, given how many hours he was spending at work—asked her dad what would happen with their regular trips to Seaside Heights.

"Where are we going to go to have fun this summer?" she asked.

"We'll figure it out," Christie said. "Maybe it won't be next summer. Maybe it'll be in two summers. We'll see."

That was the line Christie was walking from the start: letting people know he intended to make sure the Shore was rebuilt, but also letting them know it wouldn't be a quick recovery.

"It's not going to be all fixed by Memorial Day. I know New Jerseyans. I know what they're going to think: 'They'll get it all fixed by Memorial Day.' We'll try like hell, but we've got to make sure that they don't assume that's what's going to happen, because it's going to take some time for us to do it the right way," he said.

"This is too important a place in the fabric of New Jersey's culture to not rebuild it," Christie said, standing on the wrecked Casino Pier, the half-submerged Jet Star nearby. "I do not intend to be the governor who presides over the idea that this is going to be gone. I refuse to accept that. This is too much a piece of New Jersey to let it happen."

Even Bruce Springsteen, Christie's musical hero and long his unrequited love, warmed up to the governor. At a Halloween night concert in Rochester, New York, that had been delayed a day by Sandy, Springsteen—who said his E Street Band was basically a glorified Shore band—singled out Christie for praise as he thanked first responders and rescue workers, saying the governor had "done such a hard job over the past few weeks."[5] He mentioned Christie again a night later in State College, Pennsylvania. And then on Friday, November 2, when Christie went to New York to see a benefit concert organized by NBC, Christie got a hug from Springsteen. "Yeah, we hugged and he told me it's official: We're friends," Christie said. He said he wept a little at home that night due to the hug, although ten weeks later, he told an interviewer that he didn't cry and was "being New Jersey sarcastic" in telling that story. They spoke again the day before the election, when Obama put the rocker on the phone while flying to a campaign stop, and then again at the 12-12-12 Sandy benefit concert in New York, where Springsteen—and then Jon Bon Jovi—signed the cast helping mend Christie's daughter Bridget's broken wrist.

Chatter about the Obama relationship—which in some retellings was being described as a literal hug, even though the two never actually embraced—escalated to the point where Christie felt compelled to tell reporters, including an Israeli television station, that he would be voting for Romney. He had been urged to do exactly that, first on Twitter, and then in a private phone conversation with Rupert Murdoch, chairman and chief executive officer of News Corp.[6] "This shows you how broken our political system is. Because I say something nice about someone who does their job well, somehow that takes away my endorsement of Mitt Romney. Believe me, I can tell you this much: There are two people who know for sure, besides me, who I'm voting for on Tuesday: Mitt Romney and the president of the United States." He addressed the issue in Hoboken with Obama's homeland security secretary, Janet Napolitano, at his side. "If the president of the United States comes here and he is willing to help my people, and he does it, then I'm going to say nice things about him because he's earned it. And I've said plenty of not-nice things about the president over time—he knows that. And we joked about that when we were together this week," Christie said. "Anybody is upset in the Republican Party about this, then they haven't been to New Jersey. Come see the destruction, come see the loss, and then tell me if you're going to still criticize me for complimenting somebody who is the president of the United States and who has provided help to my people during one of the worst crises this state has ever faced."

Passions rose even higher after Romney held a campaign rally two days before the election on a farm in Yardley, Pennsylvania, just fifteen minutes away from the New Jersey Statehouse. At the rally, Romney said Christie was giving "all of his heart and his passion" to recovering from Sandy— but an anonymous staffer later complained to *The Huffington Post* that Christie declined a request to attend the rally. "That's completely untrue," Christie said in an Election Day visit to an elementary school. "All this other noise, I think, is coming from know-nothing, disgruntled campaign staffers who, you know, don't like that I said nice things about the president of the United States. . . . Those who fear they may be blamed if things don't go well try to look for other people to blame."[7]

Romney lost the election, with Obama capturing nearly every swing state believed to be in play, except for North Carolina. Plenty of blame from Republican quarters rained down on Christie, who had to repeatedly defend his storm response while meeting with fellow Republican governors in Las Vegas two weeks after the election. (Christie would later skip the Republican Governors Association's winter meeting in Washington.) The governor said, essentially, that Republicans are going to have to get over it.

"I am who I am. It's not that I have fences to mend. They're going to have to come to terms with it one way or the other," Christie said. "I know what I did, and I know I did nothing wrong and I have nothing to apologize for. So I don't have any fences to mend. I think over time, as with anything, an emotional race like this election was, there were a lot of people who had a lot invested, both financially and spiritually, and feelings are raw in that aftermath. I think it's certainly significantly less now than in November and December, and it's declining every month, but there are still some people who say something to me about it."

Among those seemingly willing to move on was Romney himself, who donated the maximum $3,800 to Christie's reelection primary campaign and told *Fox News Sunday* in a March 2013 interview that he does not blame Christie for his loss. "I don't think that's why the president won the election. My campaign had to kind of stop. And we were in the last week and this was the time. We were—you know, we were getting ready to hammer, hammer, hammer our message. We had to stop. But as for Chris Christie—Chris did what he thought was the best for the people of his state. And I respect that," he said. Asked by Chris Wallace if he wished Christie had been less effusive, Romney said, "I'm not going to worry about how Chris was doing what he thought was best for the people of his state. I lost my election because of my campaign, not because of what anyone else did."[8]

Yet there was some evidence that the storm, if not Christie's role in its framing, helped Obama. In a November 21, 2012, post on his *FiveThirty-Eight* blog, Nate Silver—comparing early returns with final poll estimates—said "the map shows some possible effects" from Sandy. Obama topped polling expectations across the Northeast, particularly in New Jersey—as well as in the Gulf Coast, particularly hurricane-prone Louisiana and Mississippi, Silver observed. "Could it have been that Mr. Obama's response to Hurricane Sandy was more salient in these states?"[9] The honeymoon-is-over punctuation came when the *Drudge Report* led its website with a headline ripping Christie for appearing on *Saturday Night Live* while some residents of his state were still homeless or powerless from the storm.

Christie got the *SNL* treatment twice. First, the show's November 3 opening skit included Bobby Moynihan playing Christie at a press briefing, complete with a blue fleece sporting Christie's name and job title, threatening revenge on Sandy—"We don't get sad in New Jersey, we get even!"—while a big-haired, bigger-gestured, gum-chewing Roxie Fuchinelli, played by Nasim Pedrad, provided off-color sign language in a parody of New York Mayor Michael Bloomberg's news conferences. Two weeks later, Christie himself appeared on *SNL* during Seth Meyers's Weekend Update—in what he said was the most unexpected thing to happen in 2012, even topping his long-anticipated talk with his musical idol, Bruce Springsteen.

"The Springsteen thing, you're so hopeful for it—at least if you're me; I was so hopeful for it over time, that when it eventually happened, it was great, but it wasn't as big a shock because he had said some nice things about me in the days leading up to that. So when I did see him, I figured he was going to be nice to me, we were going to make a rapprochement," Christie said. "It was not what I expected in my career."

"I was fired up for it. It was a lot of fun," Christie said. "The keynote address, candidly, was less unexpected. I knew that was in the realm of possibility. I knew that Governor Romney has great respect for me, and he likes the way I speak, so I wasn't completely shocked when he called and asked me to be the keynote speaker. But I was really shocked when Lorne Michaels called and said he wanted me on *Saturday Night Live*. That was really a shocker."

Christie wheeled in on a rolling chair, pretended to have a short temper with Meyers's questions, quoted Springsteen, and called him "more of a saint" than a poet and thanked wife Mary Pat for having "put up with a husband who has smelled like a wet fleece for the past three weeks." Christie told Meyers he wears the fleece under his suits. "I'm gonna die in this fleece," he said, to laughs. The fleece, incidentally, was a gift from a Democratic Party boss in Newark, Steve Adubato, Sr., who gave it to the governor the day after the 2009 election, when Christie made Adubato's charter school in Newark his first post-election public appearance.

"Steve Sr. goes underneath the table and pulls out this thing in plastic and flips it over to me and it was that blue fleece, with my name and title on it," recalled Christie. "And I teased him about it. This was about 1 o'clock in the afternoon, and we'd only given him about two hours notice. I said, 'How'd you find somebody to make this in two hours?' 'Are you kidding? That's how confident I was that you were going to win. I bought it beforehand.' And I said, 'Okay, then where's Corzine's? I'm sure you got him one, too. I know you, Steve, you played both sides to the middle.' I laughed, and I never saw Corzine's."

Around the same time as the *SNL* visit, Christie also talked with Romney.

"I gave him about ten days to decompress from the election," Christie said. "I sent him an email the night of the election, but I didn't want to be one of those guys all over him. I've lost elections. I know in the days after you lose an election, you don't want to really be talking to be people outside your family. You don't want to be going over the postmortem again and again. So I waited until mid-November, about ten days after the election, and I called him. We had a fifteen-, twenty-minute conversation about the race and the campaign and all the rest of the stuff. And it was like typical conversations with Mitt. He's an incredibly generous, gracious person, very disappointed that he didn't win but looking forward to the rest of his life. He already had some of that perspective in his voice— 'There's going to be a lot of interesting things for me to do with my life and my career from here. I'm disappointed, but I'm not despondent. I'm moving on.' So we had a great conversation. He's, I think, a really good person. I think he would have been a very good president, but it didn't work out. It was good to talk to him."

Christie will have other hurdles to deal with nationally in the Republican Party, if he hopes to seek federal office one day. If complimenting the Democratic president at the height of the election was strike one, then bashing the GOP Speaker of the House on the heels of a bitter defeat for his caucus in January 2013 was strike two.

New Jersey and New York, along with Connecticut, created detailed damage reports and worked with Obama administration officials and members of Congress to put together a roughly $60-billion request for recovery aid from Washington. Such appropriations are common after disasters; after Hurricane Katrina in 2005, a similar amount was approved in ten days, with additional funds added later. But sixty-six days after Sandy, with Sandy aid having taken a back seat to the "fiscal cliff" crisis that Washington had created for itself, House Speaker John Boehner unexpectedly called off a vote on the last night before Congress ended its session—reasoning, apparently, that it was too much for Republicans to bear to acquiesce to Obama's push for higher taxes for the rich and support adding $60 billion to the unbalanced budget on the same night.

Christie, who had spent parts of the New Year's holiday weekend lobbying between thirty and forty House members by phone, got an 11:20 p.m. call from House Majority Leader Eric Cantor alerting him the vote was shelved. As late as 9 p.m. that night, and repeatedly over the previous four days, he'd been assured the vote would be held. An irate Christie called Boehner four times demanding details, an explanation—but none of those calls were returned. He finally spoke with Boehner the next day, then met with reporters to savage his own party's House leader.

"There's only one group to blame for the continued suffering of these innocent victims—the House majority and their speaker, John Boehner," Christie said. "This is not a Republican or Democratic issue. Natural disasters happen in red states and blue states, in states with Democratic governors and Republican governors. We respond to innocent victims of natural disasters not as Republicans or Democrats but as Americans. Or at least we did, until last night. Last night, politics was placed before our oath to serve our citizens. For me, it was disappointing and disgusting to watch.

"Last night, the House of Representatives failed that most basic test of public service, and they did so with callous indifference to the suffering of the people of my state," Christie said.

Part of Christie's fame over the previous four years had come from his fiery, no-holds-barred attacks on opponents. But this one was different. First, few people outside of New Jersey had ever seen him do this to a Republican, being unfamiliar with his rambunctious romp through Morris County politics in the 1990s (see Chapter Three) or his biting war of words with Jim Treffinger as U.S. attorney (Chapter Four.) Also, this wasn't off-the-cuff name-calling. Christie at times stopped to choose his words and answers deliberately, as when he said—after he'd made clear he had spoken with Boehner—that he hadn't yet been assured there would be a January vote by "anyone that is credible with me about that." Christie's anger was made clear by his unusually quiet tone of voice.

"It's absolutely disgraceful. This used to be something that was not political. Disaster relief was something that you didn't play games with, but now in this current atmosphere, everything is a subject of one-upsmanship, everything is a possibility, a potential piece of bait for the political game," Christie said. "It is why the American people hate Congress. It's why they hate them."

Christie's news conference was carried live by CNN and was watched in Washington—and even more than constituents in New Jersey or citizens around the country, the D.C. crowd was clearly Christie's audience. He punctuated one flourish by saying, "Shame on you."

"Americans are tired of the palace intrigue and political partisanship of this Congress, which places one-upsmanship ahead of the lives of the citizens who sent these people to Washington, D.C., in the first place," Christie said. "New Jerseyans and New Yorkers are tired of being treated like second-class citizens. New York deserved better than the selfishness we saw on display last night. New Jersey deserves better than the duplicity we saw on display last night. America deserves better than just another example of a government that has forgotten who they are there to serve and why. Sixty-six days and counting. Shame on you. Shame on Congress."

Christie had given voice to a national frustration among voters with the political system—remarkable, given how much time he's spent working the gears and levers of that system to build up himself and his party. The move escalated suspicions for some Republicans about his party loyalty. Strike three for Christie, among some of them, was when he criticized as "reprehensible" a National Rifle Association ad in the gun-control debate that followed the Newtown, Connecticut, school massacre, which cited the armed protection provided to Obama's daughters.

"It's something that you're generally more likely to hear from a party's leaders right after that party has decisively lost a national election. Governor George W. Bush was criticized for comments he made about the Republicans in Congress when he was running for president. Bill Clinton got grief from the base of his party for trying to drag them to the center. It worked out all right for both of them," said Dan Schnur, a former Republican strategist who directs the Jesse M. Unruh Institute of Politics at the University of Southern California. "I don't think he's jeopardized his future at all. The biggest jeopardy to Chris Christie's national political prospects would be losing a reelection campaign for governor of New Jersey. But three years from now, someone who's the twice-elected Republican governor of a very Democratic state is going to look very appealing to a lot of primary voters."

Christie said he didn't get nearly the same level of blowback after his criticism of Boehner as he did after the hurricane. "It was a much different reaction to the John Boehner news conference because I think what people, even in our own party, understood was that it was just wrong what was going on, the delay in delivering these funds was just wrong."

As it turns out, though, the Boehner blast did have an impact. A week after Christie made that observation in an interview, American Conservative Union chair Al Cardenas told news outlets that Christie's broadside against the House speaker was the reason the governor hadn't been invited to speak at the 2013 Conservative Political Action Conference, or CPAC. Christie did attend in Chicago in 2012—but since then advocated for the $60 billion in Sandy funds, which Cardenas told *Politico* was "a pork-barrel bill containing only $9 billion in disaster assistance."[10] He also pinned the decision on Christie's choice to expand Medicaid in the state—which wasn't made until *after* CPAC opted not to invite him. "CPAC is like the all-star game for professional athletes; you get invited when you have had an outstanding year," Cardenas said. "Hopefully he will have another all-star year in the future, at which time we will be happy to extend an invitation. This is a conservative conference, not a Republican Party event."[11] Among the 2012 all-stars who did get invited are Romney, Sarah Palin, and Rick Perry. "He made it very hard for Republicans in the Congress at a time when we were trying to deal with fiscal restraint," Cardenas said.[12]

Christie minimized the snub. "I can't sweat the small stuff," he told a resident who asked at a town hall meeting in Montville. Plenty of people questioned the decision, given Christie's standing in the party and among independents. Some were Democrats who'd clearly been more supportive of Christie since October. But among them were Republicans, as well.

Senator John McCain's former campaign manager, Steve Schmidt, compared CPAC to the bar scene in the 1977 movie *Star Wars*. The bar, the Cantina, was filled with a collection of dregs from all over the universe, strange-looking and -acting characters who didn't fit in anywhere else.

When the hero, Luke Skywalker, walked in with his trusty droids R2-D2 and C-3PO, the bartender snarled, "We don't serve their kind in here."

Republican Representative Peter King of New York told *The Hill* publication, "If Republicans had any brains they'd stay away from CPAC. The thought that he's being penalized because he sought to get the aid for Sandy relief is disgraceful regional bias. To hold that out against him shows a narrow-minded bigotry from the party."[13]

Certainly Christie's comments didn't hurt his cause in New Jersey, where he announced in November—matter of factly, without a rally or speech—that he'd run for reelection. Christie's approval ratings moved above 70 percent. He opened his campaign with events focused on endorsements from a construction union, a public law-enforcement union, and a Democratic mayor and council, and was running—depending on the poll—either slightly ahead or slightly behind among Democrats in a trial heat against his most likely Democratic opponent in the 2013 election, state Senator Barbara Buono.

"The governor wants a big win," said Monmouth University political scientist Patrick Murray. "The governor doesn't want a 10-point win. He wants a 20-point win. And he's going to be campaigning and governing in a way that will get him that 20-point win, because he's looking ahead to 2016."

Early polls looking ahead to the 2016 presidential race show the conundrum facing Christie, should he win reelection and then seek the Republican nod for the White House. A national survey in February 2013 by the Democratic polling firm Public Policy Polling found Christie tied for third nationally among Republican voters in a field of nine could-be candidates. Senator Marco Rubio led at 22 percent. Representative Paul Ryan was next at 15 percent. Christie and former Governor Jeb Bush each drew 13 percent.

Of the nine, though, Christie clearly had the highest unfavorable ratings among Republicans—27 percent, compared with 42 percent who viewed him favorably. He was viewed more favorably by somewhat liberal, moderate, and somewhat conservative voters than by those who describe themselves as very conservative. His numbers among Iowa Republicans were slightly worse, a net +3, and he was the fifth most-preferred candidate for president. But Democrats like Christie nearly as much as Republicans do, enabling him to be the only Republican tied in a trial heat with Vice President Joe Biden and the one closest to Hillary Clinton. Among all voters, nobody came close to his national favorability ratings of a net +22, with 44 percent approving, 22 percent disapproving.

"In any of the Republican polls that I've seen, I'm always in the top two or three people for the presidential nomination in '16. I think there's a lot of people who would be willing to trade places with me in that role," Christie said. "And as for Democrat and independent support, that's no shock to me because I couldn't get elected governor in New Jersey without Democratic and independent support. So that may be unusual for some Republican Party figures around the country. Anybody who's followed my career knows that it couldn't be unusual for me or I wouldn't be sitting here. Because if you don't get some Democrats and a lot of independents to vote for you in New Jersey as a Republican, you're never going to win, just given the numbers. So it doesn't surprise me all that much. I also know lastly, on the national poll stuff, that's all very fleeting. It's quick-shot impressions of people. If I were ever to enter the national scene, then you're judged on a longer haul and you see how you do after that."

If Christie wins reelection, he's in line to become chairman of the Republican Governors Association in 2014—when thirty-six states will be electing governors, giving him a platform to cultivate even more relationships with Republicans nationally. A year after that, he'd have to decide whether to seek the presidency.

Christie said Republicans have a number of strong options for 2016.

"We've probably got a deeper bench than we've had in a long time," he said. "You've got a bunch of really good governors out there who are coming into their own, whether it's Scott Walker in Wisconsin or Rick Snyder in Michigan, Susana Martinez in New Mexico or John Kasich in Ohio, Bobby Jindal in Louisiana. There's a crop of Republican governors who I think are really coming into their own and could be absolutely good presidential candidates in 2016. And then you also have some members of Congress, whether it's Senator Rubio or Congressman Ryan, who are really good members of Congress and could have something to say on the national level. John Thune, Senator Thune from South Dakota. There's a number of those folks. I think the bench is pretty deep at the moment. So I think it will be interesting—and that doesn't count Senator Santorum, who I think is likely to come back and try to run again."

And what type of candidate would be best?

"What type of person? We should be looking for the type of person who can win. That's the type of person that we should be looking for," Christie said. "I don't think it's a whole—there's a lot of other things that go into it, but priority number one should be you can't govern unless you win, no matter what it is you believe. So you've got to win first.

"It [the party] needs a new approach, at a minimum. I don't think that we're necessarily, that our ideas are unpopular," Christie said. "But I think you've run into some very popular candidates. I've always believed that presidential races are about the candidates and is the person likeable. Is it the person you want to have dinner with, you want to have a beer with? I think that's a lot of what happens in presidential races. I'm not trying to minimize issues, but I think that in the end it's a very personal vote that people make, and they try to get a feel for that person.

"And I think that in four of the last six, we clearly have had it up against candidates who were extraordinarily personally popular in President Clinton and President Obama—for different reasons, obviously, but they have their own skills that allow them to be very personally popular.

"In between, George Bush lost the popular vote in 2000 but he won the electoral vote, and it was close enough on the popular vote that I think you could basically call it a draw. And his reelection is, I think, a reaffirmation of his personal style and his leadership style, and the fact that he won it fairly comfortably over John Kerry tells you that the public will vote for a Republican that they believe cares about them. That's what it's all about."

NOTES

1. NOTHING LEFT UNSAID

1. Clifton town hall meeting, Nov. 10, 2010.
2. Cynthia Burton, *Philadelphia Inquirer*, May 28, 2009.
3. David Halbfinger and David Kocieniewski, *New York Times*, Sept. 24, 2009.
4. Ibid.
5. Burton, *Philadelphia Inquirer*, May 28, 2009.
6. Steve Politi, *Star-Ledger*, June 13, 2010.
7. Claire Heininger, *Star-Ledger*, Jan. 17, 2010.
8. William Kleinknecht, *Star-Ledger*, May 7, 2007.
9. Ibid.

2. GIVE ME A LAW BOOK

1. Claire Heininger, *Star-Ledger*, Jan. 19, 2010.
2. Mitchel Maddux, *The Record*, Nov. 10, 2002.
3. Ginger Gibson, *Star-Ledger*, Jan. 10, 2011.
4. *Piers Morgan Tonight*, CNN, June 14, 2011.
5. Amy S. Rosenberg, *Philadelphia Inquirer*, April 17, 2011.

3. RUN OUT BY REPUBLICANS

1. Joe Territo, *Star-Ledger*, April 15, 1993.
2. Ibid.
3. Territo, *Star-Ledger*, April 20, 1993.
4. Territo, *Star-Ledger*, April 23, 1993.
5. Lawrence Regonese, *Star-Ledger*, July 28, 1993.
6. Ragonese, *Star-Ledger*, May 22, 1997.
7. Mitchel Maddux, *The Record*, Nov. 10, 2002.
8. Brian T. Murray, *Star-Ledger*, June 3, 1994.
9. Ragonese and Murray, *Star-Ledger*, April 30, 1994.
10. Murray, *Star-Ledger*, May 3, 1994.
11. Murray, *Star-Ledger*, June 1, 1994.
12. Murray, *Star-Ledger*, June 3, 1994.
13. Ragonese, *Star-Ledger*, Oct. 6, 1994.
14. Murray, *Star-Ledger*, July 8, 1994.
15. Murray, *Star-Ledger*, Nov. 12, 1996.
16. Murray, *Star-Ledger*, Sept. 30, 1994.
17. Ragonese, *Star-Ledger*, Sept. 1, 1994.
18. Ragonese, *Star-Ledger*, Sept. 2, 1994.
19. Ibid.
20. John Cichowski, *The Record*, Jan. 4, 1995.
21. Ragonese, *Star-Ledger*, March 6, 1997.
22. Ragonese, *Star-Ledger*, Jan. 25, 1995.
23. Murray, *Star-Ledger*, May 2, 1997.
24. Kevin Coughlin, *Star-Ledger*, Jan. 27, 1995.
25. Coughlin, *Star-Ledger*, April 4, 1995.
26. Murray, *Star-Ledger*, April 19, 1995.
27. Coughlin, *Star-Ledger*, May 16, 1995.
28. Coughlin, *Star-Ledger*, May 26, 1995.
29. Coughlin, *Star-Ledger*, June 7, 1995.
30. Coughlin, *Star-Ledger*, June 27, 1995.
31. Ragonese, *Star-Ledger*, Aug. 6, 1995.
32. Murray, *Star-Ledger*, April 12, 1995.
33. Ragonese, *Star-Ledger*, May 26, 1996.

34. Murray, *Star-Ledger*, April 14, 1996.

35. Ragonese, *Star-Ledger*, Feb. 29, 1996.

36. Ragonese, *Star-Ledger*, July 10, 1996.

37. Cichowski, *The Record*, July 10, 1996.

38. *Piers Morgan Tonight*, CNN, June 14, 2011.

39. Murray, *Star-Ledger*, Jan. 3, 1997.

40. Cichowski, *The Record*, Jan. 5, 1997.

41. Ragonese, *Star-Ledger*, Jan. 4, 1997, and Cichowski, *The Record*, Jan. 5, 1997.

42. Ragonese, *Star-Ledger*, Dec. 21, 1997.

43. Cichowski, *Star-Ledger*, Nov. 22, 1998.

44. Ragonese, *Star-Ledger*, Dec. 3, 2000.

45. Ragonese, *Star-Ledger*, June 1, 1997.

46. Ragonese, *Star-Ledger*, March 6, 1997.

47. Cichowski, *Star-Ledger*, Nov. 22, 1998.

48. Ragonese, *Star-Ledger*, Jan. 12, 2001.

49. Ragonese, *Star-Ledger*, June 4, 1997.

50. Ibid.

51. Ragonese, *Star-Ledger*, Dec. 21, 1997.

52. Ragonese, *Star-Ledger*, June 5, 1997.

53. Ragonese, *Star-Ledger*, Dec. 21, 1997.

4. BUSH TO THE RESCUE

1. Claire Heininger and Josh Margolin, *Star-Ledger*, Aug. 25, 2009.

2. Peter Aseltine, *The* (Trenton) *Times*, Jan. 22, 1999.

3. Chris Christie, Letter to the Editor, *Star-Ledger*, Aug. 16, 1998.

4. Max Pizarro, *PolitickerNJ.com*, Jan. 7, 2009.

5. *Hunterdon County Democrat*, Jan. 13, 2000.

6. Lawrence Ragonese, *Star-Ledger*, Dec. 3, 2000.

7. John P. Martin, *Star-Ledger*, Feb. 5, 2002.

8. *Asbury Park Press*, Dec. 8, 2001.

9. Robert Cohen and Robert Rudolph, *Star-Ledger*, Sept. 5, 2001.

10. Martin, *Star-Ledger*, Feb. 5, 2002.

11. Mitchel Maddux, *The Record*, Dec. 15, 2000.

12. The Auditor, *Star-Ledger*, March 18, 2001.

13. The Auditor, *Star-Ledger*, Aug. 26, 2001.

14. Peter Saharko, *Press of Atlantic City*, Aug. 31, 2001.

15. Peter Weiss, *Jersey Journal*, Feb. 27, 2003.

16. Associated Press, Aug. 21, 2011.

17. Kate Coscarelli and Robert Cohen, *Star-Ledger*, Sept. 11, 2001.

18. Cohen and Robert Rudolph, *Star-Ledger*, Sept. 6, 2001.

19. Coscarelli and Cohen, *Star-Ledger*, Sept. 11, 2001.

20. *Star-Ledger*, Sept. 6, 2001.

21. *Asbury Park Press*, Sept. 1, 2001.

22. *Asbury Park Press,* Dec. 8, 2001.

23. Associated Press, Aug. 21, 2011.

24. Jonathan Casiano, *Star-Ledger*, Dec. 21, 2001.

25. David Halbfinger and David Kocieniewski, *New York Times*, Oct. 29, 2009.

26. Jeff Whelan, *Star-Ledger*, Nov. 16, 2003.

27. Martin, *Star-Ledger*, Feb. 5, 2002.

28. Martin, *Star-Ledger*, April 16, 2002.

29. Martin, *Star-Ledger*, May 31, 2002.

30. Associated Press, Jan. 1, 2003.

31. *Jersey Journal*, Feb. 13, 2002.

32. Maddux, *The Record*, Dec. 15, 2000.

33. *Star-Ledger*, Jan. 12, 2003.

34. Martin and Coscarelli, *Star-Ledger*, Nov. 19, 2002.

35. Martin, *Star-Ledger*, Feb. 5, 2002.

36. Martin, *Star-Ledger*, Oct. 11, 2002.

37. Weiss, *Jersey Journal*, March 8, 2003.

38. Martin, *Star-Ledger*, Oct. 29, 2002.

39. Bob Ingle and Sandy McClure, *The Soprano State*, p. 171.

40. Whelan, *Star-Ledger*, Nov. 16, 2003.

41. Weiss, *Jersey Journal*, March 8, 2003.

42. Joe Donohue and Martin, *Star-Ledger*, Nov. 20, 2004.

43. Angela Delli Santi Associated Press, Jan. 9, 2007.

44. J. Scott Orr, *Star-Ledger*, May 30, 2002.

45. Brian Ross, *ABC News*, Aug. 13, 2003.

46. John P. Martin, *Star-Ledger*, April 4, 2004.

47. *The Economist*, April 13, 2003.

48. Laura Ingle, *On the Record with Greta Van Susteren*, Fox News Channel, May 8, 2007.

49. Amanda Ripley, *Time*, Dec. 6, 2007.

50. Michael Miller, *Press of Atlantic City*, Jan. 14, 2009.

51. Darryl Isherwood, (Trenton) *Times*, Feb. 14, 2007.

52. Associated Press, April 24, 2009.

53. Lisa Fleisher, *Wall Street Journal*, July 27, 2011.

54. Lawrence O'Donnell, *The Last Word with Lawrence O'Donnell*, MSNBC, August 4, 2011.

55. The Auditor, *Star-Ledger*, March 7, 2004.

56. Brian Donohue, *Star-Ledger*, June 25, 2004.

57. Diane Walsh, *Star-Ledger*, Nov. 3, 2004.

58. Josh Gohlke, *The Record*, May 8, 2005.

59. Ingle and McClure, *The Soprano State*, p. 175.

60. Joe Ryan, *Star-Ledger*, Sept. 27, 2010.

61. Bob Braun, *Star-Ledger*, Aug. 23, 2010.

62. Press Release, Office of Attorney General, Oct. 6, 2006.

63. Ryan, *Star-Ledger*, June 17, 2009.

64. TheSopranoState.com, Update, 2009.

65. McClure, Gannett State Bureau, July 27, 2004.

66. Lilo Stainton, Gannett State Bureau, July 8, 2004.

67. Jeff Pillets, Maddux, and Clint Riley, *The Record*, March 12, 2004.

68. Robert Schwaneberg and Dunstan McNichol, *Star-Ledger*, July 9, 2004.

69. Mike Kelly, *The Record*, July 13, 2004.

70. Schwaneberg and McNichol, *Star-Ledger*, July 9, 2004.

71. Ingle and McClure, *The Soprano State*, p. 55.

72. Ted Sherman and Josh Margolin, *The Jersey Sting*, p. 86.

73. Ryan, *Star-Ledger*, June 2, 2010.

74. David Porter, Associated Press, Feb. 18, 2011.

75. Samantha Henry, Associated Press, March 16, 2010.

76. Ibid.

77. Bob Braun, *Star-Ledger*, March 25, 2010.

78. Ryan, *Star-Ledger*, March 24, 2010.

79. Press release, U.S. Attorney's Office, District of New Jersey, July 6, 2011.

80. Sherman, *Star-Ledger*, July 22, 2011.

81. Peter J. Sampson, *The Record*, Oct. 28, 2010.

82. Sherman, *Star-Ledger*, July 22, 2011.

83. Melissa Hayes, *Jersey Journal*, Oct. 28, 2010.

84. MaryAnn Spoto, *Star-Ledger*, Dec. 17, 2010.

85. Hayes, *Jersey Journal*, Dec. 17, 2010.

86. Matthew Van Dusen, *The Record*, Oct. 19, 2010.

87. Sherman, *Star-Ledger*, July 22, 2011.

88. Terrence McDonald, *Jersey Journal*, August 15, 2011.

89. Sherman, *Star-Ledger*, July 14, 2011.

90. Sherman and Margolin, *The Jersey Sting*, P. 325.

91. Associated Press, Dec. 31, 2002.

5. TOSSING MUD AT MR. CLEAN

1. Andrew McCarthy, *National Review*, Jan. 17, 2007.

2. Karl Rove, *Courage and Consequence*, p. 508.

3. House Judiciary Committee, White House documents, Part 4.

4. J. Scott Orr, *Star-Ledger*, May 18, 2007.

5. Tom Moran, *Star-Ledger*, May 18, 2007.

6. Jerry Gray, *New York Times*, May 28, 1992.

7. Moran, *Star-Ledger*, Nov. 23, 2005.

8. Paul Mulshine, *Star-Ledger*, Oct. 23, 2011.

9. Steve Kornacki, *New York Observer*, Sept. 25, 2006.

10. Jeff Whelan and Josh Margolin, *Star-Ledger*, Sept. 8, 2006.

11. Whelan, *Star-Ledger*, Sept. 24, 2006.

12. Whelan, *Star-Ledger*, Aug, 25, 2006.

13. Beth DeFalco, Associated Press, Sept. 8, 2006.

14. Joe Donohue and Whelan, *Star-Ledger*, Sept. 9, 2006.

15. Donohue and Whelan, *Star-Ledger*, Oct. 31, 2006.

16. Whelan and Donohue, *Star-Ledger*, Sept. 9, 2006.

17. Sherman and Margolin, *Star-Ledger*, Sept. 9, 2006.

18. Moran, *Star-Ledger*, March 23, 2007.

19. Rutgers-Eagleton poll, Nov. 5, 2009.

20. Margolin, *Star-Ledger*, July 17, 2008.

21. The Auditor, *Star-Ledger*, Feb. 7, 2010.

22. Mark Mueller, *Star-Ledger*, Oct. 23, 2011.

23. Mark Mueller, *Star-Ledger*, Oct. 23, 2011.

24. Raju Chebium, Gannett Washington Bureau, Oct. 26, 2011.

25. Moran, *Star-Ledger*, March 14, 2007.

26. Paul Krugman, *New York Times*, March 12, 2007.

27. Moran, *Star-Ledger*, March 23, 2007.

28. Walter Timpone, *Star-Ledger*, May 10, 2007.

29. Transcript, House Judiciary Committee, July 7, 2009.

30. Kate Zernike, *New York Times*, Jan. 5, 2012.

31. *The Soprano State*, pp. 133–37.

32. Jim McElhatton, *Washington Times*, March 18, 2008.

33. Ibid.

34. Associated Press, June 25, 2009.

35. Ibid.

36. Letter from Frank Pallone Jr., Nov. 21, 2007.

37. John Martin and Jeff Whelon, *Star-Ledger*, Jan. 20, 2008.

38. Ibid.

39. Ibid.

40. David Goldstein, *Sacramento Bee*, March 12, 2008.

41. Raju Chebium, Gannett News Service, March 12, 2008.

42. Chebium, Gannett News Service, March 12, 2008.

43. Moran, *Star-Ledger*, Nov. 21, 2007.

44. *Press of Atlantic City*, Nov. 25, 2007.

45. Moran, *Star-Ledger*, Nov. 21, 2007.

46. Herb Jackson, *The Record*, June 25, 2009.

47. Ibid.

48. Transcript, Subcommittee on Commercial and Administrative Law, June 25, 2009.

49. Herb Jackson, *The Record*, June 25, 2009.

50. Ibid.

51. Kimberly Hefling, Associated Press, June 26, 2009.

52. Lara Jakes Jordan, Associated Press, April 3, 2008.

53. Pete Yost, Associated Press, Nov. 8, 2010.

54. Margolin, *Star-Ledger*, Nov. 9, 2010.

55. Angela Delli Santi, Associated Press, Oct. 13, 2009.

56. David M. Halbfinger, *New York Times*, Oct. 22, 2009.

57. Margolin, *Star-Ledger*, Nov. 9, 2010.

58. *Philadelphia Daily News*, Nov. 10, 2010.

59. *Star-Ledger*, Nov. 10, 2010.

60. Halbfinger, *New York Times*, Oct. 22, 2009.

61. Delli Santi, Associated Press, Oct. 19, 2009.

62. Jonathan Weil, *Bloomberg*, July 27, 2011.

63. Jim Edwards, CBS Interactive Business Network, July 18, 2011.

64. Weil, *Bloomberg*, July 27, 2011.

65. David Carr, *New York Times*, July 17, 2011.

66. Weil, *Bloomberg*, July 27, 2011.

6. SWINE FLEW

1. Jonathan Tamari, Gannett New Jersey, Oct. 9, 2005.

2. Matt Friedman, *PolitickerNJ.com*, Aug. 25, 2008.

3. Tamari, Gannett New Jersey, Oct. 9, 2005.

4. Ibid.

5. Neal Cavuto, Fox News Channel, Nov. 4, 2009.

6. FactCheck.org, Feb. 28, 2011.

7. Paul Mulshine, *Star-Ledger*, June 30, 2011.

8. *Vanity Fair*, February 2012.

9. CBS News, April 12, 2007.

10. Greg Volpe, Gannett New Jersey, Oct. 24, 2008.

11. Ibid.

12. Volpe, Gannett New Jersey, Sept. 7, 2008.

13. Michael Symons, Gannett New Jersey, May 27, 2009.

14. Ibid.

15. Ibid.

16. Symons, Gannett New Jersey, May 26, 2009.

17. Ibid.

18. Ibid.

19. Symons, Gannett New Jersey, March 4, 2009.

20. Symons, Gannett New Jersey, June 2, 2009.

21. Ibid.

22. Editorial Board, *Star-Ledger*, July 16, 2009.

23. Bob Jordan and Kevin Penton, *Asbury Park Press*, July 22, 2009.

24. Symons, Gannett New Jersey, July 24, 2009.

7. I'M FAT BUT YOU'RE UGLY AND I CAN LOSE WEIGHT

1. Michael Symons, Gannett New Jersey, June 4, 2009.

2. Paul Cox, *Star-Ledger*, June 9, 2009.

3. Symons, Gannett New Jersey, April 2, 2009.

4. Tom Baldwin and Jonathan Tamari, Gannett New Jersey, Nov. 4, 2005.

5. Ben Widdicombe, (New York) *Daily News*, Nov. 4, 2005.

6. David M. Halbfinger, *New York Times*, Oct. 20. 2009.

7. David Kocieniewski and Serge F. Kovaleski, *New York Times*, May 23, 2007.

8. Symons, Gannett New Jersey, Aug. 8, 2009.

9. Halbfinger, *New York Times*, Oct. 20, 2009.

10. Symons, Gannett New Jersey, Aug. 25, 2009.

11. Angela Delli Santi, Associated Press, Sept. 5, 2009.

12. Chris Megerian and Claire Heininger, *Star-Ledger*, Sept. 9, 2009.

13. James Ahearn, *The Record*, Sept. 6, 2009.

14. *Wall Street Journal*, Oct. 2, 2009.

15. Symons, Gannett New Jersey, Jan. 12, 2010.

16. Charlie Gasparino, *The Daily Beast*, Oct. 31, 2011.

17. Halbfinger, *New York Times*, Oct. 8, 2009.

18. Ibid.

19. Ibid.

20. Associated Press, Oct. 16, 2009.

21. Ibid.

22. Halbfinger, *New York Times*, Oct. 8, 2009.

23. Cynthia Burton, *Philadelphia Inquirer*, May 28, 2009.

24. Juliet Fletcher and Mary Jo Layton, *The Record*, July 29, 2011.

25. Halbfinger, *New York Times*, Oct. 8, 2009.

26. Brian T. Murray, *Star-Ledger*, June 26, 1996.

27. Symons, Gannett New Jersey, Oct. 8, 2009.

28. Symons, Gannett New Jersey, Oct. 2, 2009.

29. Peter Halmby, CNN, Oct. 2, 2009.

30. Halbfinger and Kocieniewski, *New York Times*, Oct. 29, 2009.

31. Monmouth University, Nov. 3, 2009.

32. Ibid.

33. Jason Method, *Asbury Park Press*, Nov. 7, 2009.

34. Josh Margolin, *Star-Ledger*, Jan. 3, 2010.

35. Joseph F. Sullivan, *New York Times*, Dec. 7, 1993.

36. Margolin, *Star-Ledger*, Jan. 3, 2010.

8. GEARING UP FOR THE THIRD BATTLE OF TRENTON

1. *PolitickerNJ.com*, June 13, 2011.

2. Bob Ingle, Gannett State Bureau, Aug. 17, 2010.

3. *PolitickerNJ.com*, June 13, 2011.

4. Charles Stile, *The Record*, June 19, 2011.

5. Michael Symons, Gannett State Bureau, Nov. 5, 2009.

6. Stile, *The Record*, June 28, 2011.

7. Peggy McGlone, *Star-Ledger*, June 27, 2011.

8. Matt Friedman, *Star-Ledger*, Jan. 29, 2012.

9. Symons, Gannett State Bureau, Dec. 2, 2009.

10. Symons, Gannett State Bureau, Nov. 18, 2009.

11. Symons, Gannett State Bureau, Jan. 19, 2010.

12. Symons, Gannett State Bureau, Dec. 3, 2009.

13 . Jeff Whelan, *Star-Ledger*, Dec. 19, 2005.

14. Mitchel Maddux, *Bergen Record*, Dec. 17, 2005.

15. Ibid.

16. Symons, Gannett State Bureau, Dec. 3, 2009.

17. Ginger Gibson, *Star-Ledger*, June 19, 2011.

18. Ibid.

19. Symons, Gannett State Bureau, Dec. 3, 2009.

20. Gibson, *Star-Ledger*, June 19, 2011.

21. Ibid.

22. Symons, Gannett New Jersey, Jan. 17, 2010.

9. PUTTING THE BULLY IN THE BULLY PULPIT

1. Michael Symons, Gannett State Bureau, Nov. 24, 2009.

2. Symons, Gannett State Bureau, Jan. 12, 2010.

3. Claire Heininger and Lisa Fleisher, *Star-Ledger*, Feb. 12, 2010.

4. Tom Moran, *Star-Ledger*, Feb. 12, 2010.

5. Symons, Gannett State Bureau, Jan. 9, 2011.

6. *World News with Diane Sawyer*, April 6, 2011.

7. Bob Jordan, *Asbury Park Press*, April 23, 2011.

8. Terrence Dopp and Dunstan McNichol, *Bloomberg News*, Nov. 24, 2010.

9. Ibid.

10. Jordan, *Asbury Park Press*, Feb. 6, 2011.

11. Jordan, *Asbury Park Press*, Jan. 24, 2011.

12. *Star-Ledger*, June 5, 2011.

13. Symons, Gannett State Bureau, Dec. 2, 2009.

14. Ibid.

15. Matt Katz and Maya Rao, *Philadelphia Inquirer*, Feb. 19, 2011.

16. Ginger Gibson, *Star-Ledger*, Jan. 1, 2011.

17. Jordan and Symons, Gannett State Bureau, Jan. 31, 2012.

18. Evelyn M. Rusli, DealBook, NYTimes.com, July 6, 2011.

19. David Giambusso and Jessica Calefati, *Star-Ledger*, July 9, 2011.

20. Charles Stile, *The Record*, July 7, 2011.

21. Moran, *Star-Ledger*, July 3, 2011.

22. Ingle, Gannett State Bureau, July 10, 2011.

23. Patrick Murray, *Inthelobby.net*, July 8, 2011.

24. *Piers Morgan Tonight,* CNN, June 14, 2011.

25. Matt Friedman and Jessica Calefati, *Star-Ledger*, July 9, 2011.

10. YOU'LL THANK ME LATER

1. Michael Symons, Gannett State Bureau, Nov. 5, 2009.

2. Jason Method, Gannett State Bureau, April 17, 2011.

3. Associated Press, April 29, 2011.

4. *Communications Workers of America, AFL-CIO v. Chris Christie*, appellate ruling, May 7, 2010.

5. Amy Ridenour, Amy Ridenour's National Center Blog, Feb. 19, 2011.

6. James Sherk, *New York Times*, Feb. 19, 2011.

7. Joshua Rauh, Northwestern University, May 15, 2010.

8. *Meet the Press,* NBC, June 26, 2011.

9. Maggie Haberman, *Politico*, June 25, 2011.

10. Associated Press, June 25, 2011.

11. Symons, Gannett New Jersey, May 22, 2011.

12. Jason Method, *Asbury Park Press*, June 2, 2011.

13. Method, *Asbury Park Press*, June 26, 2011.

14. Volunteer recognition ceremony, Oct. 26, 2011.

15. Jenna Portnoy, *Star-Ledger,* Jan. 8, 2012.

16. Press release, New Jersey Democratic State Committee, June 1, 2011.

17. Bob Jordan and Michael Symons, Gannett State Bureau, June 1, 2011.

18. John Reitmeyer and John P. McAlpin, *The Record*, June 3, 2011.

19. Charles Stile, *The Record*, June 7, 2011.

20. Reitmeyer and McAlpin, *The Record*, June 3, 2011.

21. Statement issued by Governor Christie's office, Oct. 17, 2011.

22. Bob Ingle, Gannett State Bureau, June 13, 2000.

23. *Abbott v. Burke VI*, decided March 7, 2000.

24. Megan DeMarco, *Star-Ledger,* Oct. 20, 2011.

25. John Schoonejongen, *Asbury Park Press*, Aug. 26, 2010.

26. Symons, Gannett New Jersey, Oct. 7, 2010.

27. Ibid.

28. Symons, Gannett New Jersey, Sept. 4, 2010.

29. Ingle, Gannett State Bureau, Sept. 26, 2010.

30. Ingle, Gannett New Jersey, Sept. 26, 2010.

31. Ingle, Gannett New Jersey, Sept. 15, 2010.

32. Amy S. Rosenberg, *Philadelphia Inquirer*, April 17, 2011.

33. Terrence Dopp, *Bloomberg News*, Oct. 27, 2010.

11. THE WHITE HOUSE CAN WAIT

1. Jack Newfield, "The Full Rudy: The Man, the Mayor, the Myth" *The Nation*, May 30, 2002.

2. William Mitchelson Jr., "How to Avoid Letting a 'Perp Walk' Turn into a Parade," *National Law Journal*, March 21, 2006.

3. Nikita Stewart and John P. Martin, *Star-Ledger*, Nov. 1, 2002.

4. Michael Jennings, *The* (Trenton) *Times*, Jan. 4, 2004.

5. *New York Times*, Nov. 5, 2007.

6. Quinnipiac University, Oct. 29, 1977.

7. Michael Powell, *New York Times*, Sept. 21, 2007.

8. "Mayor of the World," *Time*, Dec. 31, 2001.

9. Joe Tyrrell, *NJ Spotlight*, Nov. 30, 2011.

10. Elise Young, *Bloomberg News*, Oct. 21, 2011.

11. Chris Megerian, *Star-Ledger*, Sept. 7, 2011.

12. Magerian, *Star-Ledger*, Sept. 7, 2011.

13. Press Conference in Camden, NJ, Nov. 27, 2011.

14. *Morning Joe*, MSNBC, Dec. 20, 2011.

15. Camden Press Conference, Nov. 27, 2011.

16. Matt Bai, *New York Times Magazine*, Feb. 27, 2011.

17. Matt Friedman, *Star-Ledger*, Oct. 19, 2011.

18. Paul Giget, *Wall Street Journal*, Sept. 22, 2011.

19. John Reitmeyer, *The Record*, Sept. 23, 2011.

20. Christopher Beam, *Slate*, Nov. 2, 2009.

21. Michael Symons, *USA Today*, Sept. 30, 2011.

22. Herb Jackson, *The Record*, Nov. 24, 2011.

23. Fox News Channel transcript, Oct. 26, 2009.

24. Ginger Gibson and Chris Megerian, *Star-Ledger*, Dec. 21, 2010.

25. Symons, *USA Today*, Sept. 30, 2011.

26. Ibid.

27. Steve Peoples, Associated Press, Oct. 11, 2011.

28. State House staff, *Star-Ledger*, Oct. 14, 2011.

29. John Kraushaar, *National Journal*, Jan. 10, 2012.

30. NBC News, Oct. 11, 2011.

31. John DiStaso, (Manchester) *Union Leader*, Nov. 10, 2011.

32. *Ask the Governor*, 101.5 FM radio, Nov. 22, 2011.

33. Video, Delawareonline.com, Nov. 18, 2011.

34. Amy S. Rosenberg, *Philadelphia Inquirer*, April 17, 2011.

35. Kathleen O'Brien, *Star-Ledger*, Aug. 22, 2010.

13. "I'M GONNA DIE IN THIS FLEECE"

1. Amy Ellis and Stephen Stirling, *Star-Ledger*, Oct. 29, 2012.

2. Emily Previti, *Press of Atlantic City*, Oct. 28, 2012.

3. Jenna Portnoy, *Star-Ledger*, Nov. 4, 2012.

4. Portnoy, *Star-Ledger*, Nov. 4, 2012.

5. Associated Press, Nov. 1, 2012.

6. Michael Barbaro, *New York Times*, Nov. 19, 2012.

7. Kelly Heyboer, *Star-Ledger*, Nov. 7, 2012.

8. *Fox News Sunday*, March 3, 2013.

9. Nate Silver, *New York Times*, Nov. 21, 2012.

10. *Politico*, Maggie Haberman, Feb. 27, 2013.

11. Elahe Izadi, *National Journal*, Feb. 26, 2013.

12. *Wall Street Journal*, Patrick O'Connor, Feb. 26, 2013.

13. Cameron Joseph, *The Hill*, Feb. 28, 2013

INDEX

Rosenstein, Hetty, 223, 242
Ross, Brian, 81
Rossi, Ray, 131, 151, 181
Rove, Karl, 65, 95–96, 98
  before House Judiciary Committee, 105–6
  on U.S. Attorney purge, 99
Rowan University, 278–79
Rubio, Marco, 301, 302
Russo, John, 166
Rutgers University, 13, 113, 130, 151, 241, 255, 278–79
Rutgers-Eagleton Poll, 102
Ryan, Paul, 272, 301, 302

Sabato, Larry (Dr.), 113, 222, 262
Sabrin, Murray, 145
St. Louis Cardinals, 11, 19, 26
Sampson, Kyle, 96–98
Samson, David, 110, 173
Sanchez, Linda (Congresswoman), 112
Sanford, Mark (Governor), 138
Santorum, Rick, 303
Sarlo, Paul, 292
Saturday Night Live, 256, 261, 295–97
Sawyer, Diane, 196, 244–45
Scavone, Domenica ("Minnie"), 7–8
Scavone, Salvatore, 6–8
Schmidt, Steve, 300
Schnur, Dan, 299
Schriefer, Russ, 256–57, 272
Schulder, Esther, 86
Schulder, Jared, 86
Schulder, William, 86
Schumer, Charles (Senator), 99
Schundler, Bret, 66, 88–89, 126, 187
  New Jersey governor and, 230–32
Schwab, Charles, 250
Schwartz, Patty, 106
Scott, Eric, 158, 167–68
The Seaport Group, 67–69
Seaside Heights, 290
SEC. See Securities and Exchange Commission
Secret Service, 120
Securities and Exchange Commission (SEC), 160–63

Securities Industry Association, 63
Seitz, LeRoy, 199
self-assuredness, 1–3, 52
Seton Hall Law School, 34–35, 111, 113
Seton Hall University, 38
Shafton, Rick, 51
Sharia law, 83
Shaw, Jack, 93
Shea, Tom, 133, 146–47
Sherman, Brad (Congressman), 161
ShopRite grocery, 25
Sidamon-Eristoff, Andrew, 184
Sierra Club, 179, 241
Silver, Nate, 295
Simon, William, Jr., 145
Slotnick, Stephen, 22
Smith, L. Harvey, 91–93
Smith & Nephew, 110
Snowflack, Fred, 148
Snyder, Rick, 302
Solomon, Lee, 106–9
The Sopranos, 77
South Jersey, 282
Spear Leeds & Kellogg, 160–61
speeding ticket, 150–51. See also driving record
spending cap, 195–200
Spicuzzo, Joseph, 206
sports betting, 278
Springsteen, Bruce, 195–96, 271, 293, 296
Squawk Box, 133
Stack, Brian, 211
Star-Ledger, 52, 62, 70, 99–100, 102
  on government spending, 118
  Menendez story, 103–5
  on Pinkett, 140
State of the State speech, 279
state workers, contracts and pensions, 278
stem cell research, 132
Stepien, Bill, 114, 134, 239
  campaign manager, 152, 156, 172
Stern, Herb, 75, 84, 239–40
Stevenson, Adlai, 50
Steward, Luther C., 219
Stewart, Jon, 292
Stewart, Martha, 161
sting operations, 89–91